CODY RODEO

The Mystique of Buffalo Bill Cody and the Great American Cowboy

Lew Freedman

Blue River Press
Indianapolis, IN

ISBN: 9781935628491

Cover photo by Jason Koperski
Cover design by Kevin Essett
Packaged by Wish Publishing

Printed in the United States of America
10 9 8 7 6 5 4 3 2

Published by Blue River Press
www.brpressbooks.com

Distributed by Cardinal Publishers Group
Tom Doherty Company, Inc.
www.cardinalpub.com

Tim Ditrich is in for a wild ride on the bucking horse he drew and is about to meet the hard dirt (photo by Jason Koperski)

Curry Fielder was the best of the best all season long in the bull riding category at Cody Nite Rodeo (photo by Jason Koperski).

Table of Contents

This is where the action happens (photo by Lew Freedman).

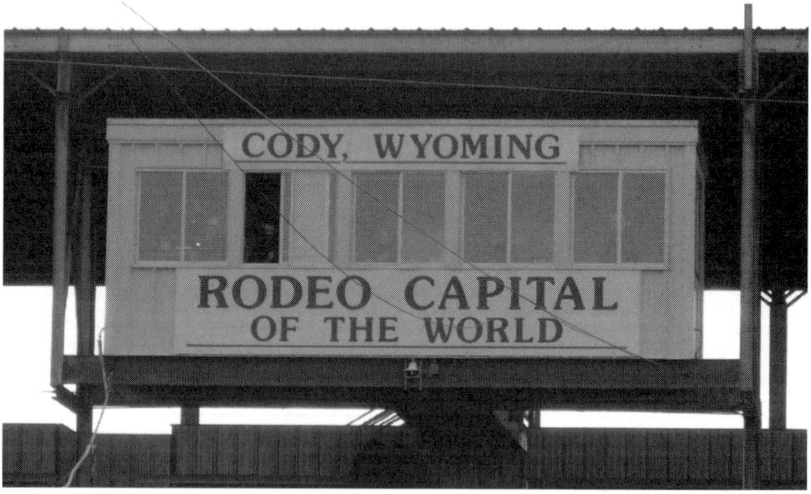

Cody calls itself the Rodeo Capital of the World because it hosts rodeo every night from June 1 to August 31 (photo by Lew Freedman).

Acknowledgements

A special thank you goes to Maury and Nikki Tate of the "Mo" Betta Bull Company of Apache, Oklahoma and the operators of Cody Nite Rodeo for more than a decade. They made it possible for the author to be live on the scene in the middle of the action during the summer of 2014.

Another thank you goes to Cody Stampede officials, especially president Al Schultz, for their help during the same time period.

Also, thanks goes to the Buffalo Bill Center of the West in Cody, Wyoming and the staff at the McCracken Research Library for assistance with rodeo historical research.

A very special shout-out of "Yippee ki yay!" goes out to all of the cowboys and cowgirls who helped out during the 2014 rodeo season.

Author Lew Fredman with a horse named Speedy.

A Personal Note

One of the rules Cody Nite Rodeo imposes on writers if they come to visit and report on the rodeo and wish to gain entrance to the staging area behind the chutes where bucking horses and snorting bulls emerge is that they must wear a cowboy hat.

I was aware of this regulation before I drove to Wyoming in time for the June 1 opening day of the 2014 season, but I had not shopped. It seemed quite likely that the selection would be better in the state that announces on the welcome signs on highways "Forever West" than just about anywhere else.

Hats and I do not get along well. They do not become me. The last time I owned a cowboy hat I was probably four years old. There is a family photograph of me at about that age wearing a cowboy hat and a western shirt and riding the arm of the sofa in my family's Massachusetts home. I mention that for a couple of reasons. The first one being that I was always a cowboy fan – thank you James Garner and Jack Kelly in "Maverick," Clint Eastwood in "Rawhide" and John Wayne in all of those Wild West flicks.

The second one being that despite that allegiance to the Wild West it didn't matter if it was a baseball cap, knit winter hat, fedora, or cowboy hat, it wasn't going to be flattering to me.

Once in Cody I shopped around. I stopped in at least six western wear stores or local shops that included cowboy hats for tourists. I met someone who was prepared to make me a snug fitting, personal felt hat for something like $500. During this time period I also sat and talked rodeo with Maury Tate, the chief of Cody Nite Rodeo just beginning his 10th season in charge.

I informed Maury that I was on the prowl for the right hat. I wanted one that was inexpensive, would not blow off my head in a strong gust of wind, and one that would not make me look like too much of a dork. He gazed at me and said, "Good luck."

The next day I returned to one of the places I had previously investigated, the Tecumseh Trading Post, which had a sale going on because owner Jerry Fick was going out of business at the site at the end of the summer after 20 years of operating in Cody.

I sprung for a marked-down-to-$20 model made of straw, summer weight. It was more flat than I would have preferred, but I was careful to avoid a high crown, knowing that I would definitely look silly in one of those.

For the rest of the summer I wore my cowboy hat nightly. It fit and I only had it blown off of my head in Wyoming's famous winds twice. I've still got it though I look at it more as an ornament or a souvenir of the season at the moment. Every time I gaze at a picture of myself wearing the hat, or pull it on and look in the mirror, even though nobody laughed out loud at me, I can't swear that I escaped the stigma of looking dorky.

But if that was the price of watching a summer of rodeo up close and personal, it was worth it.

— Lew Freedman,
December, 2014.

Prologue: Rodeo Beginnings

During the summer of 1872, Buffalo Bill Cody was hanging out in North Platte, Nebraska, one of several places around the United States he called home at one time or another during his life.

He asked around to find out what kind of excitement might be found in town to celebrate the Fourth of July. When he was told nothing much special was in the works, Cody – sounding a bit like Mickey Rooney in those old black and white movies – more or less said, "Well, let's put on a rodeo."

American rodeo, an outgrowth of Hispanic influence and the "gauchos" in Spain rather than cowboys, really began on working ranches during the second half of the 19th century. During their down time, such as it was, bored cowboys began challenging one another. They sought to cut through big talk and find out who was the best amongst them at roping, breaking broncs, and riding bulls. Most likely, wagers were made by the participants and the onlookers. It has been noted by those who have made studies of rodeo's evolution from low-key competition to serious sport to big business that cowboys basically had to entertain themselves if they were on a cattle drive.

In the book *Rodeo History and Legends*, one of those match-ups was documented. In 1869, the cowboys at the Colorado Hash Knife & Mill Iron operation competed and bet on themselves.

These were not rodeos contested at fair grounds or competitions that had tickets sold to the public for admission. These were rodeos conducted at out-of-the-way locations on the prairie or back near the bunkhouse on the ranch.

Buffalo Bill has been credited with organizing the first rodeo designed to be a competition with the public invited. This was 14 years before Cody built a retreat in North Platte

Buffalo Bill Cody was the most famous person in the world during his lifetime (Buffalo Bill Center of the West McCracken Library).

that he called Scout's Rest Ranch. He had one of his sisters, Julia Goodman, decorate the interior and that impressive mansion still stands today. The building is the main feature in Nebraska's 4,000-acre Buffalo Bill State Park.

The engaging mansion, which cost $6,000 to construct, is painted white and features green trim, is two stories tall and has nine rooms. Cody maintained a home in North Platte between 1877 and 1902.

The rodeo grounds where that first North Platte rodeo was held are just a very short distance down the road from the home. There were big doings on the site on July 4, 1882.

Cody envisioned a buffalo hunting exhibition – one of his specialties – as part of the program. He printed up and handed out 5,000 handbills advertising the Independence Day celebration called "Old Glory Days Blow-Out." Cody was astonished when the rodeo attracted about 1,000 cowboy entrants. Many call this the formalized beginning of modern rodeo, as well as the forerunner of Cody's Wild West performances. When Cody assessed the turnout, he realized he had underestimated the American public's appetite for Old West events. This propelled him to organize his 1884 Wild West debut.

Other rodeos contest North Platte's claim to being the first of its kind to lead the way to rodeo as we know it. Alpine, Texas makes its own case based on a rodeo conducted in 1882.

Pecos, Texas jumped into the fray with a July 4, 1883 rodeo. Prescott, Arizona likes to think of itself as the father of pro rodeo dating to July 4, 1888. Prescott has trademarked the phrase "World's Oldest Rodeo," noting that prize money was presented and a champion was crowned in 1888.

Rodeo evolved in many ways over many years. Cheyenne Frontier Days in Wyoming has been held every year since September 23, 1897 and now attracts about 200,000 fans a year. It calls itself, "The Daddy of Them All." The Frontier Days motto is grandiose in its own way, but does produce arguments. Conducted for most of the last 10 days in July, Frontier Days awards one of the most prestigious belt buckles that a cowboy can win.

Wendy Coe, a retired cowgirl from Cody, who now hand-sews western shirts for contestants, said, "Buffalo Bill didn't invent rodeo, but he learned to market rodeo."

Elizabeth Atwood Lawrence, who penned the treatise, *Rodeo: An Anthropologist Looks at the Wild and the Tame* in 1982, said Buffalo Bill Cody did more to uplift the broad positive image of the cowboy than anyone else in America.

"It is historical fact," Lawrence wrote, "that before Buffalo Bill, the American cowboy was far from being considered a hero...cowboys were considered at worst as armed desperados, and at best rough, rowdy, uncouth and irresponsible laborers." It was Cody, and the novelist Owen Wister, whose western classic "The Virginian" appeared in print in 1902, whose combined efforts remade the image of the cowboy, she said. "The figure of the cowboy hero was born," she wrote, "the strong, handsome man, as daring and courageous as he was noble and generous, with his unswerving chivalry, personal code of honor, and almost courtly manner."

Of Cody, she added... "It was he that paved the way for rodeo as it is known today."

Once Cody put his two cents worth in at North Platte, though, he was pretty much out of the rodeo business. Inspired by the success and interest of the rodeo he threw his energy into the Wild West tours that dominated the rest of his life.

It was during these traveling years that Cody proved his acumen and judgment as a showman and his involvement with rodeo as we know it ceased. Rodeo went on without Cody. However, in its early days events in rodeo included trick and fancy roping and fancy riding, the type of showy displays included in the Wild West. Rodeo events did not become standardized for decades.

By the late 1890s and early 1900s, rodeos were popping up all over. Any cowboy will tell spectators that without the cooperation of terrific livestock that have bucking in their blood and are bred for the task there could not be a show. A small number of horses and bulls have gained legendary status over the last century or so, a recognition that no matter how good a cowboy was he was going to have a tough time staying aboard for the standard eight seconds.

The best-known horse or bull in rodeo history is the saddle bronc horse Steamboat. No bucking horse or wild bull ever gets the attention that Steamboat still garners roughly 115 years after his first bucking trial. Steamboat is the horse ridden by the cowboy on the Wyoming state license plate. Steamboat is also the symbol of University of Wyoming athletics. The team's nickname is the Cowboys for men's teams and the Cowgirls for women's teams and the uniform logos feature Steamboat.

Steamboat is actually a registered trademark of the state of Wyoming, although one must wonder about the appropriateness of claiming a trademark on a living thing. Steamboat was foaled on a ranch in Chugwater, Wyoming and made his first appearance as a bucking horse in a rodeo in Denver in 1901. Steamboat was a rodeo horse for a dozen years. But he edged into immortality when his countenance was adopted by the state and the university.

The Wyoming license plate has featured Steamboat since 1936 and if state officials voted to change the design residents might riot. The plate is most likely the most popular ever used by any state.

The cowboys worked in the West, but it was soon discovered that rodeo was popular in the East, as well.

In 1905 the famed Miller's 101 Ranch of Ponca City, Oklahoma staged a western show at Madison Square Garden in New York City. Rodeo became a more regular thing at the Garden in the 1920s.

For many years there was discrimination against women in rodeo – and it is still an imbalanced sport emphasizing men's events. Rodeo attitudes mirrored the world at large where it was felt that women should remain in the home to cook and clean and raise children. It was said that it was unladylike to sweat and women were closed out of major rodeo competitions. Things are changing, but women are still limited to certain more "ladylike" events.

Rodeo has always been a hard way to make a living, but it may have been tougher in the 1930s than at any time. Event organizers were so cheap that cowboys realized that even if they won their event they might not make money. In 1936, this manifested itself as a cowboy strike at the Boston Garden, the main demands focusing on higher payouts.

Cowboys kept battling for increased shares of the purse. They founded organizations to represent them and bargain with rodeo operators. The first such group was the Rodeo Association of America. Another was the Cowboy Turtles Association and women founded their own organization and rodeo circuit.

After World War II, as the country settled into a new era of prosperity in the 1950s, rodeo boomed. At one time there were about 600 sanctioned rodeos held annually across the United States. Cowboys will never gain the riches of athletes who compete in the four major U.S. team sports of baseball, football, basketball and hockey, or stock-car driving. They still must pay their own travel expenses and entry fees. In that sense they are like golfers or tennis players, although there is more prize money available in those sports.

Rodeo was thriving, but there was no all-encompassing championship that the average fan could point to as the biggest bash of the season after which the cowboys would go home crowned as world champions. Rodeo got some television attention, but organizers felt what was needed was a big-deal event like the World Series or NFL championship game.

They made it happen. In 1959, a rodeo milestone was recorded. For the first time ever a true end-of-the-year championship was conducted. The National Finals Rodeo made its debut. The top 15 money winners for the year in each event gathered in Dallas. A common phrase in rodeo is that Fourth of July week is "Cowboy Christmas," because a hustling cowboy can hit several rodeos in a short period of time and be rewarded with big paydays. The true cowboy Christmas, however, is really the National Finals Rodeo, held in early December each year with the biggest payouts in the sport.

The National Finals moved from Dallas to Los Angeles in 1962 and then to Oklahoma City, where it stayed from 1965 to 1984. Since 1985 the National Finals have been contested in Las Vegas and tickets to the Thomas & Mack Center are hard to find and expensive to buy. Despite the history and reverence attached to rodeos like Cheyenne Frontier Days, the National Finals Rodeo is the biggest event on the calendar for cowboys. It is like the playoffs in the NBA or NHL, the post-season play of baseball and football.

Not just anyone can compete. Cowboys must qualify through a points system. But once in the door, that top 15 in each event has a chance to carry home the richest purses of the year. It took years, but the first $100,000 cowboy in earnings was Tom Ferguson of Miami, Oklahoma, who won $114,110 in 1976.

Ferguson could thank Buffalo Bill for undertaking that North Platte rodeo. But Cody left a bigger footprint in the community east of Yellowstone National Park that bears his name.

In the 1890s, Buffalo Bill, who had traveled through the area many times, decided to establish a hunting camp called Pahaska Teepee. He also believed the area was ripe for settlement. He pictured the creation of a tourist town with steady visitor traffic on the way to the Park or out of it.

Today Pahaska Teepee has a restaurant, gas station, gift shop and lodge. Cody, Wyoming sits at an elevation of 5,000 feet 50 miles away with the Shoshone River running through and past the community. Buffalo Bill was instrumental in its establishment in 1895. The city's population is now 10,000 and is often referred to as "Buffalo Bill's Town in the Rockies."

The grandest downtown landmark is the Irma Hotel. It opened in 1902 and is named after one of Cody's daughters. The colorful structure, which features numerous photographs of Buffalo Bill, as well as animal heads mounted on walls and western paintings in its dining room, is commonly called "Buffalo Bill's Irma Hotel."

Buffalo Bill believed that Cody would be a successful town because of its proximity to Yellowstone. However, Buffalo Bill

The Irma Hotel is still at the heart of activity in downtown Cody, more than a century after it was built by town founder Buffalo Bill Cody and named for one of his daughters (photo by Lew Freedman).

and other town fathers convinced the state of Wyoming to grant them water rights from the Shoshone River to irrigate up to 169,000 acres of land in the Big Horn Basin. The Shoeshone was dammed for hydroelectric power and irrigation and when the dam, located only a few miles east of Cody, was finished in 1905 it was the tallest dam in the world. About 30 years later Congress bestowed Buffalo Bill Cody's name on that structure. The dam overlooks a reservoir that borders Buffalo Bill State Park.

Nancy Tia Brown, Cody's mayor since 2008, and the first female mayor in the city's history, believes that of all the things Buffalo Bill Cody accomplished in his life, securing those water rights might be the most important one.

"The dam may have been his greatest achievement," she said. "That's what makes the city of Cody viable."

Buffalo Bill's presence in Cody is ubiquitous. His visage adorns a sign outside the Visitors Center. The biggest tourist attraction in town is the Buffalo Bill Center of the West. The Irma might as well be a Buffalo Bill shrine. In the early years of Cody, when it had not been much developed, Buffalo Bill tested and drilled applicants for the Wild West a few blocks from the Irma.

One story goes that Buffalo Bill was standing on the porch of the Irma in 1909 and watched a cowboy crash through the window of a drugstore. When the cowboy, whose name was Harry Webb, maintained his place in the saddle Buffalo Bill signed him for the Wild West.

On other occasions bronc riding competitions took place downtown on Sheridan Avenue.

Buffalo Bill died in 1917, about six weeks shy of his 71st birthday. The first Cody rodeo commemorating Buffalo Bill's contributions was organized by a citizen named Clarence Williams in June of 1919. In 1920, Buffalo Bill's Cody Stampede was moved to its July 4 slot. By then the Stampede had incorporated and formed a board of directors to handle arrangements.

The Stampede has endured and the 2014 version was the 95th year. The Stampede is always a stopping point for touring professionals on the circuit on July 4 and the few days leading up to the holiday.

In 1938, Cody Nite Rodeo was created, the brainstorm of a gentleman named Carly Downing, who had been a Wild West performer. Downing nicknamed his new rodeo "The Pup Rodeo" because it was aimed more at amateurs and was not designed to compete against the Stampede.

The Nite Rodeo is contested every night from June 1 through August 31. It is the only every-day rodeo in the world. There are older rodeos. There are older weekend-only rodeos, but there are no other rodeos operated for three months straight every night. That means there are more rodeos annually in Cody than in any other place in the universe.

Although the Cody Stampede is the attraction for big-name cowboys seeking big paydays, the Cody Nite Rodeo is considered the best training ground for beginners. It is also the best place for an established cowboy to obtain practice for tougher competition.

During its long and storied history, Cody Nite Rodeo has spawned many talented cowboys who have gone on to win major championships such as Chris LeDoux, Freckles Brown, Mel Stonehouse, Jim Houston, Bill Smith, Tom Ferguson and others. Perhaps better known than some of those rodeo stars are Cody Nite Rodeo competitors who became Hollywood figures – Richard Farnsworth and Slim Pickens.

There are 90 Cody Nite rodeos in a season attracting around 1,200 people nightly for a yearly attendance close to 100,000 fans. The Buffalo Bill Center of the West years ago produced a story on Cody rodeo history with the headline "Cody is Rodeo." The phrase has caught on and still occasionally comes up in conversation.

It is the uniqueness of Cody Nite Rodeo and its lengthy, reliable schedule, even more so than the Cody Stampede, which enables the city of Cody to call itself "The Rodeo Capital of the World."

Buffalo Bill Cody would have loved that label.

Standard cowboy equipment: hat, boots, gloves and rope (photos by Lew Freedman)..

Introduction: The American Cowboy

The Wild West and the Old West have become synonyms, whether they were intended to be at the start or not.

The American West was beaten into submission by "progress," such as the building of railroads, the stealing of Native-American land and the frenetic shooting of buffalo that nearly brought them to extinction. It was all part of the process of what came to be called "the settling of the West," the westward expansion from the 13 colonies.

Although this long-term adventure as part of the building of the United States — spanning roughly 1800 to 1890 — involved considerable hardship and danger, plus rudimentary, close-to-the-land living, it has morphed over time into a romantic period of American heritage.

Despite realities being much more brutal than those discussed in Dime Novels, portrayed in Buffalo Bill Cody's Wild West performances, and later shown in Hollywood movies, the American West of the past has, in most minds, become an American West of nostalgia.

Yet there still are cowboys out there. Many still ply the livestock trade on ranches in Texas, in Wyoming and Montana. They raise cattle and horses and they dress the part of a cowboy, not because it is fashionable, but because it is utilitarian. The wide-brim hats protect against the elements. Blue jeans make more sense than black dress pants. The other type of modern cowboy is the rodeo man (or gal, although there are many fewer of them).

Rodeo riders are the closest thing the other 300 million Americans get to cowboys these days. At one time just about everyone west of the Mississippi wore a cowboy hat. Nowadays, someone wearing a cowboy hat in an airport will be the object of numerous stares — not negative stares, by any means. Often those clandestine, casual looks are accompanied by smiles. You can almost hear the thinking out loud, "It's a cowboy. Cool."

The Old West is inextricably linked to the opening of the frontier. Before the United States gained its independence from England during the American Revolution – with the Declaration of Independence being signed in 1776 – much of the map of what we see today as part of the U.S. was either unexplored by Europeans or under the control of French or Spanish royalty.

Once there was a United States the presidents began instituting policies that drove the nation's boundaries ever-westward. Thomas Jefferson orchestrated the Louisiana Purchase in 1803 and then sent Meriwether Lewis and William Clark to explore the country's new territory in 1804. In one of the grandest of adventures and explorations of all time, Lewis and Clark spent two-and-a-half years on the road. They made friends with some Indians and enemies of others. They encountered growling grizzlies and snow-covered gigantic mountains. They brought back stories of what they had seen, and soon the American government had to have it.

The United States was always land hungry and would not be satiated until covered wagons bumped into the Pacific Ocean on the West Coast (although Alaska and Hawaii were bonuses). The definition of the frontier was a constantly moving target.

Just about everything that occurred defining the Old West was an offshoot of this westward expansion. People rolled west seeking to build new lives on rich soil that could be bought inexpensively or obtained for free. People hungry for gold set out to find a fortune. Hunters, trappers working the fur trade, men seeking to free themselves of city life, sought a niche in the mountains.

Wherever people went, towns sprang up. Saloons and gambling establishments were always some of the first wood-front buildings erected. Cattle barons bought up huge acreages and their workers came to the towns to blow off steam. Law enforcement was sparse, so that's how the Wild West grew out of the Old West.

As in everyday life in the 2000s, most people in the 1800s were solid citizens. The average cowboy did his job, worked hard for his wages, and remained anonymous. However, there is a major difference in the availability of information between then and now.

Today, not a day goes by without it being remarked upon how exaggeration and innuendo ride rampant on the Internet. Sorting out truth from fiction is an everyday challenge.

In the 1800s there was a dearth of information. Of course there was no electronic media, but newspapers were also rare in the West during the first half of that century. Only in the biggest towns were you able to get a reliable news source. In most places it was as difficult to latch onto truth as it was fresh fruit. Later this was compounded when European writers enamored of the stories they had read of the West, crossed the Atlantic to write their own and when New York writers boarded trains and then borrowed horses or burros to see for themselves.

The appetite for news from the West was enormous, but the same editors who wanted to hear all about it wanted sensational stuff. They were not interested in learning about the working cowboy. They wanted picturesque tales of gunfights and fist-fights — good guys against bad guys, U.S. cavalrymen pursuing Native Americans.

To some people the Old West consists of Kit Carson, Daniel Boone, Davy Crockett, Buffalo Bill Cody, Wild Bill Hickok, Custer's Last Stand, Wyatt Earp and the gunfight at the OK Corral, Texas Rangers and the motto of "one riot, one ranger," the Alamo, the blue-clad cavalry riders, Indian chiefs with brightly colored headdresses, Doc Holliday, Johnny Ringo, Billy The Kid, Jesse James, Butch Cassidy and the Sundance Kid, Bat Masterson (who became a sportswriter in New York), and above all, men with wide brim hats and boots sitting astride horses.

In the tales of the day, these respectable riders were always covered in dust. When they spoke at all, they talked in one-word sentences, but they were always polite to women, adding "ma'am" to their replies. They kept to themselves and were at home on the range with a bedroll and their trusty horse. The good guys tried to avoid trouble. The bad guys shot first and asked questions later. The Indians were savages, beneath contempt because they did not conform to the modern and encroaching world. Politicians and generals, whose vested interest was to keep the frontier expanding, assimilated the West through two extreme prisms, one holding a rose-colored glasses view of pioneer life, the other a negative view that held life cheaply (as long as it was not their own).

Probably nothing shaped these somewhat warped images of the Wild West with as much sweep and power as the Dime Novel, introduced in 1860. Originally, the publications, which were churned out by the thousands, cost 10 cents, hence the name. Also, while they touched on many topics, they became closely identified with swashbuckling yarns of the West.

There was no greater influence on the dime novels of the West than author Ned Buntline. Not only is his one of the few names of writers connected with the genre that has endured, he led Buffalo Bill Cody (whom he first met in 1869) into show business. Buntline led such an adventurous life that he should have been the subject of one of his own books.

Ned Buntline was born Edward Zane Carroll Judson Sr. in 1821 (or 1823, records are sketchy) in Harpersfield, New York. As a young man Buntline ran away to sea, was aboard ship during the Seminole War, and later was an enlisted man during the Civil War. He became a newspaper columnist and went West, where he met Buffalo Bill and Wyatt Earp. He also met Wild Bill Hickok, but that gunfighter was not enamored with his company and threatened to shoot him. That did not stop Buntline from later featuring Wild Bill in one of his novels – presumably he was out of range when the story was published.

Buntline, the king of purple prose, penned novels using the real names of these famous men while indifferently sacrificing accuracy. One of Buntline's best-known dime novels was *Buffalo Bill: King of the Border Men.* Buntline's 25 western novels romanticized the West and boosted Buffalo Bill Cody's profile. In a 2011 book collecting four of Buntline's stories, editor Clay Reynolds wrote, "A fully evolved Ned Buntline hero contains all the ordinary virtues required of the period. Handsome, athletic, capable and daring, his heroes are expert marksmen who can break wild horses in a few moments' time, find game on a barren landscape, and locate groves of trees surrounded by good grazing and plentiful grass in which to camp without trouble. They spit in the eye of danger and they laugh at threats…"

When Buntline met Bill Cody, he was taken by his regal appearance, especially on horseback (Buffalo Bill was born to sit upon a horse), his long, flowing hair, dashing clipped-tight beard, stories of his bravery and action, and his friendly personality. As historians look back upon the exciting life of Buffalo Bill it has taken some effort to separate fact from fiction. One of the chief reasons was Buntline's (and then others') carelessness with the truth. To the writers of the time it mattered most that stories of western heroes enraptured the readership. Adherence to the facts would only get in the way of a good tale. Many years later Hollywood movie director John Ford said, "When the legend becomes fact, print the legend." The phrase was part of the movie *The Man Who Shot Liberty Valance,* and it also ended up being part of the title of Ford's biography.

The dime novelists of the 1800s may not have classified their approach so neatly, but they lived by that rule.

However, by any measure, William F. Cody led a fascinating and varied life from a young age and before his death in 1917 Cody had become one of the most famous people in the world.

To summarize, in real life, Cody was born in Le Claire, Iowa in 1846, became a ranch hand, fought in the Civil War, was a cavalry scout, earned the Congressional Medal of Honor during the Indian wars, was a buffalo hunter supreme, and also rode with the Pony Express during its short-lived existence. Some dispute the Pony Express claim, but the reasons given about his age are specious because he had been on his own since age 11 after his father died and because he already had worked as a messenger for the organizers of the Pony Express. Cody was an excellent horseman who was credited with an almost continuous ride of nearly 300 miles because the men who were supposed to relieve him were not available at the designated exchange places – one of them because he had been killed the night before.

Cody discussed his mail delivering Pony Express experience in his autobiography, *Buffalo Bill's Life Story,* which first appeared in print in 1879. The Pony Express' lifespan was only 1860-61. It was an idea that had come too late and was almost immediately eclipsed by the telegraph.

"He hired me at once as a pony express rider," Cody wrote of a man he had previously known, "but because I was so young he thought I would not be able to the stand the fierce riding which was required of the messengers. He knew, however, that I had been raised in the saddle – that I felt more at home there than any other place."

In 1872, Buffalo Bill journeyed to New York City, where he was somewhat of a sensation. While there, he attended a stage show that featured him as a character. When Cody was recognized and then introduced to the crowd he received a wild ovation – the genuine article eclipsed the on-stage imposter. The show was produced by Ned Buntline and immediately thereafter Buntline began lobbying Cody to perform in his own stage shows. Cody had no real interest in becoming an actor, but Buntline wore him down and convinced him that he could make big bucks just by being Buffalo Bill under the spotlight.

"Ned Buntline was the front man for Buffalo Bill," said Bruce Eldredge, executive director of the Buffalo Bill Center of the West in Cody, Wyoming.

Cody talked his friend Texas Jack Omohundro into joining him in a play written by Buntline called "Hurrah for the Scouts of the Plains!" The play made its debut in Chicago to considerable fanfare. The duo acted in buckskin outfits and was applauded by such luminaries as General Philip Sheridan.

While Buffalo Bill was a thespian of limited talent he had a natural showman's ability to make crowds love him. That was enhanced by the strength of his resume. When Cody spoke about the Wild West he brought the voice of authority to his words. He had been there, done that and he was telling it like it was to audiences made up of suit- and dress-wearing members of the public who had never been West of the Mississippi River.

Of course, Cody wasn't telling those naïve crowds what it was really like to have whooping Indians charge at you intent on taking your life, to have bullets whiz past your head, to ride alone over the dusty, uneven ground in search of water. They didn't want to hear that stuff. They ate up the flavor of the West, the legends of the West. Before the Wild West even died out, its candlepower reduced to the flicker of a match, Americans were drinking in the myths of the West.

His personality – he was admired for his honesty – and flamboyant looks, helped him bridge the era of the Wild West to the Old West.

Buffalo Bill Cody was the right man, in the right place, for most of his life.

One day, scout, plains fighter, buffalo hunter Buffalo Bill Cody woke up and he was Buffalo Bill Cody Showman.

In 1893, at the Chicago World's Fair, in a treatise, historian Frederic Jackson Turner released a scholarly paper called "The Significance of the Frontier in American History." In it he proclaimed that the frontier was closed. What this meant was that the Indian wars were over, the western portions of the country were settled, and that the era of the cowboy and gunfighter was past. One could no longer quite so easily quit his job in a big eastern city and find the adventure his soul sought.

Buffalo Bill Cody was already filling the gap between the real Old West he had lived through and the stories of the Old West that he tried to tell in performances across the United States and Europe where he might travel with hundreds of animals and hundreds of cowboys and Indians – yes Indians. Remarkably, the Native Americans Cody had once fought he now gave jobs to in order to re-enact battles and horseback rides they once did for real.

The United States was rushing pell-mell on a path to more thorough industrialization, modernization and was emerging as a world military power. Many believed the cowboy would become extinct as readily as the passenger pigeon. The pigeons didn't make it. The cowboy survived, was revived, and despite being viewed as a relic of a bygone age, even thrived in some corners of the country.

There was something about the cowboy that Americans did not want to cut loose, did not want to bury in history. A cowboy was a symbol of freedom, a symbol of the Wild West territories in those rocky hills, crossing those barren deserts, and always aided by his faithful horse. The cowboy isn't gone, but he has been updated. Mostly, if city dudes want to experience the flavor of the West they take in a rodeo.

"Everyone has this perception that while they are seeing the rodeo shows that it's the Wild West," said Maury Tate, operator of Cody Nite Rodeo in Wyoming for the last decade. "People come here because they want to experience the West, the Wild West. That's why they come to Wyoming."

Eldredge said the myth and the mystique of Buffalo Bill Cody, the Wild West, and places like Cody, Wyoming, remain strong.

"Europeans know Buffalo Bill better than Americans under 40," said Eldredge, who was 62 when he spoke. "In Europe they teach the American West in the schools, and they do it through Buffalo Bill. Europeans know a lot about Buffalo Bill. In Germany they read books about him. It's like 'The Hardy Boys' of our generation. They were essential."

Buffalo Bill sparked this interest when he toured Europe with his Wild West extravaganzas (Cody refused to call them shows) starting in 1883 and basically spanning the last 34 years of his life. Cody's first overseas jaunt began in 1887. European communities where Cody's Wild West played typically have exhibits about those visits in their museums, said Eldredge, who has seen many of them. That nurtured interest in future generations.

"There is a great interest in the West in Europe and Asia," Eldredge said. "Many of them saw the 1950s and 1960s western TV shows. The other thing that attracts Europeans is the mystique of the West's wide open spaces. It's Buffalo Bill, cowboys and Indians, wide open spaces. In the U.S., the gun culture and horse culture never did go away. It's been modified to a focus on rodeo. Buffalo Bill picked it up from ranch hands. He blended and freshened it in his Wild West."

The Wild West performed re-enactments of real famous American events such as Custer's Last Stand (Cody met General George Armstrong Custer) and also melodramatic cowboy and Indian skirmishes. Trick shooting, daredevil riding, stagecoach pursuits, cattle roping, and other skills on display in modern rodeo were all part of the Wild West. Cody wanted to bring his audiences a sense of realism while keeping them enthralled.

Cody's goal was to entertain and educate. The Wild West, which was still, after all, show business, felt more genuine to Cody than the stage productions where he uttered lines written

Buffalo Bill Cody strikes a statesmanlike pose (left). Buffalo Bill reads a copy of the Cody Enterprise, *the newspaper he founded 1899 (photos by Lew Freedman).*

for him by others that might even seem absurd to him. Cody called the Wild West entertainment on "a high toned basis" with his cast filled out by "representations of real life in the far west by the originals themselves." Before the Wild West there had been some Wild West activity as part of P.T. Barnum's touring circus, but Cody said his performances would not "smack of a show or circus."

The Wild West may not have been the circus, but the English synonym that better describes Cody's troupe as being a show has yet to be invented.

However, before Cody toured the world by slow boat and overland train, he made a more specific major contribution to rodeo than just having his riders perform rodeo-type acts within the Wild West. He forever linked his name to the beginnings of modern rodeo.

More often than not the bulls win and throw a cowboy before the 8-second qualifying time is reached (photo by Lew Freedman).

June

OPENING NIGHT

The snorting bulls, up to 2,000 pounds of meanness, indifferent to the name or reputation of any rider who dared to climb upon their broad and muscular backs, cut through the swarm of wannabe dreamers. The cowboys' $25 entry fees announced to the world they believed they could balance atop the beasts for eight seconds. The bulls said no.

Rodeo bull riding is an unholy, unnatural pairing of men with try and will coursing through their veins and hearts with bulls that were born into the sport through sophisticated breeding that trains them to despise anything heavier on their backs than a mosquito.

Eight seconds doesn't sound very long. In bull riding it can be an eternity. It is the demarcation line between success and earning a score and defeat and being blanked. The lithe and wiry men with boldness in their souls climb aboard for a ride that packs more turbulence than an airliner in a thunderstorm.

However long they last they are coping with a different sort of thunder, a bull that stomps and paws the arena dirt, a bull that spins like a top, or a bull that sprints across the grounds, stops on a dime and flips the rider over its head – and only by the grace of god do the tossed riders avoid getting hooked by a knife-sharp horn as they fly by as if hurled out of a third-story window. This is bull riding, cowboys trying to surpass seven-point seconds, versus bull, itching to dump the human as fast as possible. Sometimes the bull attempts to stomp a cowboy lying helpless into the earth.

In the first competition of Cody Nite Rodeo of the 2014 season, the bulls seemed in mid-season form. They didn't need to practice, only react, if one of those dudes nestled his butt onto the bare skin to attempt a qualifying ride.

Just surveying the list of animals chosen to burst out of the gate on opening night, it seemed as if they had been named by someone with a sense of how to instill terror into a potential rider. Among the names sported were Shake N Bake, Shake It, Smack Daddy, Pity Party and Hot Wire. If the cowboys really paid attention to the bull's names their courage may have been shaken. Of course, all would chuckle over the bull named Eat More Chicken, as if that bull had an endorsement contract with Chick fil A.

There were 14 riders of dubious sanity but enormous fortitude who signed up to ride.

Cody's rodeo grounds are situated a few miles west of downtown, on the road to Yellowstone National Park. Just about the absolute, stuff-'em-in capacity is 6,000 folks with standing room. That number is not approached during Cody Nite Rodeo performances, but over the three months of rodeo the crowd is consistently in the 1,200-and-up range.

One by one the bulls tortured the riders. Kyle Osborne, no time. Mark Dorendorf, no time. Cody Culver, no time. On and on it went — bulls in command, tossing humans into the air with a shrug of shoulders, a duck of the head, a thrust of the rear hooves or a dizzying spin move. Down cowboys went, and up they sprang, off-balance, but hustling to escape an ornery bull that might be looking to get in another lick, almost like hitting after the bell in a boxing match.

Thirteen riders did not get to count to eight. Only one, the aptly named Native-American rider Machiah Not Afraid, conquered his bull and the clock. He scored 82 points for the win and helped the entire human race escape embarrassment.

Scores cap out at 100 points. Half a rider's score, if he lasts the eight seconds, is based on his form, and the other half is based on the bull's effort. The rider can control his fate only so much. The bull is in charge, and doesn't give a damn about points and scores and clocks.

Harkening back to its 1930s roots as amateur rodeo, Cody Nite Rodeo does not make a cowboy rich because payouts are limited. The low entry fees — designed to encourage participation — guarantee small purses. For winning an event on a given night, the nightly champ might bank $200 or less. However, the experience a cowboy or cowgirl collects while either pursuing a colorful hobby or as prelude to competition on the pro circuit is priceless.

Bull riding is the last event of the night every night. It is like the main event on a boxing card. By implication it is said these are the heavyweights. Saddle bronc riding is called the classic event of rodeo because the range cowboy was often asked to tame and break wild horses by staying on as long as he could.

Yet bull riding has evolved into the glamour event of the sport, probably helped along by the fact that since 1992 the Professional Bull Riders, Inc. has operated its own series. There is no pro barrel racing league or bareback riding outfit. Famed rodeo cowboy Ty Murray, a champion bull rider, was instrumental in creating the pro circuit. Bull riding carries the whiff of danger and risk, things that apparently appeal to something dark in the hearts and minds of Americans. Murray had the vision to see that some rodeo fans were bullophiles and wouldn't mind skipping what in their minds were preliminary events. The PBR has been a success.

It probably has also weaned many prospective cowboys from bucking horse events because they are convinced riding bulls is manlier and will impress more girls. Not that many contestants say that out loud.

On any given night the dilettantes are difficult to tell apart from dedicated bull riders with a future because the luck of the draw determines the bull assigned. A spectator in the house for the first time – and a huge percentage of Cody Nite Rodeo fans are tourists who may never have seen a rodeo before and may never see one again — can't tell one flailing cowboy in mid-air from another. The test of the long season sorts them out and proves whose mettle should be most rewarded. Check back at the end of August, folks, then you'll know who is for real.

In the meantime, the Cody Nite opener crowd commiserated with the beaten cowboys top to bottom – except Not Afraid, who wasn't. Not Afraid, from Hardin, Montana, adjacent to Crow Indian territory, has been a notable track runner and played football. He used his all-around athleticism to walk away with first prize – and then never returned the rest of the season.

That's Cody Nite Rodeo, too. Sometimes passers-by are the equivalent of ringers. Other cowboys are there for the duration.

Those nasty bulls, though, didn't seem to be going anywhere, except back to their pens beneath the grandstand, their few seconds of work complete.

★★★

The United States is a nation of sub-cultures. What's of paramount importance in your house may not matter one whit to your next-door neighbor. You may live and die with the Alabama Crimson Tide football team, but the guy next door to you may have attended Auburn. People have their passions, sometimes shared by the community at-large. In Cody that unifying passion, the thing more people care about than anything else, is rodeo.

Two nights before opening night of Cody Nite Rodeo 2014, Maury and Nikki Tate,the ones entrusted to make sure the show runs on time, threw a party at the Irma Hotel. In attendance were sponsors, long-time supporters, officials, judges, timers and behind-the-scenes people who make the show tick. Cowboy hats ruled.

Wendy and Casey Coe, married locals, together run a western shirt-making business called Quarter Circle Jug Custom Shirts. Wendy hand-sews shirts and, recognizing that many cowboys are just scraping by, charges the ridiculously low fee of $20 for a colorful shirt.

"These young kids can't afford $50 or so," she said.

Their business is located in the heart of the downtown shopping district on Sheridan Avenue – where they live above their store – and within a 10-yard walk in every direction are shops selling rodeo shirts for much higher prices. The Coes, regulars at Cody Nite Rodeo, were excited about the pending season.

"What's life without rodeo?" Wendy asked rhetorically. "Life is not worth living without rodeo. I have loved the Cody Nite Rodeo my whole life."

The Coes are retired rodeo competitors. Casey is 47, but Wendy will only admit to being "way over 21." They are retired less because they are too old for the grind than because rodeo told them it was time to get out. When asked if she had incurred many injuries, the gabby, but show-no-signs of age Wendy replied, "A lot." She rattled off the big ones so quickly it was hard to keep up with the math. She may have said she broke her right wrist 12 times. She did say, "My left wrist I've only broken five times. My left hip, I only broke it once. I had a torn rotator cuff. Bones don't heal as well as they used to."

Casey spent his younger days in Roseburg, Oregon and around Wyoming. He said he started twirling a rope when he was eight or nine.

"It was part of life," he said. "You grew up in a community where cattle are part of life. You can't just walk up to a cow and say, 'I'm going to brand you.'"

Nope, you had to rope it. Casey's injuries, to his back and head and many other body parts, led to retirement from competition, but not from watching.

It is no accident that many rodeo people limp. They all seem to be unfailingly polite. Even men your own age are likely to call you "sir," never mind the cowboys 30 years younger.

Casey shares his love of rodeo with his Cody neighbors and the cowboys that flood the town in summer. There are many couples in rodeo – cowboys and cowgirls who effected a marriage merger after meeting at the arena. They also raise their little ones to believe in rodeo. However, you don't have to be related to riders to be adopted by the clan.

"A rodeo family is different from any other group of people you meet," Casey said. "Everyone is family."

This was evident amongst some of the low-key revelers at the kick-off party, which seemed as much reunion as introduction to the season because long-time regulars had gone months without seeing one another.

Sid McFarland of Montgomery, Alabama was in the house. He was wearing a shirt that would have done Wendy proud. It had longhorns all over it. McFarland is a rodeo clown, who has worn the greasepaint for so long and been coming to Cody for so long he could fool people into believing he was a contemporary of Buffalo Bill.

"I love coming to Cody," McFarland said.

Maury and Nikki Tate schmoozed with all of the guests. Once the rodeo commences, Maury is the on-site supervisor of the stock. Nikki is more likely to be found in the gift shop peddling souvenir T-shirts and sweatshirts, but she handles

Rodeo operator Maury Tate (finger pointing) talks to some cowboys before the start of a rodeo (photo by Lew Freedman).

arena administration sometimes, too. Their daughters, Cydney (16) and Hadley (13), grew up around rodeo and are part of the operation, helping out in little ways and competing periodically – just not on the bulls. It is very much a Tate team effort, but during the rodeo performances it is Maury out front and the most visible.

Nikki knows the history of Cody Nite Rodeo well. Cody's weather is fickle. It is in an arid climate, but the winds can be disruptive and being surrounded by mountains sometimes there are weird climate deviations from the norm. Occasional postponements might be expected. Not so, Nikki said.

"Practically never," she said, though pulling out one example of what it took to call off a night. "We once got seven inches of snow." In summer, it should be remembered. "Other times there was so much water and mud we feared for the health of the animals."

Just what you need: a rootin'-tootin'-snortin' bull with a pulled hamstring. You treat him, Doc.

Lest anyone think that Nikki exaggerated about a summer snowstorm, Casey Coe said that on July 3, 2002, he remembers the temperature being 85 degrees when he was out selling cotton candy. "The next day, for the Stampede, there was that much snow," he said, spreading his hands about six inches apart, "the great snow on the Fourth of July."

Nikki's and Casey's stories were fascinating meteorological tales, but they were talking about different fluke snowstorms.

★★★

Competitors drive their horse trailers around back of the rodeo grounds to park on a roomy dirt lot. After they check in (having initially signed up by phone), they release their horses from their trailers and let them stretch their legs.

There was a time when Nikki Tate asked entrants to come to her Cody home to sign up. Then it dawned on her she could forward phone calls to her house and do a laundry as she worked.

One early arrival was Dusty Moore, a team and calf roper, who was straightening his hat on his head and saddling his horse. From Douglas on the eastern border of Wyoming, 21-year-old Moore was a college rodeo man who competed for Panhandle State. Since his father managed ranches, Moore had been around cattle his whole life and first swung a rope at age two. Family pictures support the memory.

"Rodeo is something I always wanted to try," Moore said. "Now I rodeo year-round."

In calf roping, the cowboy is on horseback and both he and the calf sprint out of chutes alongside one another: the calf running out of habit, the cowboy in pursuit with a rope circling above his head. The aim is to lasso the calf, secure the other end of the rope on the pommel of the saddle, then dash to the calf, and use shoulder and arm strength to upend it before tying three legs together. And the cowboy must do it as quickly as possible.

While the bulls and bucking horses explode from gates on the near side of the arena, any event involving sprinting horses is begun at a far end, giving the cowboys, horses, and calves maximum room to maneuver.

When Moore travels outside of the West, like any true cowboy he wears his hat. He gets stares and comments such as "'Oh boy, you're a cowboy.' They see the hat and they want to take my picture."

Nearby, another 21-year-old loosened up her horses, Nitra and Badger. Molly Jo Collins is from Alpine, Texas, a town with deep rodeo roots. Collins was in Cody for the duration, working by day, riding in the breakaway roping for women by night. There is plenty of rodeo in Alpine, she said, "but not every night. Cody is a pretty amazing place."

Bryce Bott, 17, from nearby Powell, is a calf roper. His older sister Kooper is also a roper, and his mom Kate rodeoed in high school and college. Bott warmed up by taking throws at a stationary artificial calf. He said he began coming to Cody Nite Rodeo when he was 12 and probably started absorbing rodeo in toddlerhood.

"You use your whole arm," Bott said as he flung a rope. He did not have any complicated plan for the evening. "Hopefully a win."

The scene outside the grandstand on the opposite side of the arena where the public parks, was considerably different. This is where tour buses disgorge visitors in a paved lot adjacent to the box office facing Yellowstone Avenue. A walk-up, one-day ticket costs $25. Tourists often purchase tickets in advance in travel packages. Locals can buy discounted season passes. The price may vary.

One very large, notable attraction out front was Mongo, a 2,000-pound, four-year-old bull. Every night of Cody Nite Rodeo Mongo had a job to do. Mostly it involved standing around looking impressive, but also not throwing a temper tantrum when customers paid $10 to sit on his wide-as-a-Winnebago back. The mere sight of the monstrous Mongo frightened some rodeo goers away. Others pouring in the front gate stopped and stared, fascinated by his girth, demeanor and availability.

As soon as fans' tickets were ripped and they ogled Mongo, they were approached by bull fighters Justin Josey and Zack Flatt, both from Oklahoma uttering the phrase, "Want to sit on the bull?"

Bull fighters have the most dangerous job in rodeo. Dressed in colorful get-ups with clown makeup on their faces, they are life-savers. Bull fighters are like Secret Service agents willing to hurl their bodies in the face of danger to rescue a cowboy. They are the human shields between angry bulls and thrown riders and bucking broncos and their victims. When riders go splat they are not really prepared to defend themselves against a blind attack. Bull fighters step in.

A father and daughter from France get into rodeo spirit by sitting on 2,000-pound bull Mongo (photo by Lew Freedman).

Flatt and Josey hung with Mongo as salesmen. Flatt estimated that between 10 and 25 people a night paid up to sit on docile Mongo. Where else can a cowboy wannabe take a picture on a 2,000 pound bull at so little risk?

Mongo resembled a 300-pound football lineman who is a gentle soul off the field. Mongo was bottle fed and has no grudge against people. Mothers and babies, teens and senior citizens, brothers and sisters, two at a time, sat astride Mongo's very broad back. Mongo believed in economy of motion. The tethered Mongo stood in his spot an hour at a time and only barely moved. Once in a great, great while he shrugged his head. Sometimes he unblushingly went to the bathroom on the spot, or he drooled, but those seemed more like involuntary activities than anything else. One Mongo quirk is a liking for lollipops.

Among the very first Mongo sitters of the year were 28-year-old Chicago resident Kelly Barichello and her father Sylvan, who was visiting her from France. Instead of taking an elevator to the top of the Sears Tower, they followed Horace Greeley's advice and went West. Growing up in France, Kelly Barichello said they learned all about the Old West in school. "It is one of the first things I think of when I think of the United States," she said.

These two average-sized adults climbed on Mongo together. Mongo never twitched.

"I was very scared," Kelly said of the perhaps minute-long up-close-and-personal visit with Mongo.

Yes, it was their first rodeo. That was true of many customers from foreign countries. However, many of the American tourists said they had long wanted to attend a rodeo, but hadn't made it until now. A woman named Sally from Washington, D.C., offered a sage observation, "There's some cowboy in all of us."

Also welcoming spectators onto the grounds were clowns Sid McFarland and Tony Martoglio. It was a two-clown special. Sid and Tony, in their 60s, have been pals for nearly 40 years. Neither works full-time on the rodeo circuit anymore and only occasionally do they share a show. With their gaudy clown costumes they were a sight and a delight. Fan after fan asked to pose for pictures with the Bozo-like duo.

Sid asked where they were from. He kept a running tally, writing state names and country names on his hand with a Sharpie, and then put the information to show-business use later.

★★★

That first Buffalo Bill Cody-instigated rodeo that took place in North Platte, Nebraska occurred on the Fourth of July, July 4, 1882.

Looking back, the rodeo cowboy of 2014 would say, "That figures."

No day on the calendar is more red, white and blue than July 4, the nation's birthday and no sport in the United States is more patriotic than rodeo. It is likewise probably no accident that the week of July 4, highlighted by the day of July 4, (excluding National Finals Rodeo days in December), is the biggest holiday on the calendar for the rodeo cowboy.

July 4 and the days surrounding it during the hot and dusty summer, is ironically referred to as "Cowboy Christmas." The calendar is stuffed with major rodeos with the Cody Stampede ranking right up near the top in importance and payouts.

Cowboy Christmas may come just once a year, but cowboy patriotism is a year-round thing. You can't go near a rodeo anywhere, anytime, without flags-a-wavin', red, white and blue décor smacking you in the face, the National Anthem playing, and maybe some other patriotic tunes, too.

Wyoming is a conservative state politically and it wears red, white and blue all of the time. So it is no surprise, not in any way out of kilter, that Cody Nite Rodeo is as much of a patriotic convention as it is spectator sport, the site of as much heavy-duty flag waving as anyplace you can visit on Flag Day.

Although the Cowgirl Up Rodeo Drill Team gets a couple of nights a week off, on most nights the show doesn't begin in the arena until the red, white and blue-clad local girls bound into the grounds in perfect formation, each carrying an American flag trailing in the breeze in precise time to a patriotic song, sometimes Neil Diamond's "Coming to America." It is a slick production that concludes with one rider sitting astride a horse in the middle of the arena holding one flag tall as the Star-Spangled Banner plays.

The Cowgirl Up squad started in 2011 and participation has been as high as 18 riders, though the number of riders varies. It may be tougher than the rest of the world thinks to find appropriately fitted, red, white and blue sequined outfits.

Sometimes a bareback horse has already been loaded into a pen for one of the first riders of the night and it kicks and bangs hard hooves against hard slats. The kicking is never in rhythm with the song, always a smack, smack, smack in the horse's own time.

The master of ceremonies/public address announcer sets some of the patriotic tone, commentary in alignment with the visual production and the flags galore.

"People can't believe how patriotic Cody Nite Rodeo is," said Kade Rogge, who began the season as the man on the microphone. "That's cowboys. That's our mentality. Americans want a hero, especially right now and I think cowboys can be that hero."

In addition to John Wayne and his swagger on display in myriad movies, literature has played a part in the making of the cowboy as hero. Owen Wister's esteemed novel, "The

Virginian," released in 1902, and set in the rugged corners of pre-turn-of-the-century Wyoming, has served as the prototype offering of the rugged, do-right, individual western man of the period.

The wonderfully crafted book is considered the true classic western novel, and fans of the Old West see many of the elements, from reluctant gunfights, to romantic aspects, in "The Virginian" that they saw in future books and movie plots. As this honorable gent contends with the circumstances he is thrust into – naturally he doesn't seek out trouble, but is ready when it comes to him – it is easy to see how this Virginian became the Everyman good-guy cowboy. He was the man with no name decades before Clint Eastwood was the man with no name in the movies.

Maybe it is so, as Rogge said, that the modern rodeo fan remains hungry for heroes of any sort, but not a night goes by when Cody Nite Rodeo fails to recognize veterans in attendance with some applause. That certainly acknowledges that those in the nation's armed forces risking their lives are bigger heroes.

But for everyday life, cowboys will do, and the cowboy as good guy dates back more than a century, so at the least the cowboy is on a long winning streak.

"I think that cowboy mystique is still pretty strong," Rogge said. "I really do. Kids still dress up for Halloween as cowboys. I think the cowboy was the pioneer superstar."

Besides the National Anthem, other patriotic songs may bust out over the loudspeakers, from "God Bless America," to "God Bless the USA."

While it was probably true that cowboys always bled red, white and blue, it wasn't really until post-World War II that rodeo events per se became so rooted in patriotism. Concurrent with the rise of rodeo on the national scene and its increased exposure, rodeo became increasingly patriotic. Heck, if the National Finals Rodeo wasn't held indoors at the Thomas & Mack Center in Las Vegas, there would probably be a jet flyover.

Recently, a story posted on the NFR Insider for the National Finals Rodeo, addressed the connection between rodeo and patriotism, reading in part, "A person would be hard-pressed to find a more patriotic group than the world of ProRodeo. From fans, contestants and personnel, to sponsors, administration and organizers, patriotism runs strong through the Western world and the professional rodeo industry."

Wrangler, the western wear clothing manufacturer, is the title sponsor of the NFR, but it also oversees the Wrangler National Patriot Program which since 2009 has raised many hundreds of thousands of dollars for soldiers in need and their families. World bareback riding champion Kaycee Feild is the front man-cowboy for the program and has traveled the world visiting with active duty soldiers, almost like a one-man USO program.

So Cody Nite Rodeo being invested in patriotic themes is merely being consistent with rodeo on a national scale. The cowboys at Cody Nite do everything but salute just before busting out of their gates.

It didn't take very long into the action on opening night for Sid McFarland, the clown, to inform spectators what was expected of them as cowboys roared out of the chutes on half-crazed horses and on fired-up bulls.

He explained that he would help them identify extra special rides and even if their novice eyes did not readily let them know what they were seeing, a top-notch moment should not pass unremarked upon. This is especially important in rodeo because sometimes the athletes walk or limp out of the arena with nothing but applause as their reward. If a cowboy doesn't make eight seconds on the back of a bounding beast he cannot record a score and that means he is not going to win any money. Zilch. There is no such thing as appearance money in rodeo. You come, you pay your entry fee, you conquer, or you strike out. Rodeo entrants pay to play. They must earn every cent.

"We like audience participation," McFarland declared. The point being, even if he had to lead the fans, McFarland made sure a cowboy at the very least got a hand. At McFarland's signal and employing his signature phrase, "And the crowd goes wild!" Sid pumped up the volume. About that foot stomping – the pounding of feet on the grandstand, Sid said, is called "Wyoming Thunder." That is not to be confused with anything somebody smokes, the recent legalization of marijuana for personal use in Colorado just over the border notwithstanding.

Bareback riding was first and it didn't even take eight seconds for a cowboy to get in trouble. When the bronc flung him his hand caught in the rope, so he was left dangling on the side of the horse while being dragged. A few seconds longer and he would be a more urgent candidate for Tommy John surgery than any baseball pitcher. Bull fighters Zack Flatt and Justin Josey dove in and helped free the hapless rider and as soon as he was clear a representative of the Yellowstone Sports Clinic provided aid.

The cowboy was OK. His shoulder was still attached at the hinges. But his mishap was the first and an immediate reminder that rodeo is not a kind and gentle sport. It is a sport – especially the bareback and saddle bronc riding and bull riding – for young men with large cajones. Football players have it easy compared to rodeo riders. Never a night goes by in the long season when a cowboy doesn't limp or crawl off the stage. And if medics are keeping score, it is rare that someone doesn't demand major assistance. The body can only take so much jouncing and rodeo cowboys test that threshold every night.

Dusty Moore, Mr. Panhandle State, was last out in the tie-down roping. A squirrelly calf burst out of the starting gate and headed pell-mell the length of the arena as Moore and his horse erupted from a parallel gate. As Moore sought to run down the calf he had his lasso twirling above him. Moore's aim was dead on. He looped the rope over the calf's head, pulled the rope taut, and the calf came to a halt. Moore leapt from his horse, heaved the calf on its side and tied three legs together. Tick, tick, tick, tick. Bummer, the calf broke free, erasing Moore's slick six-second clocking.

It is not easy to rope a sprinting steer while balancing on a galloping horse and throwing a rope, and not all that many people in 21st century America do it for either a living or sport.

During a lull in the action Sid the Clown read his hand, the notes he took at the front gate as fans filed in. "Where are the people from Germany?" he yelled. A pocket of fans yelled back. He ran through France, England, New Zealand and other lands far, far away. "Where are the people from California?" Those fans took their turn shouting. "Welcome to America," McFarland said.

In Wyoming, people from California are sometimes viewed as being from another planet, never mind another state.

Young Bryce Bott's turn came up in the tie-down roping and his time was 14.0 seconds. Not great, but not bad, on this night not good enough to win, but good enough to place in the top three. Reminding the spectators that Bott was just 17 and still in high school, Rogge said, "If you've come to see the rising stars, you've come to the right place. We've waited all winter for this."

The next event in the show was breakaway roping. It is a women's event not contested on the pro circuit. Breakaway roping is similar to tie-down calf roping without the tie-down. Riders and calves come out of the gates. But when the rope loops around the animal's head it then breaks free. That's when the clock stops. The women are not asked to climb down from their horses, tip over the calves, and tie the legs.

"This is the most dangerous event in rodeo," Sid the Clown announced at risk to his health with his old-fashioned humor. "It's full of women drivers." Men laughed and women booed.

Molly Jo Collins got her chance to break the ice early. She was the first one out in the breakaway roping. She guided her horse, pulled close, let fly with the rope and gloomily watched the calf shrug it off. No score.

A notable in saddle bronc riding was Colt Chlarson. A New Mexico rider who in 2013 broke his leg in the arena, Chlarson missed a chunk of the season, yet rallied to finish third overall in the point standings. A red head who wore thick glasses (not a common sight in the rodeo crowd) and a distinctive black cowboy hat with a feather stuck in it, Chlarson was brash by nature, but harmless brash, not offensive brash. He gave off the vibe of enjoying life every minute he was awake and of being slightly annoyed that he had to slow down to sleep once in a while.

When people sum up cowboys with commitment to rodeo, who are not touring on the pro circuit, and who are accepting minor-league payouts in exchange for experience, Chlarson is

An artistic view of saddle bronc rider Colt Chlarson at Cody Nite Rodeo (photo by Lew Freedman).

one of the guys who come up on that Facebook page. He was scrimping on expenditures with such fervor that he and a couple of cowboy pals were living in tents at one far corner of the back parking lot. The Hilton it was not.

Chlarson began this season the right way. Although his score of 69 on a scale of 100 wasn't very high, he won the first night's rodeo.

Another competitor in saddle bronc, 16-year-old Grady Eckley, wasn't as fortunate. He was thrown by a horse named Rooster and when he popped up from the ground he was holding his arm. It appeared Rooster's wake-up call was stomping on Eckley's arm. It was pretty much a one-and-done season for Eckley.

Even though it was June and the longest day of the year was on the horizon in three weeks, the lights were turned on for Nite Rodeo. That was prescient. A few events into the performance the sky darkened and the wind whipped in over the top of nearby Cedar Mountain. Rain began falling. Luckily it lasted only 20 minutes.

In-between events Sid kept the atmosphere lively. That's what rodeo clowns do. They make sure there is no down time, that there are no dead spots in the show, if it is taking a few extra minutes for a cowboy to prepare his horse or the livestock to be readied. Clowns must have deep repertoires and be able to wing jokes or stories off the cuff. McFarland asked how many fans were at their first rodeo and many hands went up in the air.

A few minutes later, filling time, McFarland took control of the air waves from Rogge again. "My wife lost 35 pounds in one day," he said. "She shaved her legs." Some laughter. "Do you know the difference between Congress and Hollywood?" he asked. "Hollywood only has Three Stooges." Much more laughter. Congress' approval ratings are below sexist jokes apparently.

McFarland's got a million of 'em. He has a storehouse of one-liners that pre-date the Carter Administration, can be a little hokey and are not far removed from vaudeville.

Barrel racing was a chance for the women to shine. Only there was a twist to the event where horses sprint around three red, white and blue 55-gallon drums disguised as barrels. One of the best around was a 12-year-old Cody girl named Anna Allshouse. To encourage youngsters to compete, one nightly event is junior barrel racing, for girls 12-and-under. But Allshouse is precocious in her abilities. So while still eligible for the juniors, which she also regularly entered, she went head-to-head with adults, too.

"She knows what she's doing in the saddle," gushed Rogge. "Just one look tells you that." Allshouse's uncle Larry, who sometimes roped, said, "She grew up on a horse."

The three barrels were placed around the arena, just far enough out of the starting chute for a horse to work up a good head of steam. At a barrel, riders must rein in, steer the horse around while ratcheting down the speed, much like braking a car on a turn, then let the horse loose to cross the arena sideways, rein in again, and then guide the horse to the far end of the arena to circle the third barrel. After that it is an all-out sprint to the finish.

Horses must be savvy enough to get the picture while not being spooked by the sight of barrels seemingly in their path – a hazard with a young or inexperienced horse. The rider must be one with the horse, communicating the need for speed and the need for caution at the right moments. From afar barrel racing doesn't look hard, but it is the sum of several moving parts and the smoothness of the run against the clock proves it is much more challenging than a casual fan might believe.

Allshouse made the first race of the season a statement race – she was going to be a factor in the ladies division. Her time of 17.38 seconds gave her the nightly victory. Second place went to Hadley Tate, the boss' daughter, who was only 13, in 17.64. In this sport, every tiny mistake made is costly on the clock.

Entrants in junior barrels run almost the same course but the barrels are moved in slightly to make it a little bit shorter. Allshouse won that race, too, in 16.90.

Those rip-roaring bulls had their moment as the grand finale. Sometimes, as a distraction, a dummy is set up in the middle of the arena in the hopes a ticked-off bull takes out his fury on a cloth replica sacrifice in place of a human body. Sometimes bulls run right past those dummies and sometimes they hit them full blast like J.J. Watt sacking the quarterback. A bull named Smack Daddy smacked this dummy and sent it soaring.

Shake N' Bake's rider lasted about one second aboard. "Unridden is Shake N' Bake and he's proud of it," Rogge said.

The bull named Blind Side did blind side rider Cody Culver, who was swiftly tossed.

"Look at that animal!" said Rogge. "Two thousand pounds of fear and intimidation!"

The thorough decimation of the riding corps by the bulls made one wonder if anyone would ever pay to sit on Mongo's back after a rodeo. Those fans probably would have fear and intimidation coursing through their veins.

Wendy and Casey Coe, those rodeo super-fans, were indeed in the house for opening night and quite satisfied by the exhibition.

"It's rodeo and it starts my summer off perfectly," Wendy said.

★★★

GUNFIRE IS A GOOD THING

There aren't many modern towns in the United States where gunfire attracts people rather than repels them.

Cody is one of them, at least in summer. Cody may be the rodeo capital of the world, but it classifies as a western town in other ways, too.

Buffalo Bill Cody is not identified with gunfighters of the 19th century, except those he met or befriended. He was a Civil War fighter, an Indian fighter, a cavalry scout, and a buffalo hunter, but he was no quick-draw artist.

Still, as part of the "Wild West" and heavily invested in the Buffalo Bill Cody mythmaking business, the community of Cody strives to keep alive the American West of legend. Since one can hardly rely on gunfighters with genuine grudges to stalk one another on Sheridan Avenue at high noon, the populace is blessed with a team of faux gunfighters to take up the slack.

The Cody Gunfighters were birthed in 1996 as entertainment for the annual Buffalo Bill Ball. But rather than become a one-time-only extravaganza, the Cody Gunfighters have been expending ammunition ever since, Monday through Saturday during the summer months on a blocked-off street adjacent to the Irma Hotel.

The Gunfighters don't shoot anybody on Sundays. That's their code of the West.

Don Bash, 60, is the leader of the pack. Bash, has spent 25 years as a re-enactor in various places, a good portion of the time as Wyatt Earp. "Everybody says I look like him when I dress like him," Bash said.

However, he plays Wild Bill Hickok with the Gunfighters, and he has that mustache that fits the character. Bash has lived in Cody for seven years and joined the Cody Gunfighters right away. His background is that of many American males of his era. As a youth, he was deeply immersed in the golden era of cowboy television, when shows like "Maverick," "Have Gun Will Travel" and "Rawhide" ruled the airwaves. He did not always have a special role in the melodramatic skit that plays out for tourists.

As a Cody newcomer Bash originally had to be a desperado in the skit, but now he gets to be a hero. "I was one of the bad guys," he said. "I put in my time."

The show runs about forty minutes. That leaves the crowd plenty of time to be bussed across town to rodeo. Seats are only $2 and the money goes to charity. It's also possible to stand behind the crowd and watch for free. Cast members sell posters of themselves in character for $3, again with proceeds going to charity.

In 2013, the Gunfighters were actually Buffalo Bill-less, which is pretty much unforgivable in Cody. The new 2014 Buffalo Bill was Roger Harrell, 52. He had the proper wavy Buffalo Bill hair, the proper Buffalo Bill mustache and goatee, and the proper buckskin jacket. He was definitely a reasonable facsimile of Buffalo Bill at a similar age.

Some basic elements of the skit stay the same each year, but not all. The name of the 2014 skit was "End of the Trail." It didn't take a genius to ferret out the likelihood that the end of the trail was going to apply to some unlucky soul. Each evening cast members hauled false front buildings onto the street, a saloon with tables and chairs, a bank, and a jail, which did have a door.

A couple of hundred fans lined the street to obtain a glimpse of the cowboys and cowgirls. Characters included Wild Bill Hickok, Buffalo Bill, Wyatt Earp, Johnny Ringo, Butch Cassidy, the Sundance Kid, Calamity Jane, Belle Star, Fifi Larue, Doc Holliday, and Little Britches. A few members of the cast were slightly more anonymous or made do with made-up names.

Wild Bill Hickok, Bash, acted as master of ceremonies.

"We're going to blow off a bunch of gun powder and have some fun," he announced. As a hint that this play would take on overtones that somewhat shy of Broadway drama, Wild Bill provided instruction. "When you see a bad guy we want

Six nights a week in summer the Cody Gunfighters stage a melodrama with actors impersonating real-life Old West characters. Left is Don Bash as Wild Bill Hickok and right is Roger Harrell as Buffalo Bill Cody (photo by Lew Freedman).

you to boo and when you see a good guy we want you to cheer. Butch, Sundance and Johnny Ringo, they're bad. Rotten."

Spectators jumped at the 6 p.m. firing of a shotgun. Essentially, it was the starting gun, as in a track meet. However, there was also a demonstration for the benefit of youngsters in the audience, accompanied by a short lecture on gun safety. The heavily armed participants all shot blanks, but blanks sound like the real deal and they are not as innocent as movie western fans think.

Johnny Ringo placed a soda can on the ground and stepped back a few yards. He aimed and fired and it turns out that blanks can still blow a hole in aluminum cans and send it flying 15 yards.

The show was campy, with dialogue definitely not written by Eugene O'Neill. The style and general outlook of the show was old-fashioned and family-oriented and might well have been something acted out onstage in the 1800s.

Johnny Ringo shot the Sundance Kid in the butt. As Sundance lay "wounded" in the street, out ran Dr. Feelgood, carrying his black bag, ready to perform surgical magic if necessary. He asked the patient, "Did you sign up for Obamacare? Do you have any insurance at all?"

Like so many other Americans, Sundance was uninsured. Doc seemed preprared to give the patient a gulp of whiskey to kill pain, but instead he drank from the bottle. Then the good doctor withdrew a pair of pliers to perform the operation.

Out of nowhere, diverging from the plot, such as it was, a cast member yelled, "Photo op!" All players leapt to their feet, formed a line and smiled for tourists wishing to snap pictures. A few clicks and everyone returned to his role, including any previously dead or wounded characters.

The bad guys crossed the line of badness and Wild Bill, Buffalo Bill and Wyatt Earp rescued monies stolen from the bank and damsels in distress. Plugged by sharp shooting, the bad guys dropped to the pavement and lay still. Swiftly, several females in the cast, including the aptly named Bandit Queen, raced to the bodies and rifled their pockets. Wild Bill asked what they were doing. "Shopping!" shouted the Bandit Queen.

The End. As the show concluded, the actors once again lined up for photo opportunities.

Bash said he had probably participated in 1,600 re-enactment shows in a variety of locations. He grew up in Topeka, Kansas and lived in Southern California. Besides Wild Bill in Cody he had played Doc Pain, (presumably the opposite number of Doc Feelgood), a crazy sheriff, and Ike Clanton (one of those bad guys).

"It's a blast," Bash said. "You get to meet people from all over the world. We try to mix it up. I'll do an outlaw once in a while." Bash is also a member of the Single Action Shooting Society, in which scenes are staged, individuals have their own "handle" and shoot-'em-ups take place on weekends. Doc Pain originated with SASS. "I have a lot of books on gunfighters. There's a lot of research that goes into it." He's even been an extra in western documentaries and visited high schools to speak about the Old West.

The gunfighters made their own movie, Bash said, called *The Life and Times of Calamity Jane*. The rookie Calamity had a lot to live up to. Among four new actors in 2014 was the woman playing Calamity Jane.

Bash thinks Harrell is the sixth Buffalo Bill. One of Harrell's predecessors joined the real Buffalo Bill in the hereafter. Bash said the guy looked exactly like Buffalo Bill and was pretty much Cody's official Buffalo Bill for years. Although this sounded a little like one of those western tall tales, Bash said that Buffalo Bill so resembled the genuine article he was banned from a Buffalo Bill Cody lookalike contest in Colorado.

It should be noted, he said, that the gunfighters once had a Calamity Jane who was the spitting image of the real Calamity Jane, too. However, there are not nearly as many historical photographs of Calamity Jane as there are of Buffalo Bill. Buffalo Bill was neither camera shy nor a recluse and after his early years he was in the public eye so much, in so many ways, for so long, that there are multitudes of Buffalo Bill photos.

Calamity Jane — whose real name was Martha Jane Canary — was born in 1852. She was friends with Wild Bill Hickok, fought Indians, was a frontierswoman, and lived until 1903.

She had her own photo ops, but Cody got around much more, performing before millions during his showman career.

Even more remarkable than the gunfighters' show is the Old Trail Town exhibit virtually next-door to the rodeo grounds.

Old Trail Town never existed as an entity, was never part of Cody as a neighborhood, but represents the passion of one man, who essentially created a mini western town out of whole cloth on a two-acre parcel of land. While Old Trail Town was not a real trail town, it is also not fictional.

The late Bob Edgar hauled in the old-time buildings from all over the West and planted them on the site. The cabins, saloons, furniture, old wagons, a hearse, animal heads of harvested beasts, and old stores, all date to the 19th century and are evidence of the way it really was.

Inside those 22 buildings, connected by boardwalks, are artifacts of the period. Curley's Cabin features a picture of General George Armstrong Custer on the wall. There are rifles, photos, old clothing, copies of Harper's Weekly and Indian beads. The Henry Rivers Saloon door, circa 1888, has bullet holes in it, proof of just how dangerous getting a drink could be in the past. Crack shot Edgar also took shots at bar walls and ceilings and performed such sorcery as shooting cards out of the hands of willing victims.

There are mentions of Butch Cassidy and the Sundance Kid, popularized by the movie of the same name that starred Paul Newman and Robert Redford. The Hole in the Wall hideout talked about in the film was in Kaycee, Wyoming and a building from there was relocated to Old Trail Town. Butch and Sundance also hid out in Red Lodge, Montana, 75 miles north of Cody.

Edgar died at 72 in 2012, but during his life he was an historian, archeologist, author, naturalist and sure shot. He was born near Powell, about 25 miles from Old Trail Town, and grew up in Cody. He also owned a cabin in nearby Meeteetse. Photographs of Edgar when he is not wearing a cowboy hat are at a premium. Famed western artist James Bama, who lives in Cody, painted Edgar more than once. Edgar

Another western attraction in Cody is Old Trail Town (above), with buildings from the 1800s hauled to the site and erected.

The namesake character in the movie Jeremiah Johnson *had his remains transferred to Old Trail Town. When he was reburied, actor Robert Redford, who played Johnson in the film, acted as a pall bearer.*

Photos by Lew Freedman.

wore a beard and it was still black in most Bama portrayals, though gray before he passed away.

While some might think that transporting buildings intact to the site (which is a museum open to the public) was challenge enough, Edgar also became invested in moving bodies. Before he died he had a little cemetery going adjacent to his town.

While there are bronze tribute statues to mountain men such as Jim Bridger and John Colter, the cemetery is notable for at those at rest, particularly the Jeremiah Johnson played by Robert Redford in the movies. The movie Johnson's real name was John Johnston and his nickname was John "Liver-Eating" Johnston. Johnston was a mountain man, although he also scouted for the U.S. Army.

The "Liver-Eating" appellation stemmed from a minor battle with some Blackfeet Indians in the 1860s or 1870s, Edgar said. Johnston ended up in hand-to-hand combat with one warrior, rolled down a hill, broke his leg, and then crawled back to the other men with blood dripping from his knife. He told the others that it was "Indian liver" and asked if they wanted a bite, according to Edgar. The veracity of the tale is in question.

Amongst western movie aficionados, "Jeremiah Johnson" is a favorite. It was released in 1972 and remains popular with the rental crowd. The real Johnston, who spent much of his life in Montana and the Rocky Mountains, lived his last years in an Old Soldiers Home in Lancaster, California and when he died in 1900 he was buried in a veteran's cemetery in Los Angeles.

Following the release of the movie, a teacher and a class of 25 seventh-graders in California campaigned to move Johnston's body away from the hubbub of Southern California traffic to the region where he had been most active.

Edgar responded and soon after Johnston was disinterred and his body shipped by train to Cody, although it was misplaced along the way for a couple of days. "We finally got him back OK," Edgar said. A new coffin was made for Johnston's remains.

When Johnston was reburied in June of 1974, Redford was on hand and served as a pallbearer in the service. Edgar estimated that about 400 people turned out for the event, a ceremony he called touching. Another estimate put the crowd size at 2,000.

Later, sculptor Peter Fillerup created a bronze statue over the grave that shows Johnston riding a horse and waving a rifle above his head.

William Garlow Cody, Buffalo Bill's last surviving grandson, was born in North Platte, Nebraska at Scout's Rest ranch, but later became an attorney in Cody after graduating from Harvard Law School. In Cody he founded a radio station that is still going strong today. He died in 1992 and had his ashes spread at Old Trail Town and a headstone there memorializes his life.

This Bill Cody was actually born Garlow. His mother was Buffalo Bill's daughter Irma, for whom the famed Irma Hotel in Cody is named. However, she died in the flu epidemic of 1918, as did his father, and this young Bill was partially raised by his grandmother Louise, Buffalo Bill's wife, until she, too passed away when he was nine. Later in life Garlow was approached to endorse Daisy Air Rifles because of his Buffalo Bill connection and the company insisted he legally change his name to Cody. He did so, though at one point he said for all he knew it had already been changed as a youth when his grandmother took him in.

After Johnston was buried at Old Trail Town, Edgar either heard about or was informed about some other old scouts, trappers and buffalo hunters who had once roamed the region and whose graves were forgotten or in danger of falling into disrepair. So others' bodies were transferred to Cody. One was a scout named Jack Stillwell, who at one time had been a friend of Buffalo Bill Cody's in North Platte, and who later was a caretaker for Cody's home in Cody. Although Stillwell died and was buried in Cody, it was not well-known.

"He didn't even have a headstone," Edgar said a few years ago.

He does now.

Edgar was cremated and his ashes were spread at various places of import during his life, but some were reserved for Old Trail Town.

A rodeo fan at the Cody Nite grounds training a good pair of binoculars to the East can see Old Trail Town from the grandstand and the headstones and sculptures of the western figures of the past without ever moving from his seat.

★★★

BRONCO ANDY AND BRONCO COLT

Clown Sid McFarland took center stage on the dirt for a moment and welcomed the Cody Nite Rodeo crowd with a bellowing, "Cody, Wyoming, where the pavement ends and the West begins!"

Nice slogan, especially as the West is what the spectators crave.

Andy Mumm was a Cody Nite Rodeo fixture. In 2012, he won the bareback riding championship. In 2013, he was the runner-up. At only 25 he was thinking about a long future as a pro rodeo cowboy, life after Cody Nite preparation.

Mumm has black hair, blue eyes and regularly wore a green and black shirt that was one of Wendy Coe's custom creations. His thick mustache would have fit right in with the Cody Gunfighters. Mumm, from nearby Powell, was accompanied by wife Sarah, and two-year-old D.J., a little bruiser who seemed to possess more energy than any of those rough horses dad rode. He was on the go constantly and if not watched vigilantly he might well have made it into the arena through the competitors' door. D.J. might not yet understand the nuances of the sport, but he did know that wearing a cowboy hat had to be part of his costume. When Mom confiscated the hat as punishment for renegade behavior, D.J. threw a tantrum. Otherwise D.J. was the most adorable cowboy behind the chutes.

Mumm had been riding horses for six years. He had tried bulls but had given them up.

"I just got bored with bulls," Mumm said. "They come and spin. They're vicious. They want you off their backs so they can stomp you. Horses, they mostly kick."

Bulls do give off a more menacing appearance. It runs in that family of animals. Their facial expressions are perpetual scowls. The wonderful long-gone newspaper columnist and novelist Robert Ruark, who wrote brilliantly about an African safari, once summarized the look of a Cape buffalo as being a beast that always looks at you as if you stole his lunch money. Rodeo bulls look just as skeptical.

Mumm gripped the bareback rope with his right hand and when the gate opened he was atop Spring Flame, hoping for eight seconds and an official score. He got it, riding the kicking and bucking horse long enough for 73 points. That was the winning total that night, and while Mumm did not exactly clean up – he won $140 – victory was a good omen.

"My ride was flying by the seat of my pants," Mumm said. "On the fourth or fifth jump he straightened out. You don't think about what a horse is going to do. You put your mind on blank."

Andy Mumm shows this horse who is boss (photo by Lew Freedman).

A few minutes after the horn sounded signaling a good ride, Mumm dismounted with the aid of two galloping pick-up men easing him off Spring Flame. Mumm walked off the dirt and held out his right arm for inspection. It was still shaking from the adrenalin of the ride.

"The arm's there for balance," Mumm said. "Our true lift is in our hips." Mumm has ridden enough bareback horses to know that the cowboy doesn't always come out on top and sometimes the cowboy can't even walk off without assistance. He has broken ribs, dislocated shoulders and broken an ankle.

"There's thirty grand worth of titanium sitting in my right ankle," he said.

Mumm must be a hoot to be around when he steps through airport metal detectors. On the other hand, a nightly win total of $140 doesn't pay for a plane ticket to anywhere of great distance on the United Airlines route map, one of the small number of airlines that serves Cody.

Most cowboys drive their own cars or ride together in groups in pick-up trucks to other rodeos several hours away. Mumm is one guy who makes quickie rodeo appearances in Montana or farther west in Wyoming. Typically, these cowboys don't even stick around for the entire rodeo. They ride and "as soon as we get off our horses, we're gone." That's because they face another four-hour ride home. When you are banking small Cody Nite payouts it makes more sense to get back on the road than to bunk in a hotel.

"We actually pay to get in here," Mumm said, halfway laughing about low-income cowboys. "Fun. That's the only reason we're here. This is our style of life."

Big Bryce Bott, who has as much beef on him as the calf he chases with a rope, won the tie-down roping and collected $180 for his triumph. Prize money is not equal. It matters how many entrants there are in each category.

"I didn't throw the most beautiful toss," Bott said of his roping victory. "I got to the calf, jerked him down how I like it and tied him. The calf kicked, but I just kept moving."

There are two kinds of rowdy bucking horses in rodeo. There are Andy Mumm's kind in bareback competition, and there are Colt Chlarson's kind in saddle bronc riding. Chlarson says he is from New Mexico and Arizona and been riding horses on ranches since he was a little kid.

Recognizing that many Cody Nite Rodeo competitors are cash poor and can't live luxuriously in town during the height of the tourist season, Maury and Nikki Tate provide some options. Some season-long cowboys roll in with their own RVs. But there is also a concrete-block-wall bunkhouse which can hold a handful of stayers and in 2013 Chlarson lived there.

"I showed up with $50 and a broke-down pick-up truck," he said.

In 2014, his season-long home was a tent at the far end of the parking lot, an even less-glamorous housing choice. Chlarson oozes confidence, but there is no such thing as a bullet-proof cowboy and he knows that, too. Five days into the 2013 season he broke his leg riding and "tore the heck out of my ankle." He sat out a couple of weeks, which probably wasn't long enough to really heal, and returned to nightly action. Chlarson wore tape on his wrists, wore a vest, shin guards of a sort, and knee braces. The protection just may have been holding his body together.

Well aware that he was going to get thrown some nights Chlarson said he tries to immediately put failed rides behind him.

"Hell, it happens," he said. "I just shake it off. It's always the next one. Some nights it's a steak dinner and some nights it's not."

Chlarson has been a working ranch cowboy and has tried bull riding and team calf roping, but saddle bronc riding is his niche. Or maybe the appeal is just being able to still say he is a cowboy in the year 2014 when so few Americans can make that claim. Chlarson wears his hat around town and when he travels. He holds up his blue jeans with a belt buckle earned somewhere. On this particular night he showed off an award for the "Shoshone Labor Day Wyoming Rodeo Saddle Bronc" title of 2013.

"I get weird looks all of the time," Chlarson said of traveling in non-cowboy company. "Mostly the people seem to like it. I think the cowboy lifestyle is still revered. 'It's awesome. It's fantastic.' That's what people think."

It is also Colt Chlarson's identity. He is not a college student. He is not an accountant. He is not a guy who occupies a desk 9-to-5.

"I'm a cowboy," he said.

Chlarson is that from the boots covering his toes to the hat covering his head.

★★★

COLEMAN WHITE

At the age of 53 Coleman White was a season-long Cody Nite Rodeo joke, one that was OK to listen to if you were a one-night-only fan, but which could wear you down if you were a nightly regular — or if you were Coleman White.

Lucky for him, each time the master of ceremonies on the microphone reminded the 1,200 in the grandstands that White was old enough to be a member of the AARP (the American Association of Retired People), he was too busy to listen.

That's because he was prepping for his nightly event, an appearance in the tie-down calf roping. White was there for the summer and that meant that although the jokes were spouted about 90 times, his mind was on business.

White started roping when he was 16, but he wasn't always a rodeo traveler. He grew up on a ranch owned by his mother's family near Fort Worth, Texas. In competition, just about every night he wore a black hat, a blue shirt and blue jeans, almost as a uniform. Tall and lean and with a few weather-beaten lines in his face he fit the basic description of a cowboy as perpetuated by innumerable extras in movies.

"My heritage is ranching," White said.

And when he wasn't ranching he worked in carpentry.

For years White also dabbled in rodeo around Fort Worth, where there are plenty of them. He had no itch to accumulate frequent driver miles and said his rodeoing was roughly confined to perhaps an hour-and-a-half radius. For the longest time he was a rodeo cowboy the way some guys are basketball players.

"I was like a guy who played pick-up basketball on a Saturday night," White said.

Coleman White of Fort Worth, here warming up his horses, won the season-long calf roping championship (photo by Lew Freedman).

But he attended enough rodeos to listen to cowboy talk about the great wide world of rodeo out there across the land. About six years ago, past the age when many rodeo bucks retire, White became weary of listening to stories and thought he should make some memories outside of Texas.

"I heard about Cody Nite Rodeo," White said one night sitting in the grandstand before competition began. "You hear these grand stories of every town. I told myself, 'I am going to take a road trip more than 20 miles from my house.' I had stayed local, but I heard about all of the great cowboys who travel the country and make it to the National Finals Rodeo."

In 2013, White loaded up his horse trailer with a couple of animals and headed to Cody. He stayed for about 40 days worth of competition and had the time of his life. He came back in 2014 planning to stay longer.

"This year, the Lord willing and my horse don't limp, I'll be there for the whole season," White said.

For all of his years on horseback and all of the rodeos he competed in, this was something different. Not only did White thrive on the nightly competition, he took a job herding cattle in the nearby Beartooth Mountain Range.

"I felt like a cowboy for the first time in my life," he said. "There were about 500 head of cattle. I realized I had only ridden my horse to 1/100th of its potential." He rode in the hills. He rode across rivers. He rode off the craziest of cliffs. He rode over downed timber.

"I'd strived to be a cowboy my whole life," White said. "I got to ride in the mountains and from pasture to pasture. There were a lot of variables with cattle."

It was a compressed education on the move. His favorite horse, Speedy, excelled in the arena. White found he could hang with the best ropers despite his age. Some of the other cowboys, like Bryce Bott, were young enough to be his grandson. No matter. The choice to go out every night was a winning strategy. Cody Nite Rodeo is a long season and piling up points can lead to belt buckle victories in June, July and August and then in the end-of-year finals.

The comedian and film-maker Woody Allen once said half of life is just showing up. Showing up and showing persistence can bring a worthy payoff at Cody Nite Rodeo.

"I'm going to compete," White said. "I'm here to beat them."

One thing White did know as well as anyone else was tie-down roping. Maybe he was a little bit slower than some of the 20-somethings, but accuracy was half the game and showing every night contributed mightily in the standings.

Prepping at one far end of the arena as the calves were loaded into chutes, the riders readied their horses just a foot or two away. Once that calf gate sprang open, the rider and horse gave chase.

"In the few seconds before you go," White said, "you need to make your horse relax." Some calves, the wrong pick of the litter, don't take off immediately. Others gain smarts and play harder to get. The random matching of cowboy and calf can make all of the difference.

"Some calves don't know how to go when the gate opens. I am watching my calf go left or right. I try to wait a second or a second-and-a-half. In a matter of seconds there are like 10 different things you've got to do. I have 100 percent focus on that calf and I am thinking, 'I own you.' I get my rope up and kick my horse with my feet. The chase is on. Ideally, there will be three or four swings of the rope before I let it go."

Essentially, White said, he is trying to control three uncomfortable situations simultaneously, a darting calf, a turning horse and "a limp noodle rope."

Closing that gap with the calf is critical. The roper wants to be close enough that when he flings the lasso it floats over the calf's head. If it doesn't connect he is toast, getting a zero for the ride. If the rope loops over the calf's head and is pulled tight that calf has the brakes put on for him. The other end of the rope will be tied to the pommel on the saddle. A well-trained horse like Speedy will help the roper once he jumps off and runs to the caught calf by slowly backing up and tightening the rope.

After the roper reaches the halted calf, he flips it over with sheer strength and ties three legs together with a shorter rope, usually carried between his teeth. The calf must stay tied for six seconds or the score will be zero.

There are many more basketball players in the world than calf ropers and that distinction is something that appeals to White.

"It makes me different from 99 percent of the people in the world," he said.

Unlike bull riding, bareback riding and saddle bronc riding, injuries to ropers are not as common or severe. "I've never broken a bone," White said. "And I've never had stitches. Wait. I might have broken this finger." He held up the second finger on his left hand. Imagine a 53-year-old cowboy in good health.

The AARP one-liners aside, White did not see an end to his competitive rodeo days coming soon. Cody Nite Rodeo lent him new life. Plus, there was always the Texas Senior Pro Rodeo Association.

"There is a 75-and-over division," White said. "There was an 85-year-old guy competing."

Not that White was looking ahead or anything.

★★★

SID MCFARLAND

When Sid is in the arena he is going to be one of the loudest voices rodeo fans hear. It is him and the master of ceremonies. The MC explains to people what they are seeing. McFarland, job description "clown," makes them laugh when cowboys aren't making them watch spellbound.

McFarland was 62 during the summer of 2014, and he said it was the 40th anniversary of the first time he came to clown at Cody rodeos. Originally from Montgomery, Alabama, McFarland has been a firefighter, worked for Husky Oil, and served in the military as a combat firefighter for the Department of Defense in Iraq in 2007, but rodeo has dominated his life.

Years ago when he was rodeoing all over the country, he ran into Cody Nite Rodeo stock provider Jim Houston, who asked if he would like to spend the summer in Buffalo Bill country. McFarland gave it a try and liked it very much. He lived in Cody full-time between 1977 and 1986, working at least part of the time for Timber County Outfitters in the Absaroka Mountain Range.

"To a lot of people, especially then, the Cody resident wears a six-gun and has shootouts," he said.

Well, only some of them.

McFarland, who is now gray-haired and heavy-set, made his debut in rodeo when he was 16 in Wetumpka, Alabama. He climbed on a bull, was thrown straight up in the air, but despite the hard landing, "I was hooked from the get-go."

Rodeo clowns are an outgrowth of circus clowns in greasepaint, garb and role playing, and up until recent decades they also held a duel job that was much more dangerous than the average clown. They doubled as bull fighters. Today bull fighters, who also wear silly clothes and makeup, own the serious job of protecting the riders. Rodeo clowns focus on acts, jokes and the show business side of the performance.

The days when McFarland signs on for an entire summer of Cody Nite Rodeo are long gone, but he committed to appearing the first couple of weeks of competition and returning for the championship finals at the end of August.

McFarland stuck with bull riding until 1975, but in 1969 he began easing into the clown-bull fighter role. The first time he dressed the part McFarland was helping out a rodeo friend in need who "threw me some makeup." He dabbed it on and a clown was born.

Most certainly becoming a clown extended McFarland's rodeo longevity. Without the switch away from bulls he would have retired long ago.

"Age does something to your body," McFarland said. "I'm there for the comedy. From the neck up I still have every move I ever had. I only come back to Cody now because it used to be my home. I have a lot of dear friends here, and I get the chance to go into the mountains."

Age can affect the future use of body parts if they have been injured and McFarland has not escaped the arena floor unscathed. In 1978 he smashed his left arm and needed rods inserted to make it work again. He has been chased over arena fencing by a bull and injured a heel.

McFarland, whose son Trent is a rodeo clown as well as a professional nurse, has the science of applying face makeup before rodeos down so well he can paint his visage in 10 minutes. Probably not even the most glamorous of Hollywood babes can match that. Of course, even McFarland will concede that he can't equal the Maybelline and Covergirl models in the looks department. But can they make thousands of people laugh? McFarland has worn the same clown makeup face since 1975.

"I don't change a thing," he said.

First McFarland applies a light coat of cold cream. He follows with a layer of face paint, white, and then he adds red and blue squiggles. Powder holds the makeup firmly in place, and the final touch is a bright blue wig. Two-thirds of the way through the rodeo when barrel racing starts, McFarland races back to his trailer and touches up any makeup that might have smeared during the evening's activities.

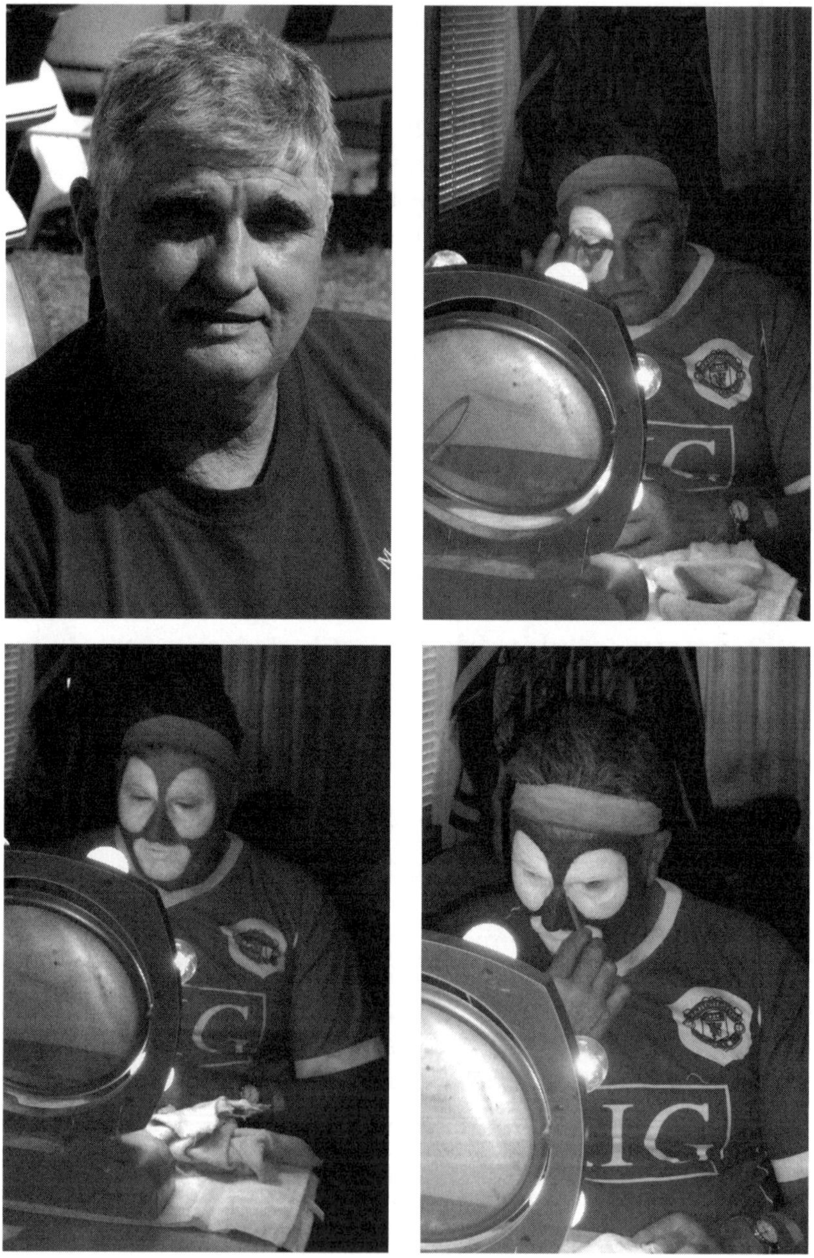

Veteran rodeo clown Sid McFarland of Montgomery, Alabama puts on his makeup in a series of photos posed before an old fashioned Hollywood dressing room mirror (photos by Lew Freedman).

"I guarantee I've worn more makeup than 99 percent of the women you'll ever meet," he said.

Over the years McFarland has evolved into a philosopher of comedy. He has performed before hundreds of thousands of people, so he knows a little bit about timing and delivery. He also knows that sometimes having loud and colorful props in the act can pay dividends. Although McFarland did not bring it with him, he owns a fire-truck-clown car. No, it's not the old standby clown car that holds a dozen people. McFarland's truck, which cost about $15,000, reads "Engine Co. 1-½ on the side and features a hood that blows off, strobe lights and sirens. The vehicle lurches up and down and has a flamethrower giving off heat out the rear.

"In show business, you have about a five-to-eight-second window of opportunity to wow people," McFarland said. "It (the truck) wows them. The purpose of a rodeo clown is to fill in any gaps in the production. It's part of a continuous energy of motion. It might be your 50th straight performance, but for somebody sitting in the stands it's their first. You may not have the best cowboys or livestock, but you've got to make the people think it is. I'm not in the rodeo business. I'm in the entertainment business."

It is extremely doubtful that when he was 16 and dreaming rodeo dreams that young Sid McFarland ever imagined he would utter such words.

"You've got to give the people something they can't see on TV," he said. "I'm the modern-day version of the court jester. Comedy is 90 percent about delivery."

To anyone who suggests that some of his jokes are politically incorrect, McFarland's reply is, "People should never take seriously what a clown says."

Those probably should be words to live by. Like so many people who have indulged a passion as a career for decades, it is difficult to step back and reflect on so much time passing.

"Travel sounds glamorous," McFarland said, "but not if it's just rodeo to rodeo. It's like being a long-haul trucker. Cowboys live for the day. Tourists used to say, 'You must have a wonderful life. You travel and only work two hours a night.'"

That's an oversimplification. Life on the road away from family and family occasions can be wearying. Rodeo participants may visit marvelous places that are high on recommended spots to see before you die, but they don't really see them. They blow into town, head to the arena, compete, and leave, sometimes without even spending a night.

Yet McFarland still gets the adrenalin rush from being on stage and being part of the rodeo. It's not clear how long he will keep going. Does he have the desire to play Sid the Clown for another 10 years and make it to the half-century mark?

"That's the million-dollar question," McFarland said.

McFarland sat in his trailer, the one he drove 1,865 miles from Alabama to Cody, telling his life story. Some black-and-white pictures of rodeo days gone by hung on the walls. One was a mock wanted poster of McFarland, saying the reward for his apprehension was $5,000.

"They caught up to me a couple of times, but I escaped," McFarland said drily as he finished applying his makeup at the old-fashioned starlet dressing-room mirror with the light bulbs ringing the edges. After one last look, he got to his feet and walked to the door. It was time to make the people laugh.

★★★

ROPES, WIND AND CLOWNING

Leslie Robertson, 23, stood at her horse trailer behind the arena, prepping her animals for the evening's competition. She is the daughter of a former barrel racer, and she has competed in that event as well as breakaway roping.

Robertson is also the mother of young children and hadn't been able to compete much over the last couple of years. She was trying to get back into things. Originally from Idaho, she lived in Cody, so there was rodeo all summer to use for regaining top form.

Her take on barrel racing is to let the well-trained horse do his thing and not try to micromanage.

"I visualize when I'm in the chute," Robertson said. "You have to be patient. My mom always taught me that you prepare yourself for the arena, so whatever happens is your fault. If I blow a barrel, it's my fault not my horse's fault. You exit the

The biggest rodeo event for women is barrel racing, where the competitor guides a sprinting horse around three barrels spread out around the arena (photo by Lew Freedman)

arena the same way you entered – with a smile on your face. If you are frustrated, later you slam a door."

It was not going to be easy for the getting-back-into-shape Robertson or anyone else to contend with the big gun in town. Fifty-six-year-old Terri Kaye Kirkland from near Billings, Montana, has been near the top of the sport for a long time. She is a four-time National Finals Rodeo qualifier (2003-2006). That's the major leagues. Kirkland was in this minor-league neighborhood for a purpose.

"This is a perfect setup for someone who wants to rodeo and to season a young horse," she said. On this trip, she brought four horses to Cody for a couple-day stay, horses she raised and named Awesome, Alibi, Alpha, and Abe. Kirkland said they resembled mischief-seeking puppies and chewed on things. Alpha chewed on a blanket. Alibi knocked down a fence

Kirkland has been seasoning horses her whole life. She first sat on a horse at 18 months and said the first horse she owned was a pony. It didn't take much to hook Kirkland on rodeo when as a little girl she won four ribbons riding her pony.

"I love the horses," Kirkland said. "I'm really competitive. It's my addiction, but a healthy one. There's a lot of hard work that goes into it; perseverance and patience and an ability to learn from our mistakes and others'. You can learn from everybody."

The next night Kirkland won the barrel racing in 16.75 seconds. Times under 17 seconds were a rarity all summer. Perhaps only a half-dozen times over three months did a barrel racer break that barrier. Any time posted under 17 seconds was smoking.

"The first and second barrels were beautiful," Kirkland said. "The third barrel was not what I wanted. We're going to go back home and work on the third barrel. I'm very grateful that I won it, but I'm a perfectionist."

Wyoming is one of the windiest places in the United States, National Weather Service stats crews and other organizations agree. Several Wyoming cities make top-20 lists. Cody, with its population just under 10,000, may not have had a large enough population to qualify for the lists, but anyone who spends much time in the city understands that on any given day the wind may just start roaring. In the winter that wind produces the big chill. In summer, it can produce a big pain in the butt for rodeo.

Unless pieces of distant buildings are blown into the arena, or unless the wind carries huge amounts of rain, Cody Nite Rodeo pretty much ignores wind velocity. It might be best to note that a couple of months after the rodeo season ended, while the citizens of Cody were indulging in Black Friday shopping the day after Thanksgiving, one wind gust was recorded at 82 mph. About 25 miles down the road toward Billings, a wind gust was recorded at 117 mph. So if someone asked a local, "Is it windy around here all of the time?" they may receive an answer as simple as, "Yes."

While Kirkland barreled to her victory, the wind blew a hurricane at the grounds, stirring up a dust storm. It came roaring in over Cedar Mountain strongly enough to send cowboys scurrying for jackets and some spectators scurrying for cars.

"Where I come from," McFarland told the crowd, "when it's this windy, it's a tornado."

While the clown may have had to hold onto his oversized, yellow stovepipe hat, the wind did not disrupt his repertoire.

"I liked school," said McFarland when his microphone was amped up during a break between events. "I stayed in the 12th grade for three years."

Although heads ducked to avoid the full blunt of the wind and cowboy hats apparently relied on Super Glue to stay on heads, Maury Tate kept the action going.

A hardcore group of boys, all less than 12 years old and all with dreams of riding the big bulls, always turned out for the junior steer riding. Brothers Zain and Kade Fitzgerald, Caden Gines, Jayson Lowden and Lukasey Morris were the top contender.

"Let me tell all of the parents, if you've got a 12-year-old that's misbehaving, bring him down here and we'll take care of them," said MC Kade Rogge.

Adult saddle bronc rider Jordan Couch tamed his horse for eight seconds and posted a solid score of 70 points. Only being tamed did not resonate with the horse named Crush and after Couch dismounted on the fly, Crush looked around for something to crush. He stared at McFarland and charged him. Old Sid could still move when he had to, darting to the fence and clambering most of the way up.

"Horse afire!" he declared. "Don't run over the fat man out here, dude."

Not that McFarland was frightened enough to lose his voice or his thought process. He kept on talking to the crowd.

"What do you want me to do, make a woman disappear?" McFarland said. "I already made five wives disappear."

★★★

ON TOUR AROUND CODY

With Rose Hughes at the wheel and Greg Pendley guiding, the Cody Trolley Tour provided a full semester's worth of history about Cody and the environs in a little more than an hour.

"Our motto is to give us an hour and we'll give you a hundred years," Hughes said.

Before the sights were shown, a tape was played over the trolley's airwaves. It was Buffalo Bill Cody's voice talking about the Congress of Rough Riders of the world. The audio was recorded by Thomas Edison. Now that's atmosphere.

Information was imparted in light-hearted tones by Pendley and Hughes, but there was much to be learned.

"This is the hand that touched the hand of Clint Eastwood," Pendley said, raising his arm in the air. It was clear that shaking hands with the actor well-known for his western movie roles during his visit to the Buffalo Bill Center of the West was one of Pendley's favorite memories.

Pause.

"We have more antelope than people (in Wyoming)," Pendley continued. It might be so. Wyoming is 50th in the United States in population with fewer than 600,000 citizens. It was not clear who the official census-taker of antelope is.

Pendley is probably the equal of Buffalo Bill as Cody salesman.

"If you notice, you can't go through the East gate of Yellowstone National Park without going through Cody," he said. "That was Buffalo Bill's idea." The Pahaska Trading post, formerly Buffalo Bill's hunting camp, is located just outside the East gate. "Pahaska means long-haired chief."

The tour ran past the rodeo grounds and on to the Buffalo Bill Dam. However, the trolley did not continue to the top of Cedar Mountain, elevation 7,890 feet, where Buffalo Bill Cody was supposed to be buried.

Pendley is one of those outraged Cody citizens who felt some kind of deal had been cut with the devil when Buffalo Bill was allegedly buried on Lookout Mountain in Golden, Colorado.

One place on the route was the Tecumseh Trading Post, a Cody fixture for two decades, but going out of business at the end of the summer. As there seems to be with every building and every individual around Cody, there is an Old West connection here.

Jerry Fick has owned a trading post in Cody for decades, but his fantastic hand-carved western miniatures are being shipped to a museum in California (photo by Lew Freedman).

Jerry Fick, 71, a member of the Lenape Indian tribe, was born in Reading, Pennsylvania and came to Cody in search of cleaner air. The white-haired Fick, a singer with several different bands over the years, spent most of his life collecting and gathering Old West artifacts and displaying them while at the same time carving miniature western figures and inserting them into an ever-growing history diorama.

Fick began making the figures before his 10th birthday and between his own work (most of it) and acquiring some others, amassed more than 7,000 of the couple-inch-high miniatures. He was always interested in anything about the American frontier and he has scrapbook articles written about him and his family that date to 1954 because of their collecting itches.

Born about 10 miles from where Daniel Boone was born, Fick said Boone "was my hero."

Fick's collection included lead, rubber and plastic figures, but he carved thousands of two-and-a-half-inch tall mini-men, then created scenes around them from frontier forts to genuine battlefield scenes. His men were made from white pine, and he carved most of them with a short-bladed utility knife.

Fick opened his first trading post in Pennsylvania around 1964, and he never stopped adding to his collection and diorama. At one time the collection was set up in an old barn. Over the years Fick sought out and collected arrowheads and other artifacts. "Indian chiefs used to come to see it," Fick said.

Besides selling everything from cowboy hats to Indian headdresses, including hand-sewn buckskin jackets – all of which were made by him – Fick displayed his collection in glass cases surrounding the back room of the trading post. As he aged, Fick wasn't sure what he was to do with his things. Family wasn't interested enough to keep the trading post going. In recent years Fick fended off offers to put him out of business by selling out.

"I didn't think the next generation wanted to keep it up," Fick said. "It's been fun, but it's been a lot of trial and sacrifice. It wasn't an easy thing to keep going. As a family we worked together. They sacrificed to help. It was my dream, though, and none of this would have been accomplished without almighty God."

Then opportunity walked through the door in early 2014.

Ken Behring, a rich philanthropist who once owned the Seattle Seahawks football team, has late in life become active in building and stocking museums. Behring opened the Blackhawk Museum in Danville, California in 1988. Its primary purpose was to house a vast automobile collection.

Behring became so enamored of Fick's trading post, the miniatures and the display items, that he bought the entire package and over the summer relocated it to Danville, set it up again, and worked out a deal for Fick to make periodic lectures in California. That's why the doors were closing on the trading post. Everything was leaving.

Behring made a fast take-it-or-leave-it offer and Fick decided to part with his things.

"No regrets," Fick said as his tenure in possession of the artifacts grew short. "It was practical. It was a tremendous amount of upkeep. You had to be devoted to it, and you give your whole heart."

Trucks moved the artifacts and the miniatures out during the late stages of summer and Fick watched it all depart.

"It is sad," Fick said of watching his carvings and collectibles depart. "I've been doing this for so many years. It's my life's passion."

Yes, he said, he did shed a tear. It was watching a chapter of his life close, a life that to some extent he thought was lived in the wrong era.

"I lived in two worlds my whole life," Fick said. "I lived 200 years ago in the day-time." Sometimes he dressed in period clothing, picked up a flintlock rifle, and slipped into the woods and back in time. "It was not a hobby."

Calling Fick's passion a hobby is oversimplifying. Somehow in 70 years of living, Jerry Fick produced two centuries of memories.

★★★

BACK ON THE GROUNDS

Cowboys will be cowboys – meaning that when they are not riding horses or bulls or whirling ropes they are thinking about cowgirls. One young lady has dismissed cowboys as being guys with just one thing on their minds and she was not referring to Cody Nite Rodeo glory.

As it so happened Dusty Moore and Luke Newsom had spent a chunk of the prior night at a bar looking for romance. They met a couple of young women who seemed to be quite taken with the idea of them being cowboys.

Luke Newsom worked as a pickup man, helping bareback riders and saddle bronc riders dismount after their 8-second rides were finished (photo by Lew Freedman).

Newsom, a pick-up rider from South Dakota, detailed this as he began to explain how he happened to incur a scrape on his chin.

"She wanted to go for a ride," Newsom said of his new friend. So he took her back to the rodeo grounds where he keeps his horses and at about three a.m. they went for a ride. "My horse wanted to go back to its trailer." They fell. Newsom cut his chin.

Moore, a roper, was also present with a young maiden. However he was not injured during his romantic endeavor. Good thing too. Master of ceremonies Kade Rogge teased Moore each rodeo night when introducing him to the crowd as "a multi-sport athlete." Recently, Rogge had taken to announcing that Moore was also a gymnast.

Moore was in no position to refute the slander just before his ride, so he could not communicate to the crowd that this was fiction.

"I am not a gymnast," Moore explained to someone who had heard him called that several times. He sighed. "Tonight I'll probably be a cheerleader."

Darned if he wasn't right. However, Rogge said it pretty quickly and there wasn't a huge amount of reaction, as if most fans didn't really hear. They cheered for Moore as he roped.

When a cowboy gives it his all and is still bucked off by a horse or a bull the description "try" is applied to his effort. The word "try" is a compliment and a synonym for giving one's all. "Try" is a trait to be admired, but is also a consolation prize when the try runs short of the eight-second clock and no score goes on the board.

Just about every night spectators express enthusiasm for junior steer riders. There is something about a frail looking, smooth-cheeked youngster stepping into the arena with the big boys that elicits a sympathetic streak in the fans. It is understood that they are watching beginners.

When a young cowboy comes through on his 500-pound, still-growing steer – staying on for six seconds, not eight – the fans lap it up. Lukasey Morris ripped off a great ride and scored 75 points. "And the crowd goes wild!" proclaimed clown Sid McFarland. So did young Morris. He threw his arms in the air and then ran into dad Jimmy's arms for a celebratory hug.

Most of the time when 12-year-olds get chances to perform on a stage under bright lights it is in a school play. This was a larger forum.

Other riders following Morris did not fare as well. "He's got a lot of try," announcer Rogge said as one youngster dusted himself off and headed out of the enclosure.

Dusty Moore seemed to have a hot hand in tie-down roping. He lassoed the creature, took the calf down and tied off three legs in 9.7 seconds. Then he was informed that his horse broke too soon and he was wacked with a 10-second penalty for the infraction.

"You mean he's leading and he got a speeding ticket?" Sid the Clown said.

Coleman White was a little slower, but minus a penalty his time was 13.7 seconds.

"That's for all the old guys like me," McFarland said.

White was on a hot streak. He clocked an 11.2 the next night and won Tuesday, Wednesday and Thursday. The 2013 season's points runner-up, he was on his way to amassing an early June points lead.

"It takes a really good horse, mental focus," White said, "and I drew a good calf."

Young Anna Allshouse was rolling in the barrel racing, too. She posted a 17.14-second winning ride that edged Jes West by 1/100th of a second.

On her first night, Leslie Robertson collected a no-score because her calf sped out of the chute and her horse never could get her close enough to rope. The next night, though, things went smoothly and she posted an 18.94-second clocking. Robertson was breaking in her horses.

The mixing-and-matching of duos in team roping was fascinating because the lineup was so volatile. There were brothers and sisters, fathers and daughters, husbands and wives, boyfriends and girlfriends, friends and friends, strangers and strangers. The ideal pairing was always of long-time partners.

One regular team was Pam Vanek and Eric Fleming, fiancés, due to be married in July. In team roping one rider throws the rope for the head of the running calf and then the other rider, known as the heeler, tries to loop a rope around the back legs. On the fly that is a challenge and sometimes the header stops the calf and the heeler might only snare one leg, resulting in a penalty. A swing-and-a-miss results in a no-score. Just another case of how rodeo is unforgiving. At Cody Nite

Rodeo, you get one attempt and if you miss you strike out. Of course, you can always come back the next night.

Vanek roped the head, but Fleming missed the heels. "It's going to be a long drive home," lamented announcer Rogge.

There was an almost audible sigh in the grandstand from couples who had been there, done that when it came to spousal discussions.

One spectator was Buffalo Bill Cody in full regalia. Roger Harrell came to watch following the Cody Gunfighters performance and hadn't had time to change. Somewhere else a Buffalo Bill look-alike wearing buckskins might occasion comment, but fans took it as a matter of course that Buffalo Bill would be in their midst. Asked if he was going to have a speaking part, Buffalo Bill said he was just in the house with friends. One of those friends was Wyatt Earp, but nobody bugged either of them for an autograph.

Saddle bronc horses are skittish by nature and can act as ornery as the bulls before they are let loose from the chute. They try to kick the gates down, but just when fans work up empathy for the rider they are shocked when the gate swings open and the horse just stands there. It may have blown off all its steam in the chute. The cowboy needs the animal to buck and kick to contribute his share to a top score, so this is bothersome.

Sometimes gate handlers slam the door again and the cowboy must again run through his pre-ride ritual. Others try to talk the horse into behaving like a bucking horse before another "ready, set" countdown begins. The cowboy goes through several emotions while this transpires. First he is psyched to ride. Then he is perturbed because the horse acts so flaky. Then he is let down because the horse won't go.

"I just try to keep calm," said rider Colt Chlarson when this sort of thing delays his start. "I don't get impatient. You can't because it's not going to do me any damned good. It kind of pisses me off, but the main thing is to get on the SOB before he acts badly."

Colt made his ride a good one. It looked like a safe eight seconds to the naked eye. "It felt like a minute," he said.

Even the most casual of rodeo spectators at Cody Nite, those first-timers from Austria or Norway, or even New Jersey, clue in to the fact that bull riding is the featured event. Bull riding is last on the program, so everything else leads up to this man versus beast contest.

The bull riding is also played up big to set up the action. Just before the competition began Cody Nite Rodeo sound man Milburn played a tape of the well-known boxing introduction popularized by announcer Michael Buffer. "Let's get ready to rumble!" rang out across the arena.

One thing the humans did not want to do is rumble with the bulls. That was a sure-loser strategy. Just staying on their backs was a tough enough assignment. Sometimes the bulls were as nasty as the bucking horses in their chutes. It was a sight to see when a bull reared up and attempted an escape over the fence. That shook up the guys behind the chute, though some swatted the bull with their cowboy hats. No, Mr. Bull, you aren't supposed to start bucking until you are out on the dirt.

Rider Wyatt Lehman of nearby Red Lodge, Montana, and a full-time summer rodeo worker by day, was confronted by a bull that sought to soar out of the enclosure. It was hard enough to sit on a bull for eight seconds when it remained more or less horizontal with the ground, but impossible to even start with a bull on hind legs. Lehman, like most cowboys, seems put out by an animal that he can't ride, and almost giddy when he stays on.

"It's what I'm passionate about," Lehman said. "Eight seconds is a paycheck."

Proving that personality traits were not factored in when the bulls were named, some of the orneriest had relatively benign names. The one called Funnel Cake caught Sid the Clown's interest. Funnel cake is a treat to eat at the State Fair, not a bad-boy bull to ride.

"Funnel cake?" McFarland shouted. "What kind of name is that for a bull?"

It turned out that it didn't matter what the bull was called, if he was too tough to ride he still made his point.

Whiplash, Skid Mark, Hatchetville and Hitler (truly unfortunately named) sounded rough, but they were no more belligerent than Cheeseburger or Money Talks. Nobody knew in advance which bull would be content with heaving his rider skyward and which bull might turn and try to gore him to pieces.

That's where the bull fighters came in. They were the protectors of the off-balance and possibly woozy riders. Bull fighter Justin Josey jumped between a downed rider and snorting bull and nearly was gored.

"If you don't move a little bit faster, you're going to find out what a 2,000-pound depository feels like," McFarland teased with a dose of sobering advice shielded by the one-liner.

Rider Aaron Anderson was thrown and chased by his bull, one named Skid Mark that didn't know how to apply the brakes. Jake Adkins didn't fare much better on Whiplash. Or off of Whiplash. "Here, kitty, kitty," McFarland joked.

"It's been all bulls so far," Rogge told the crowd, as if they hadn't seen it with their own eyes.

The riders tried to stay aboard while grasping a rope, but nothing really helped.

"What's that rope called?" Sid the Clown asked.

"It's a bull rope," Rogge said.

"No, it's not," McFarland retorted, summing up a dispassionate viewpoint of what it takes for bull riding. "It's an idiot string."

At the end of the program sometimes bull fighters showed off their dexterity, elusiveness and athleticism by tempting bulls to run right at them. The goal was to stay one step ahead of mayhem.

Zack Flatt recognized the difference between bulls on the loose like Tornado and bulls tethered in one spot like Mongo. But bull fighters are showmen as well as life savers and Flatt's slick trick was to lure a bull into a charge and then at the last moment take a couple-step running start and hurdle the bull's head.

The results were a pounding heart for Flatt, a "where did he go" reaction from the bull, and gasps and applause from the fans. The daredevil move paid off again.

★★★

THE BULL FIGHTERS

The bull that nearly ran Justin Josey out of the arena, the one that even alarmed Sid McFarland, did catch Josey off guard. Josey zigged, making a move to slip around the bull, but instead of zagging the bull zigged too.

"I kind of paused, and he went with me," Josey said. "I was kind of screwed. He hit my thighs and shins. I was against the fence, and he was hitting my whole body. I was thinking, 'Get him the hell off of me.' But it probably looked worse than it was."

Josey is 19 and six feet tall, a former football and baseball player, but at 150 pounds he is going to be significantly outweighed by every rodeo bull. So he has to rely on smarts and spryness to stay clear of horns.

Josey is from the same area of Oklahoma as Cody Nite Rodeo operators Maury and Nikki Tate. When he finished high school in 2013 and didn't know what he wanted to do they offered him a chance to try life as a bull fighter.

"You've got to be quick on your feet," Josey said. "You've got to read bulls and try to get to the shoulder (so the bull isn't coming at you straight on). I tried it and I liked it."

Not everyone back home in Oklahoma believed that Justin becoming a bull fighter was the coolest idea. Some people had the passing thought that he might have gone crazy.

"I've heard that a few times," Josey said. "They don't really understand it, so they get scared. If it's a dumb bull you can mess around as much as you want."

Being a rodeo bull fighter is probably one of the riskiest professions in America, on par with working in law enforcement or being a commercial fisherman in the Bering Sea. After all, the entire reason for the job's existence is to protect others at the possible expense of your own health.

On many nights before the Cody rodeo Josey could be seen squatting down or seeking a private corner in the area behind the chutes to pray for just a minute. He was not alone. Flatt usually did the same. Asking for protection from a higher authority than the manufacturers of four-pound, plastic shell vests with stuffing worn under floppy shirts seemed like a wise way to cover the bases. Josey admitted that he was nervous each night before the first bull hit the arena.

"Then I get over it," he said.

While not all bull fighters wear makeup, Josey and Flatt both did. Their outfits were colorful, designed to attract the attention of the bulls, and if their shirts flapped in the breeze that was OK too, since that meant the cloth was being sacrificed on horns instead of flesh. The clothing and the color were designed to turn the bull fighter into the primary target and shift the attention of an angry bull away from a vulnerable rider.

"If I need to take a hooking before a rider, I will," Josey said. "I'm target No. 1 or No. 2. I'm just trying to get the bull's attention. That's the biggest part of the job once the rider is thrown."

While quite athletic, at the beginning of the 2014 season Josey was still a raw bull fighter. The long Cody Nite Rodeo season works to a young competitor's advantage. The daily schedule compresses hard-won experience. Josey was still learning, but instead of his education being spread over weekends on the rodeo circuit he was cramming at Cody Nite school every day.

"You know, it's great experience," Josey said. "You see so many bulls. You never know what's going to happen. It beats a day job. There's no paperwork. You get to do something you like every day instead of dreading going to work. Some of the bulls are nice. Some won't do anything. Sometimes they use up all of their energy in the pen. Some are all bark. But they are bred to buck."

Still, Mongo is in his own class, standing out front every day with patience, barely reacting when little children and babies are placed on his back. Mongo doesn't snort. He stands stock still as Josey, Flatt or others steer the curious his way.

"Mongo is just a gentle bull," Josey said. "You can just walk up and pet him."

Not only were Josey and Zack Flatt partners for the summer, they were also roommates, living in the on-premises bunkhouse inside the fencing just a few yards from the arena floor.

Bullfighters play a key role in keeping angry bulls away from thrown riders (photo by Lew Freedman).

At 25, Flatt was the more experienced. He had put in an entire season of bull fighting in Cody and was starting to build a name for himself. At the end of the season he was certain he would earn his Professional Rodeo Cowboys Association card. This identification is essentially a union card that gives the bearer the power to enter rodeos anywhere. It indicates he has passed tests under fire and is a certified pro. It opens doors to be able to make more money.

Flatt, also from Oklahoma, has rodeo in his genes. His father Wesley fought bulls.

"I was watching rodeo since I was born," he said. "It's kind of inbred in me. I always wanted to be a bull rider. I thought it looked like fun, and it was fun when I did it. Daddy didn't want me to ride. He didn't want me to get hurt."

His father's reservations meant Flatt had to wait until he was 18 to ride a bull. He got on his first in Alberta, Alabama. He just about proved his dad right, too.

"On my first ride I got thrown, and I got hit in the head with a horn," Flatt said.

At 5-foot-9 and 185 pounds, Flatt is built like a defensive back, and he has the spring in his legs of a basketball guard. He possesses muscular arms, brown hair, brown eyes and is soft-spoken. Passionate about staying fit, he exercises regularly, running through Cody streets, performing plyometrics. At one time Flatt aspired to become a Navy Seal, and he did serve in the Navy.

"You're going to get hurt if you're not in shape," he said." It takes a lot of energy to get around that bull. Someone who is in shape can fight 50 bulls."

After his debut ride went south Flatt rode other bulls in Virginia and North Carolina. It was a whole different feeling to stay on for eight seconds, hear that buzzer and fans clapping. Cowboy body language tells the story of a bull ride. When he is thrown the cowboy practically mopes out of the arena, brushing off dirt, walking with a slight limp, head down. When he rides well, he's got his head up, a spring in his step and a smile on his face. He might even wave to the cheering crowd with the hat he just picked up following his dismount.

"There is no better feeling in the world than having control over something that big, athletic and strong," Flatt said. "You conquered him."

Yet Flatt drifted away from riding bulls into fighting bulls, by 2011 going halves. Now it's all about bull fighting. Sometimes the bulls win. Flatt has incurred a broken hand, stitches in the back of his head and torn up a knee and an ankle.

"Just some little stuff here and there," is the way Flatt described that injury history. But bull fighters don't get hurt as often as bull riders or bucking horse riders.

"If you ain't competing, you ain't making money," Flatt said. "As a bull fighter, you're guaranteed a paycheck." Still, Flatt's father, who well knew the phrase "It's not *if* you will get hurt, but *when*," had good reason to worry.

"I always said I didn't want to fight bulls, that I wanted to ride," Flatt said. "I was back in Oklahoma and I needed some extra money, so I tried bull fighting. I didn't know what I was doing."

Flatt has tried to soak up bull knowledge non-stop. Aware of the need to be nimble, Flatt has also thought well beyond the basic physical requirements of staying sharp.

"I always thought that I could look at them in the back pens and know how they would behave," he said. "I studied them. Some of them can't wait to get away from you as fast as they can. They want to go eat some hay. They don't want to be bothered. You can always pick out the one that's going to be mean. They look at you like those guys in the cage fights. Now I try not to look at the bulls until they're in the chutes."

When Flatt tells civilians about his rodeo job they sometimes have a difficult time wrapping their heads around it.

"I think they're just intrigued by it," Flatt said, "and they're curious about what it's like."

Flatt said he still has nerves at the start of the bull riding competition, but they don't last long.

"It's 95 percent mental," Flatt said. "It's a head game. You've got to have that mentality. There are all of these what-ifs. You don't want to think, 'What if I stumble? What if I'm too slow getting out there?' Once it starts, it's all reaction."

The profession of "bull fighter" means something else in other parts of the world, where matadors ply their trade in corridas and wield swords to kill bulls in the arena with the aid of picadors on horseback. Rodeo bull fighters do not carry swords, nor do they wave capes. They also do not regularly get as close to bulls as matadors, with some exceptions.

There are freestyle bull-fight competitions where the best rodeo bull fighters go head-to-head scoring based on how they handle the bull. This is showmanship and daring, not specifically required during a bull riding competition where the top priority is keeping the rider safe. The showy jumps that Flatt engaged in at the end of a Cody Nite Rodeo bull fight are crowd pleasers more than rescue measures, though there are times when the bull fighter must move swiftly to escape harm. Taller bull fighters with longer legs can have an advantage if they are taking a run-up, Flatt said. You can't jump the bull from a standing start and if it closes in you've got to react differently.

"You read the bull and stay close, inside, where he can't move his head quickly enough to get you," Flatt said. "Sometimes you've got to grab hold and touch him. If I have to grab the horns I'm going to."

That same skill may be applied to help a rider.

"I can tell with a lot of guys within two or three jumps that he's gonna come off," Flatt said. "Some get bucked off in a second or two and those who let go or who get ejected fast can be hard to get to right away."

It can be a grind fighting bulls every night of the summer and Flatt admitted he was tired at the end of the 2013 season. He loves fishing and Wyoming is a good place for that, but he was wrong about being burned out.

"After two weeks off I didn't know what to do with myself," he said. "This is the best place anyone can come to get better."

Wyoming is also a place that appreciates cowboys and rodeo. Even if Oklahoma is also a rodeo state, Flatt said cowboy acceptance and understanding is greater in Wyoming, a place of wind, rocks and mountains.

"This whole state is a cowboy state," he said. "It's not like back home. You can't even just jump on a four-wheeler and go out and check your cattle. You need to get on a horse."

And avoid being bucked off it, he should have added.

★★★

THE MAN WITH THE MICROPHONE

Part of Kade Rogge's job was promoting Cody Nite Rodeo by driving around at noon in the rodeo's red Cadillac that features longhorns attached to the grill and with a loudspeaker blaring.

The message broadcast was a simple one: Come to Cody Nite Rodeo tonight.

With its bright color and decals and decorations, the car was flashy. Not too many cars, even in Cody, Wyoming, have horns mounted on the front and talk to you as they drive past. Indeed, the car resembled one of those monsters frequently described as rhinos by the late author Hunter Thompson.

The Cody Nite Rodeo car driven around town rounding up customers for the nightly event all summer long (photo by Lew Freedman).

It seemed possible that the odometer had made a few laps. When asked how many miles the vehicle had on it, Rogge said, "It says 88,000" in a tone of voice that left it up to the listener to decide if that was accurate.

Rogge talked rodeo as he cruised from the rodeo grounds to downtown, in and out of parking areas, past the lunch-time walkers, into camping grounds. When Rogge wasn't talking up rodeo over the loudspeaker he played Glen Campbell tunes. "Rhinestone Cowboy" and "Galveston" were favorites.

Behind the wheel Rogge wore a cowboy hat and a University of Wyoming Cowboys shirt. People waved to him and smiled as he drove along at 20 mph or so. The car is its own advertisement with "Cody Nite Rodeo" emblazoned on the sides. As he drove through more crowded areas Rogge flipped off the music and amped up his speech. He told people to come on out to the rodeo.

"Hello people," Rogge said. "Welcome to the Rodeo Capital of the World. Don't forget us tonight. See you at the rodeo. It's a cowboy town. You're here. C'mon down."

The car was definitely an attention-getter. There might be numerous automobiles parked on the streets from different states at the height of the tourist season, but there were none quite as colorful.

"This car is pretty famous," Rogge said. "It's been on A&E (the Arts and Entertainment Network). A moving billboard is what this is."

Still in his 20s, Rogge has been around rodeo since soon after he could walk.

"I started team roping when I was seven," Rogge said of his youth. That was his step-father Merv May's specialty. Rogge, from Rupert, Idaho, competed in high school rodeo and college rodeo and did some steer wrestling too. He competed at the University of Montana Western and Southern Idaho College.

Rogge's father, Ron, and his step-father, are auctioneers, and he has that speedy gift of gab, too. So when it was suggested he try rodeo announcing in 2010 Rogge thought it made sense. He announced at some rough stock schools, did high school rodeo, and then found himself in some regional demand. In 2012 he made his debut at Cody Nite Rodeo.

"A microphone never bothered me," he said.

Moving from high school rodeo to Cody Nite is a big step, and Rogge found the every-night experience to be just as worthwhile for him as it is for cowboys.

"It's like getting paid to go to college," Rogge said. "It's a tryout for the stock, for the contestants and for me. There is no other place in the world like it. I am so blessed."

Rogge has not completely yanked free of roping, but said his rodeo involvement is about 90-10 talking now. He was chasing that pro card from the PRCA to join the ranks of touring pros at higher profile rodeos.

The rodeo grounds announcer does more than introduce the next contestant in each event. Rogge is also charged with helping to charge up the crowds. He provides background information, explains the rules, and plays straight man for the rodeo clowns' jokes as the sound man punctuates the exchanges with sound effects or music.

"I'm the director of emotion," Rogge said. "I'm supposed to feel it first, so you can feel it." That might mean juicing up the excitement level in general, letting spectators know if they didn't recognize they had seen something special, or just commiserating with a contestant who had a bad ride. "The fans have no idea what the rules are. You have to adjust to your crowd."

The MC has to adjust to the clown of the day, too. It was Sid McFarland every night for the first couple of weeks, but soon enough a new clown would come in with his own style to fill the role for a while.

"I don't mind messing around a little with the clown," Rogge said. "They're all a little bit different, but they're all good guys. Some of the nicest people in the world are the rodeo clowns. I coordinate with the clown and the sound man for those aspects of the show. You've got to work together and be clicking. This is my first year with Sid, but Sid is really easy to work with. Sid's style fits my style and my style fits his. I'm going to make fun of him a little bit, and he's going to make fun of me."

Just comes with the territory. McFarland has been in rodeo for about 35 years longer than Rogge and seen it all.

"He's a show himself," Rogge said. "I can really just follow him. You don't find that every day. With other clowns you never know what's going to happen. We're not out there to entertain ourselves."

Rogge's Cadillac tour of town lasted about an hour. It was an everyday thing, six days a week, since the turnover of the tourist crowd is so quick. Here today, gone to Yellowstone tomorrow. He had to lasso those spectators while he could.

★★★

IT WAS A DARK AND STORMY NIGHT

You could almost hear Dusty Moore going, "Arrggh." Sure enough, Kade Rogge introduced him as that multi-sport athlete again.

"Talk about a great athlete," Rogge said. "Dusty Moore is also a professional cheerleader at Panhandle State University."

Sid McFarland chimed in. "Does he shave his legs?"

It was a cold and windy night, which happens even in June in Cody, Wyoming. Most fans had been warned and entered the grounds carrying blankets or wearing layers. One woman said aloud, "I need my winter clothes."

McFarland checked off spectators from Holland, Australia, and Cowtown, New Jersey, which just happens to be somewhere they have conducted weekend rodeos regularly since 1929. As the name implies, they know rodeo in Cowtown, which is located about 45 minutes from Philadelphia.

Mongo was his usual self before the program began, and a woman named Margaret Wilson from Queensland, Australia hopped on his back and yelled, "Yipee ki yay." Then she screamed because Mongo shook his head.

Someone suggested that perhaps Zack Flatt goosed Mongo, provoking his earthquake-like movement. Flatt vehemently denied complicity. "He just coughed," Flatt said. "I'm completely innocent." Mongo, whose facial expression never changed, appeared to be proclaiming his innocence, too.

This was not Wilson's first rodeo. She said she attended rodeos in Australia, "but they call them stampedes."

Cole Klease, 58, another Australian in the crowd around Mongo was that rare foreign visitor at Cody Nite Rodeo – a repeat customer from two years earlier on a previous United States vacation. He too had checked out small "stampedes" in Australia, but said Americans do rodeo right.

"I just love the fanfare," he said. "Americans put the music into it. They get you involved. If you walk away from it without a smile on your face you can't be helped."

Klease didn't seem to mind the unfriendly weather. Since most of the fans were not around 24 hours earlier it did not seem appropriate to point out that they should have been there yesterday when the sky was blue, the wind was absent and the temperatures were mild. After people were seated rain began pelting down so hard on the metal roof of the grandstand it became difficult to hear Kade Rogge's commentary at times.

Coleman White's winning streak ended when he missed his rope throw. You can't make 'em all.

Colt Chlarson stayed hot in the saddle bronc riding, letting a little of his own flamboyance shine through after dismounting and receiving a top score of 77 points. The dirt turned muddy as the downpour continued and the cowboys went home with soaked-through hats and shirts. They were muddy cowboys, not rhinestone cowboys. Despite that, Chlarson held his concentration.

"I don't think about the small stuff," he said. "It was get down and get dirty. When I left the chute everything was a little slippery, but I saw everything before my eyes. After the eight seconds it was, 'Where the hell are the pickup men? Let's get off.' When you run back to the chute after that, it feels good."

Jennifer Lewis of nearby Meeteetse was one of the top barrel racers all summer (photo by Lew Freedman).

Pickup men of the night Harold Adema and Matt Scott rode in and helped lift Chlarson off the horse named Whopper. Rogge informed the spectators what they were doing. "We call them the cowboys' pickup truck," he said.

A wet course is not favored by barrel racers. They worry that the comparatively delicate forelegs of their sprinting horses can be damaged by a slip or by stepping into a hole. There is definitely a risk to riding all out in the rain. Sometimes when confronted with ugly weather barrel racers forfeit entry fees rather than putting the trained horses they love into too-tough situations.

Generally, Jennifer Lewis of Meeteetse, some 35 miles from the grounds, despises a sloppy course, but this time she chose to race and completed the loop in 17.25 seconds to win the night.

Merval Not Afraid, kin to Machiah Not Afraid, who won the bulls on opening night, competed in the bulls on Tornado, but didn't make the eight seconds. That didn't stop Rogge from praising him for having "the coolest name in bull riding."

As had been the case pretty much all week, the bulls had the upper hand over the cowboys. McFarland summarized the situation with gallows humor. Sid the Clown proceeded to tell the crowd about the cowboy who had been seriously hurt on a bull ride.

"They put him in the hospital," McFarland said, "and I went over to visit him. He was in room 101, 102 and 103."

Drum roll.

It was a good night in the breakaway roping. Rogge told fans that Sara Arthur's light brown model was "one of the most beautiful horses in the fleet." Molly Jo Collins broke through with a 7.8-second time and McFarland welcomed the sight by shouting, "And the crowd goes wild!"

When a different breakaway rider was assessed a 10-second penalty for leaving the starting line too soon, McFarland pulled out his standby speeding ticket line. However, it led to a story: Sid was stopped by a policeman for driving too fast. The officer of the law asked, "Are you drinking?" Sid replied, "Are you buying?"

Kooper Bott, Bryce's sister, was the cowgirl with the mostest in the breakaway, roping her calf in 3.2 seconds. And the crowd not only went wild, it added some foot-stomping Wyoming thunder.

Spectators couldn't avoid the sogginess because the wind blew sideways at times. The wind was wild enough that some cowboy hats flew off, testing those perfect-fit models. But fans that stuck it out to the end hurried out the door with that smile on their face that Klease, the Australian tourist, predicted.

★★★

THE BOSS

The 2014 season represented Maury Tate's 10th year as stock provider for Cody Nite Rodeo through his Mo Betta Rodeo Company of Apache, Oklahoma.

The phrase "Mo Betta" seems to resonate with Tate, who was 48 during the season and has been around rodeo most every minute of those years. He also owns "Mo Betta Bulls" and before that he ran a company that sold shirts made by the Mo Betta Clothing Company.

Tate was 21 in 1987 when he tired of showing up at rodeos to discover that other competitors were wearing the same shirt. He didn't like that. A woman named Ruth McDaniel, a friend of his mother's, was a seamstress, and he convinced her to make shirts for him.

Boy, did they take off. Within five years Tate had a hundred seamstresses turning out shirts for him and before he sold the company that number reached 125. His original thought was to dabble in western wear so he could ease into a career after he retired from rodeo competition.

While the shirt company proved to be a resounding success it left him on the periphery of rodeo, not as involved as he had been. Tate sold the shirt company in 2003, and he actually hit a point where he no longer owned a single horse.

Tate grew up in rodeo, riding bulls from the age of seven on. In fact, Jimmy Morris, a former bull riding champ who was working Cody Nite Rodeo over the summer, said that when he was a youngster Maury's mother was the local rodeo association's secretary.

Tate attended Western Oklahoma State and turned pro as a calf roper in 1987. He won some championships, but he started the shirt company and that gradually took up more of his time and energy. The shirts sparkled enough to earn widespread attention. They were colorful and had style and Tate hit it big when country and western singing star Garth Brooks discovered them and other country singers, including Tim McGraw, began wearing them, too. He also made T-shirts. Mo Betta was the signature. Tate's shirts were featured in *Western Horseman* magazine and in *People*, too.

Although today Tate has re-focused his attention on raising rodeo-caliber livestock, there are probably some people who don't even realize he did anything but make the snazzy shirts. A google search turns up some readily accessible advertising that features Tate's daughters Cydney and Haley and some rodeo figures from Cody Nite Rodeo.

It wasn't until after he retired as a competitor that Tate really heard much about Cody Nite Rodeo. A friend clued him in and a decade ago he became the stock supplier for the long summer rodeo with his wife and partner Nikki.

Although Tate's general supervisor is the Cody Stampede Board of Directors and he contracts with them to provide the

Maury Tate has operated Cody Nite Rodeo for a decade (photo by Lew Freedman).

animals, once the rodeo gets underway in June it is basically his to run. It may be small, but it's crazy time-consuming.

"We're the committee," Tate said. "We're the contractor. We're everything. Here you have to do every bit of it. We're unique. There are a few rodeos out there that have rodeos every weekend, but none that are every night."

Given that the Cody Nite Rodeo tradition predates his own birth, Tate recognizes that he is the custodian of quite a tradition.

"World champions have started out in Cody," he said, ticking off names that flashed into his mind.

Included were some big-time rodeo pros with fantastic resumes. Among them are Chris LeDoux, Dusty Tuckness, Kanin Asay, Jim Houston, Shane Proctor, Cody Custer and clown Justin Rumford.

The basic mission of Cody Nite Rodeo is not to develop future world champions or professional rodeo stars, but "It's a learning place for kids who want to get better," Tate said.

Tate can remember when he was one of those hungry young teens who wanted nothing more than to hit the circuit as a rodeo cowboy. Some kids dream of becoming firemen or policemen, of joining the Army, or of playing professional team sports like basketball or football. Not Tate.

"When I was a kid growing up," Tate said, "all I wanted to do was rodeo for a living and be a professional cowboy."

He was a pretty good one, too. In 1991, Tate, who is old enough to be going bald, won the Dodge National Circuit Finals tie-down roping championship.

The champs are byproducts, who gained their first exposure to serious competitive rodeo and rode off into the sunset to become big names. It's an aspect of Cody Nite Rodeo Tate is proud to promote, though in the same manner as in any other sport rodeo goes through a winnowing-down process.

Many are drafted into the minors, but never play Major League baseball. Many are college stars in football, but don't make it in the National Football League. The same applies to Cody Nite Rodeo. A select group can look back and say they got a start in Cody. Sometimes they make cameo appearances in Cody again, either at the Stampede, if they make the cut for that prestigious rodeo, or if they are passing through and wish to enjoy a nostalgic Cody Nite visit.

Over the years competitors have shown up from all sorts of unexpected places to compete, said Tate, naming Brazil, Japan, Australia and Germany, among others.

"In our world (rodeo)," he said, "it's just known as a place to come."

Tate has helped perpetuate that reputation. After a knee injury cut short his competitive rodeo days and he divested of the shirt company Tate partnered with former pro football player Jeff Zgonina to raise bulls.

Zgonina, who had a 17-year NFL career and also coached with the Houston Texas, said he began studying breeding as a hobby when he was an active player as his "escape from football."

The Tate livestock featured at Cody Nite Rodeo comes from the lines of the original horses and bulls the partners began breeding more than a decade ago. Tate spends a chunk of the year in Cody, but still calls Oklahoma home. He said it is too cold to spend the winter in Wyoming. The animals that star in the summer shows are also vanned back to Oklahoma for the off-season, too. They must not like cold weather either.

★★★

PARK COUNTY NIGHT, JUNE 7

Once a year the locals get a break and pay just $5 to enter the rodeo grounds. It's a thank-you from the organizers. There is usually a good crowd and for this rodeo 2,500 people turned out.

It also turned into double-clown night. Sid McFarland was accompanied on the dirt by his pal Tony Martoglio, the local guy. Attendance was so good that programs were being sold at the back gate where the competitors entered. That practically never happens, except during the Stampede, said gate guard Dwight Cabra.

But if you wanted to hang with Mongo you still had to go to the front. Richard Watts, a Cody resident, brought two-year-old Linsi and four-year-old Carl to the rodeo and the kids were eating up the sights and sounds. Carl developed a strong affinity for Mongo — maybe too strong.

"They're really into this," Watts said. "Carl wanted to take Mongo home with us, but we have a two-bedroom apartment. We can't even have a dog."

Not even Mongo's most ardent admirers could envision him in an apartment. The bull that was usually as immobile as a boulder might actually blow his cool. Imagine the furniture damage.

Park County Night was heavily promoted on the radio and Buffalo Bill Cody read one of the ads. This came as news to Cody Gunfighter Buffalo Bill Roger Harrell, who was not involved. "It must have been another Buffalo Bill Cody," he said. Those are the hazards of the impersonation trade. There are imposters everywhere.

A troupe of gunfighters came to Park County Night, still in show attire. After all, they are Park County residents. Yet even in full regalia rodeo fans just acknowledged them as part of the scenery. Somehow it didn't seem likely that if Buffalo Bill, Wyatt Earp and other western figures showed up in Times Square they would blend so readily.

Do you ever get stopped for autographs and chitchat, Andy DiPiazza, alias Wyatt Earp/Johnny Ringo, was asked?

"If we walk down the street downtown it happens," DiPiazza said. He rode bulls and bareback horses long ago, was even into junior steers as a youth. He does notice during the gunfighter skit that some youngsters think it's real and "They cry when I get shot. They ask, 'Are you OK?'"

Tarin Clausen, 20, played Little Britches in 19th-century period costume. She was in Cody for the summer, working in a veterinary practice as an intern, guiding horse rides on weekends for Cedar Mountain Trail Rides while living in a barn, and attending Cody Nite Rodeo every night she could. Clausen wished she owned a horse, but didn't. One thing about those one-to-two-hour trail rides: "You can see all of Cody," she said of climbing via horseback to higher elevation.

It's not as if Clausen was an actress back home. In real life she was headed into her junior year at Northwest Missouri State studying animal science as part of pre-vet training. Clausen didn't know a thing about Little Britches.

"I don't know if she's a real person," she said.

She is not. Little Britches was a character in a group of novels.

"I love the skit," said Clausen, the youngest actor in the cast. She thinks that's why the kids in the crowd gravitate to her. It is not because of her oratory. Playing a saloon girl with a very limited speaking part does not gain her much attention. "I only have two lines. The little kids just melt my heart."

Clausen wasn't looking to add any more lines, either. The entirety of her prior career on stage consisted of playing Little Bo Beep in pre-school.

What brought her to Cody, though, was family. She had visited before to see relatives and wanted to stay longer. The summer of 2014 was staying longer. Clausen was about as a loyal a rodeo spectator as anyone who didn't have a son, daughter, father or mother in the competition. Sometimes she rushed over wearing her frilly Gunfighters' dress. Mostly she had time to change into blue jeans.

Clausen learned quickly what the good rodeo fan – and indeed what the good sports fan – knows. Every night of competition is different from the night before. Rodeo is live theatre, but it comes without a script, unlike the gunfighters' show. The lines for Wild Bill Hickok don't change. The horse, the bull, the bucks and the heaves change every night for the cowboys.

The competitors may change from night to night at Cody Nite and some of the livestock they draw will be different from one night to the next. That's part of the challenge. One thing rarely changed, however.

Just about every night Andy Mumm came to ride in bareback he stayed on for eight seconds and put up the best score. This night it was 74 points and he was the winner. It was only early June, but Mumm was already looking ahead to July 4 week, Cowboy Christmas. Why not? He was on a hot streak and hoped he still would be. "You can do three rodeos in a day if you want to," Mumm said of the holiday.

Dusty Moore, evading Kade Rogge's embellishment of his athletic career beyond rodeo for once, had a good night, winning the tie-down roping.

Curtis Wilkerson was not as fortunate in the saddle bronc riding. His horse was named Big Hunk and the horse did not want to make friends. Wilkerson was tossed head over heels, and in a rare sight, the horse fell down. Both were able to rise on their own. "If Curtis keeps falling only forward he'll never sprain his ankle," reported Rogge. Wilkerson probably spent the rest of the night wondering if that was a dig or a compliment.

Colt Chlarson, who had been tearing it up in the saddle bronc division, fared worse than Wilkerson. A horse named Snickers threw Chlarson and it had the last laugh. Chlarson landed flat on his back with a thump. A mob of folks rushed out to help him when he didn't get up right away: Yellowstone Sports Medicine staff, bull fighters who were not able to rescue him from his hard landing and clowns, surrounded him.

Chlarson walked out of the arena wobbling a little bit. It was a good sign that he was moving under his own power, but it turned out Chlarson had broken his collar bone, and doctors informed him that he might be sidelined until August. Recovery time figured to be four-to-six weeks. He hated the notion of living in a sling.

Chlarson was not a happy cowboy. "Hell yeah, it's depressing," he said a day later. "I just bucked off and landed on my left shoulder. I heard the snap when I hit the ground. At first I was scared I broke my neck."

Chlarson had been dominating the saddle bronc class and thought he had a good chance to win a season-long championship.

"Things were starting to happen," he added morosely. "I'll just have to lie around to pass the time. I went straight to the hospital. I've been hurt worse, but I know when I'm hurting."

Getting ready to ride, Andy Mumm psyches himself up for a bareback competition (photo by Lew Freedman).

Hurt worse? Well, yeah. Chlarson had been through ankle, rib and foot injuries. Now he was a 2014 Cody Nite Rodeo statistic, too.

Sid the Clown unveiled a more ambitious-than-usual stunt. He explained to an avid audience that he had brought in the McFarland rocket launcher for their viewing entertainment. It would be fueled by a mixture of ten pounds of dynamite, ten pounds of nitro, and 25 pounds of horse manure. Hmmm. The rocket, he announced, would shoot 10,000 feet into the air and spell out "Rodeo" across the sky. "People will see it in Yellowstone," he said. "People will see it in St. Louis."

On the first try, the rocket, propelled by a plunger, soared about two feet. McFarland stood in the middle of the arena scanning the sky. The rocket was behind him. He gave it another try and the plunger blew up. End of skit.

Common sights at rodeos are horses and bulls with no desire to fade into the background and return to their corrals after disposing of a rider. It's almost as if they feel they deserve extra applause, so they circle the arena at a gallop, taking a victory lap.

A bull named Tombstone seemed unlikely to ever go home. Pickup men Harold Adema and Luke Newsom did everything but whisper in the bull's ear. They rode next to Tombstone, hemming him in while trying to guide him through the open gate. The bull wanted no part of it. Adema whipped out a rope and looped it over Tombstone's head. Tombstone yanked the rope out of his hand. Then Luke roped Tombstone.

Zack Flatt darted into the arena, picked up the loose end of Adema's rope and handed it back. Tombstone was twice-roped and still gallivanting around. The bull also seemed twice as ticked off as it had been when Jeff Guy tried to ride him. Now Tombstone was steaming and came up with a revenge plan. Tombstone dropped to his belly and began rolling around in the dirt. It was mind-boggling to witness. Tombstone was staging a sit-down strike.

It took the pickup men, the power of their horses and the strength of the ropes to get that bull back to its feet and lead it to the pen. Tombstone resisted every step of the way, digging its hooves into the ground.

Afterwards, Newsom tried to analyze what the crowd saw.

"The bull was extra hard to handle and we were on green horses," he said of the inexperienced mounts he and Adema rode. "It happens sometimes. But a guy should be able to drag a bull in by himself. I was frustrated. Both of us were. Some bulls won't go back in the chute, but they just stand there. You always get a shot. It's our job to handle the situation as smoothly as possible.

"You've just got to read the situation, so it's easiest for your horse and the bull," Newsom said. "He just wasn't cooperating. Some bulls if you rope them, they come right in. Not him."

★★★

WYATT, SKEET AND THE BULLS

Not so long ago Wyatt Lehman was a high school football player who weighed 240 pounds and whose main goal was to knock the stuffing out of ball carriers. Now he weighed 200 pounds and his main goal became avoiding having the stuffing knocked out of him while riding a bull.

Lehman, from the Bridger-Red Lodge area in Montana, just across the border from Wyoming and north of Cody, went to rodeos as a kid and knew that after he wrapped up life as an offensive and defensive lineman in high school he wanted to change sports.

"I always dreamed of being a bull rider," said Lehman, sitting in the vacant stands at the rodeo grandstand during a quiet afternoon. "I got started at 17."

His father Jay ranched and farmed, and the family, including mom Jennette, had pretty solid roots in Montana. When Lehman was a little boy he was already thinking ahead to the days when he would sit astride 2,000-pound bulls.

"I tried to ride my hound-dog, and I split my lip," he said. "I don't know how long I stayed on."

It could have been eight seconds.

"Bull riding is a passion of mine," Lehman said. "They don't scare me. I'm sticking to it."

Leaner than when he played football, Lehman stands 5-foot-10. The ideal bull rider size in his mind would be "a little bit shorter and a little bit lighter." Unless he is going to subsist on diet Jell-o, however, there are limits.

A Cody Nite Rodeo worker by day, he was a bull rider by night and rarely missed taking a turn. Sometimes he paid for his persistence, limping off the dirt. Sometimes he got thrown faster than he thought possible. But Lehman always got back on.

By 2011 Lehman was into bulls rather than hound dogs. He had chaps and a rope and was armed with tips from a friend. When he started, Lehman rode with his cowboy hat on his head, but he later switched to the new fashion amongst safety-conscious cowboys. He wore a black helmet every day at Cody Nite Rodeo, one that resembles the type of full head protection National Hockey League goalies use.

It didn't take long for Lehman to learn that bulls are completely unpredictable. When a cowboy climbs on the platform behind the bucking chutes he surveys the scene. He takes a look at the bull. He checks his rope. Only then does he climb over the fence and lower himself onto the bull's back. Lehman still recalls his first bull ride.

"I came out of chute No. 3 (in Cody) on a big, old brindle bull," Lehman said. "On the second of two jumps he threw me higher than the bucking chutes. I landed flat on my back."

Lehman's second bull was not much nicer. In fact, it was probably meaner since the instant Lehman gave the ready sign to open the gate the bull flipped out.

"When I nodded he turned right around, spun around, and cracked my wrist against the latch," he said.

Lehman may have shed weight, but he still has a hefty build. He has been determined to master bulls from the start, but he did not make an eight-second score in 2011. Nor did he record one in 2012.

"I didn't make eight seconds until last year (2013)," Lehman said. "I'm still learning. I'm getting the hang of it."

By the standards of the stars of the sport, not getting on a bull until 17 makes you a latecomer. Many rodeo youngsters start out riding sheep, or mutton busting as it is called, when they are eight or so.

In December of 2014, a few months after the Cody Nite Rodeo season ended, The New Yorker magazine printed a feature story "The Rodeo Children." It was about the Youth Bull Riders World Finals in Abilene, Texas where the best child riders compete. They are still too young to ride full-grown bulls, but do get a head start in the sport over people like Lehman who wait until they are practically adults to begin riding.

One thing the article talked about was how rodeo is "the most dangerous organized sport." As those who follow rodeo closely are aware rodeo participants get hurt at a much higher rate than football players. The story noted that bull riding is riskier than ever because the animals are being bred more scientifically and they are better buckers. That was becoming evident by the day at Cody Nite rodeo as rider after rider ate dust while a hulking bull pranced around eyeing him as road kill.

As the young, hustling, pint-sized cowboys grow they move up to larger animals, such as calves and steers. Lehman was riding the big-'uns, but he didn't have the same deep background as other the young lads, so he was more or less trying to go from zero to 60.

Lehman remembered his first eight-second ride as a glorious moment at Cody Nite Rodeo. The bull ran, hopped, jumped and circled but could not dump Lehman. The other cowboys and workers knew how much he had been through, so when he conquered the bull kudos rang out.

"I remember the hats flying," Lehman said. "There are a lot of people here that believed in me." It meant a great deal to him when he won an event for the first time, even if it paid only $200. "I was excited. I put all of this time and effort and money into this."

A proud cowboy, Wyatt Lehman worked for the rodeo by day and rode bulls by night (photo by Lew Freedman).

Lehman understands people at home, people in the family and casual acquaintances whisper, "You're nuts." He shrugs off such sentiments. "It's not about being nuts. It's making your dream happen. It's never going to be easy, on no bull. You can't have the mindset that you can't ride him even if it is the raunchiest bull out there. Instead, it has to be, 'I can handle this sucker.'"

Lehman said he owes a lot to Nikki and Maury Tate. He called Maury "like a father figure. He keeps me going. There are times I get discouraged. There are people who are doubters and haters. If I ever make it in bull riding, I'll find some way to pay Maury and Nikki back."

By the start of the June 1 campaign he estimated he had been atop 300 of the big animals. Lehman was primed to ride 90 more over the summer. He had shown the stick-to-it-iveness that it takes to make headway in the rough sport, and he had shown enough savvy to believe he could continue to improve and get somewhere in rodeo.

"If I get it all figured out I can be pretty good," he said.

Dressed in a black shirt and jeans, boots on his feet and a felt cowboy hat on his head, Lehman looked the part of a rodeo cowboy and he walked with that certain western strut that seems to come naturally to the men of the Wild West.

There are a lot of Average Joes in the crowd each night. Some have never seen rodeo. It's unlikely that most have ever tried any event in the sport.

"There are some people who will watch this and be inspired by it," Lehman said. "And some will watch it and say, 'I'll never do this.' I already know that when I retire from bull riding I'll have trouble getting out of bed."

Bodies do take a beating in bull riding. Lehman, who helped feed the livestock days thought the bulls had a pretty good life. All they had to do was work for eight seconds at a time, then "go back to their pens and eat and drink. I see bulls all day long. I have no grudge against any bulls. You can't know what they're thinking. I just love Mongo. He's just been around humans a lot. He got to trusting them."

Acknowledging that saddle bronc riding is the classic event in rodeo, Lehman seems to be a member of the modern school of thought suggesting that bull riding has eclipsed riding horses as the most glamorous event.

"What goes through my head when the gate opens?" Lehman said. "I try to keep centered and try to keep moving. You are trying to move with him. You get some of the best bulls out here and when they have done it for a few years they figure out ways to get riders off. If I was ever to be reincarnated I want to come back as a bucking bull."

Lehman is both sincere and politically correct when saying he likes to stay on the good side of bull fighters. Bull fighters give it their all no matter who is riding, but maybe it is an insurance policy to be friendly with them, as well.

"I like to get to know them and show my appreciation," Lehman said. "After you've been thrown sometimes you don't even have time to stand up. Sometimes I'm doing the bear crawl on the ground to get out of there. I've been worked over. I've been tossed."

Lehman recognizes that there is an entire cross-section of society that doesn't believe bull riding is a completely sane occupation and thinks participants should do something else for a living.

"People ask, 'Aren't you scared of dying?'" Lehman said. "I'm not scared of dying, but you can die walking down the street. You've got to look past it (the danger from bulls) and hope the good Lord is with you."

Many bull riders pray for their health and safety and Lehman is one of them.

"I do pray," he said, "but not when anybody's around. I look up at the sky and thank Him that I am here another day."

Lehman is a regular on the backs of those bulls, but he is not the only one who hadn't been doing it for a lifetime. It seemed as if the young and the reckless cowboy of 2014 couldn't call himself a real cowboy unless he tried riding bulls. Some of the young riders romanticized the sport, became enamored of it by watching television. They thought it was all about guts, and they have a point, up to a point. You can't jump into bull riding without some innate gumption. But it takes more than guts to make a go of it.

Bull riding know-how is hard-earned. Skeet Chadwick, 18, migrated to Cody for the summer from New Mexico to ride more often. He joined Colt Chlarson at the end of the back parking lot living in a tent, marking him for-sure a low-budget cowboy.

Chadwick was full of fun and youth and optimism. He was still learning about the world, not just bulls. He was a "Yes, sir" guy with a Huck Finn appearance. Some freckles dotted his face and a cowboy hat was tilted back on his forehead.

He first rode a bull at 13. His mother was a barrel racer, and he has a brother named Dalton who is "a danged good bull rider." Chadwick said he is religious. "Everyone says I've got a lot of heart and try," Chadwick said. "I'm a Christian man. I have watched the bull fighters and the riders since I was a young man." As if he is not still one.

Chadwick appeared in rodeos in New Mexico, Arizona, North Carolina and Wyoming. He stood 5-foot-11 and weighed a deceptive 185 pounds. He did play some football and found it to be good for conditioning.

Very early in the Cody Nite Rodeo season Chadwick took five stitches in his forehead. Maybe that's why he didn't pull

Skeet Chadwick preparing his gear for a bull ride (photo by Lew Freedman).

his hat down so tight in front. "I came out sitting back and I got thrown into the bull's head and caught a horn," he said. "I took a day off and felt fine."

Chadwick knows he is still learning what it takes to ride to eight seconds consistently. On one of his early rides he was thrown at 7.9 seconds. That's not an estimate. The clock was official.

"When I first started I was making it two seconds maybe," Chadwick said. "To do well you've got to have some nerve and lots of heart. If you ask me you need a lot of faith and skill. Being fit and balanced plays a role. Then it comes down to muscle memory. A lot of people go, 'Geez, he's crazy. He's not all there in the head.' It's astonishing to them that someone would want to attach himself to a 2,000-pound animal."

Chadwick had been attached to bulls named Widow Maker and Mash lately, but was still going after it.

"We're all pulling for the New Mexico kid," Kade Rogge announced.

Chadwick drew Funnel Cake. The rodeo clown of the day, Andy Burrelle, hadn't encountered that name before.

"Oh, that sounds delicious," Burrelle said when the bull was introduced.

Funnel Cake was actually obnoxious to Chadwick. Things went badly. The bull had barely exploded out of the gate when Chadwick was tossed, and he was nearly nicked by a horn before he scrambled to his feet.

Bull fighter Zack Flatt sliced in-between the defenseless Chadwick and the angry Funnel Cake. It was a subtle move for a fan to absorb, but Flatt's move probably saved Chadwick from injury. The ride lasted four seconds.

"It felt like 10 minutes," Chadwick said.

★★★

YOU NEVER KNOW

This is live, unpremeditated action. The cowboys and cowgirls think they know what they are doing. They also have faith in their own horses. They just don't have any idea what the bucking horses, the bulls or the calves might do on a particular evening.

The tie-down roping usually has a crowded field, but even on nights when only a handful of ropers sign up it is a quality field. The regulars are very regular. But every once in a while a new face pops up and tries to break through with a Cody Nite win.

Wyatt Rising probably thought he had the same chance as everyone else entered in the tie-down roping June 9. Saddled and ready to go, it turned out he was saddled with an uncooperative calf. When the gate flung open his calf seemed to be responding to the starting gun in the Olympic 100-meter dash.

Rising got his horse to bear down for the chase and waved a rope over his head, but he could never catch up to the unleashed calf running pell-mell the length of the arena. The calf was so excited to run it didn't know when to stop. It just put its head down and kept those little feet going. Typically, calves that do a run-out, just dash through an open gate at the other end of the arena. Not this baby.

Rising's calf turned on the after-burners, ran all out, and banged its head flush against the wall at the opposite end of the arena. Someone forgot to say whoa.

One of several clowns who entertained fans during the 2014 Cody Nite Rodeo season was Andy Burrelle (photo by Lew Freedman).

"That calf is a sprinter," observed Andy the Clown. "But he isn't a hurdler."

Bryce Bott had a calf he could catch and notched a time of 12.6 seconds. Coleman White was forced to endure fresh jokes about being in his 50s.

"He gets to take time off because he is a member of AARP," said Burrelle who hadn't been around for Sid McFarland's AARP teases of White.

Every rodeo clown is different, and Burrelle brought his own act to Cody Nite Rodeo.

For one of his featured acts Burrelle appeared in mid-arena wearing a red sport coat and toting a whip. He bantered with Rogge. "I've got a whip because I thought I was coming to the circus," Burrelle said. "I was going to become a lion tamer. You know how I knew I was coming to the circus? I'm talking to a clown."

Rogge retorted, "You're the one wearing makeup." Burrelle cracked the whip and somehow caught himself in the butt.

When introducing a different act Burrelle dressed as a pot-bellied jockey and again talked about race horses with Rogge.

"I'm familiar with quarter horses," Rogge said.

Burrelle brought out a tiny little pony. "This is an eighth of a horse," he said. "You've been watching that Triple Crown with California Chrome? Well, this is Oklahoma Rust."

Another competitor who put in the time night after night was young Anna Allshouse in the barrel racing.

"She makes a living in this arena taking money from grownups," Rogge said.

Certainly, her college fund was growing. Allshouse's 18.09-second run won the night.

Burrelle, 37, is a converted bull fighter. In the old days bull fighters and rodeo clowns were one and the same. Burrelle still wears the face paint, but he has been edging out of bull fighting.

"Thirty-seven is old for a bull fighter, but not for a clown," he said. "It's like in football. You start to lose a step."

As he morphed into a different rodeo persona, Burrelle needed practice. In his own way, his changeover gained him a kinship with the novice bull riders despite his longevity in the sport. Burrelle kept bringing out new material, trying it out on the Cody Nite Rodeo audiences. He likened his appearance in Cody to a comedian taking low pay to perform on an open microphone night at a comedy club.

"It's good practice," Burrelle said. "It's trying stuff out Off-Broadway. If it doesn't work at one of those big rodeos, they won't invite you back."

Not surprisingly, when Coleman White clicked off a 10.5 clocking, definitely good for points, Burrelle was back on his case again with AARP commentary. "Boy, that old guy is good," Burrelle said. "It makes me want to sign up for an AARP card."

One after another the junior steer riders had a tough go. "Don't worry everybody," Burrelle said. "It's just like Little League. Tell 'em to walk it off."

Zain Fitzgerald was able to stick on board for six seconds.

"I think the Wrangler officials need to check his behind for Velcro," Burrelle said.

In the team roping Dan Vanek and partner Willy Gould blistered the course. When they finished the clock read 0.00. Nobody is that fast. A 0.00 would come under the heading of "You want to see it again?" It was somewhat like the old joke told by the great pitcher Satchel Paige about fellow Hall of Famer Cool Papa Bell's speed. Bell was so fast, Paige said, when the hurler roomed with him the outfielder could turn off the light switch and be in bed before the room darkened. The 0.00 actually represented a malfunction of the clock but provided joke fodder for Burrelle.

"Look at that time," he declared. "That's the fastest I've ever seen. Zip."

The genuine time was fast enough. The duo clocked 5.5 seconds and won the contest.

Burrelle appealed to the crowd for suggestions for a birthday present for his mother-in-law. He recommended a free bull ride, but lamented, "She didn't even use what I bought for her last year – a cemetery plot."

Bull riding was next up and Rogge set the stage. "This is the most dangerous game in rodeo right here," he said.

For the first several days of Cody Nite Rodeo, bull rider Jeremy Jacobs had difficulties staying on. Ten days into the season he scored a 77 to win a round. He studied video of his rides and felt he was overriding and getting out of position — the rodeo equivalent of a baseball player checking tape to see what he was doing wrong in the batter's box.

Jacobs wore chaps with dollar signs on the sides, made for him by an encouraging uncle.

"He was a little bit of trouble in the chute," Jacobs said of the bull that helped him win money. "Every once in a while it will get really slow out there and you can see things unfold. Your adrenalin is going, but the time feels much longer. All day I was thinking about my ride, how I was going to set myself. I was anxious to get going. It felt good."

★★★

PAUL FEES

When Paul Fees was a kid growing up in Arizona he was a rodeo fan. Some of his cousins were rodeo participants too. Fees, 65, drifted away from the sport to other things in life, but in 1981 he became an historian at the Buffalo Bill Center of the West in Cody and spent the next 20 years working at the Center.

The white-haired Fees bears a passing resemblance to the late actor Richard Farnsworth. In 1994 he became a member of the board of the Cody Stampede. Rodeo reclaimed him.

"I became interested all over again," he said.

Fees knows his Buffalo Bill history and his rodeo history. The Stampede continuously holds its place amongst the top outdoor rodeos of the summer, but it was not always flush.

"There were some fallow times," Fees said. "About 40 years ago board members had to borrow money to keep it going. Now it's as good as ever. The board at the time had to make the choice to go big-time. Cody is always one of the top 20, by whatever measure."

That was the beginning of prize money growing to irresistible numbers like the roughly $400,000 paid out today. Cowboys are going to go where the money is when they have a finite amount of time and there are competing rodeos.

The board puts in about $25,000 for each Stampede event, and while there are variations, it costs about $300 per event to enter and that money also goes toward prize money.

Cody Nite Rodeo and the Stampede are linked. Fees said Jackson, Wyoming; Cowtown, New Jersey; and Kissimmee, Florida come to mind as towns that have weekly rodeos, but Cody maintains its unique place as the only place with daily rodeos.

"There are no others like it," Fees said. "Others — North Platte, Nebraska, for one — have tried."

The most important element that allows Cody Nite Rodeo and the Stampede to flourish, Fees said, is the tourism produced by the hundreds of thousands of people that come and go on the road to Yellowstone National Park. Not everyone who travels through Cody knows about the city's rodeo heritage, nor do they all have the time to stop. But many, many do, and that's why so many people in the stands at Cody Nite Rodeo raise their hands when asked if this is their first rodeo.

"The tourism has made the Stampede and the Nite Rodeo as successful as they are," he said.

Tourism, plus the continued mystique of the American Cowboy?

"Oh, you bet," Fees said.

Fees is another of those guys who was weaned on TV westerns and he has never forgotten them. He just wishes there were more new cowboy shows on the tube now.

Fees sates most of his rodeo thirst through his Stampede board work and at the rodeo, but periodically over the summer he drops in on the Nite Rodeo, just to see how its running and to catch a little action.

Some days there is more going on than others. Bareback rider Andy Mumm checked in for his usual event and glanced at the entry sheet. Surprise! There was only one entry.

"It's just me against me," Mumm said.

And Mumm, who had been streaking through the competition, didn't even win. He missed his mark on the horse, placing his feet wrong, so he was disqualified. He made it eight seconds, but it didn't matter.

"I wasn't lifting with my hips," Mumm said. "I couldn't keep my feet up."

Not every day is going to produce the perfect ride. Mumm recalled a bareback ride where the horse seemed determine to scrape him off its back by riding dangerously close to the fence. Mumm had to choose between dismounting in one piece and forfeiting the ride. He brought down his free hand and illegally took hold of the rope with two hands.

"It's better to double grab and stay healthy," Mumm said. "There's another day to ride."

After one good ride Mumm said, "That felt like a 56." Meaning in his mind it was a lousy ride, even if he stayed aboard. He recalled a 93-point score in Casper in 2006.

Some spectators, like Andy Mumm's 2-year-old son D.J., get the rodeo fever young (photo by Lew Freedman).

"I don't think there will ever be a 100-point ride," Mumm said.

Maybe not, but for decades that was said about a perfect 10 in gymnastics and then along came Nadia Comaneci at the 1976 Summer Olympics. There are 300-score perfect games in bowling, and pitchers can throw a perfect game in baseball. Will judges ever allow a 100-point rodeo score to occur?

In the next event, Brandon 'The Music Man' Milburn upped the ante a bit, giving each barrel racer a tune to compete by, and it was usually an action-packed song. "Twist and Shout" played for a rider. "Rio" for another. The women may or may not have been psyched up, but it didn't matter. Anna Allshouse, the 12-year-old who was born after all of the tunes were composed, ran a composed race, finishing in 17.83. It was the second time in a week Allshouse won by a hundredth of a second.

Clown Andy Burrelle climbed on a bucking horse and told everyone he was going to hypnotize it by waving his keys and win the event. He was quickly thrown.

"I saw it on YouTube and the guy made it look easy," Burrelle said.

Night after night the darned bulls tormented riders. On a typical night there were 10 bull riders and on a typical night nine or 10 of them lost out to their bulls. If these opponents were professional basketball teams the bulls would be the San Antonio Spurs, and the riders would be the Philadelphia 76ers.

Every once in a while someone showed up that no one knew and plunked down an entry fee. One night the humans chipped away at the bulls' insurmountable lead. While six riders went down Clayton Ahlgren on Blind Side and Wyatt Bartels on S'More stayed on and scored identical 77s to share first place.

Bartels was built more like a cross-country runner, so thin that if he turned sideways he would be a shadow. But not only did he stay alive for his eight seconds Bartels rode the highlighted bonus bull so that all shoppers could purchase Cody Nite Rodeo T-shirts or sweatshirts for $5 off.

The 18-year-old was the hero of the moment just for saving rodeo fans a few bucks.

★★★

ROPIN' AND RIDIN'

It is not unusual to see a cowboy or cowgirl limping at a rodeo. Generally, it means that they were bucked off a horse and landed wrong, twisting an ankle, or something of that nature.

So although people sympathized when Kooper Bott stepped out of her car and relied on crutches to reach the sign-up house for Cody Nite Rodeo only some knew that she needed to lean on them because a prior automobile accident injured her back and hip.

Bott, 19, had been a student at a junior college in Casper, but was planning to transfer to a four-year school in Texas to join the rodeo team. She got the idea to obtain a cosmetology degree and then travel the rodeo circuit offering services between rides to cowgirls who worried about their nails and appearances. Bott had been studying radiology, but realized that was the wrong major for her.

"I'm not a huge fan of hospitals," she said. "I don't like needles."

The accident (not her fault) had been an all-around nuisance, but each night Bott paid her entry fee and competed in the breakaway roping after tossing her crutches aside as if she had just swum in some eternal spring and been cured. Riding was probably not part of her rehab, but at least she didn't ride a bucking animal which more likely would have pulverized her already wounded body. Did the doctor approve of her activity?

"They didn't tell me I couldn't," Bott said.

Bott, the older sister of Bryce Bott, was another rodeo kid. She started tying goats when she was in the fourth grade, was a rodeo queen and also showed horses. Horses were some of her best friends.

"I'd get bored if I didn't have my horses," Bott said. "I wish they could be in my dorm room." Possibly a roommate would object in such close quarters.

Bott was one of the consistent daily contenders in breakaway roping. Often a family member, usually her mother,

Cowgirls lined up awaiting the results of the breakaway roping event (photo by Lew Freedman).

filmed her runs so she could study them and improve. On some nights there wasn't much that she could do better and she won the round. Other times the rope bounced harmlessly off the streaking calf.

"You have to have a good horse to start with," Bott said. "They need to be able to brake really hard and stop. They've got to make slide stops in two seconds. For the rider there's a huge mental part. There are a lot of other good ropers out there and you can't get psyched out. My mom always told me, 'Get blood in your eye.'"

Bott knew that with her hip problem breakaway roping was one of the only events she could safely enter. She hoped to stay competitive all summer and still heal well enough to start college rodeo in the fall. In 2012, Bott, who said breakaway is still her best event, started team roping. It is always advantageous to compete with the same partner every rodeo, but at the nightly Cody Rodeo more often mixing and matching occurs. Sometimes the Bott siblings roped together, but not always.

"It kind of sucks when you can't practice with your partner every day," Kooper Bott said. "The teams that do have more togetherness. When I started I was just really slow and not very good."

Horses are athletes, too, and not all prefer a heavy diet of hay and oats and other healthy stuff. Bott's horse Cracker Jack seemed to crave the types of foods that might be arrayed in the same grocery store aisle as its namesake. Cracker Jack, Bott said, likes nacho cheese chips, Rice Krispie treats, and is also into the hard stuff like curly fries.

"He even ate my mom's ham sandwich," Bott said. "He's a garbage gut."

Meanwhile, her horse named Roy has a total chips addiction. If someone is leaning on a fence and shakes a bag of chips the horse runs across the pasture aiming to stick its nose in the bag.

"He wouldn't eat a protein bar," Bott said.

It was suggested that Roy might make a fine candidate to act in a Super Bowl commercial for a chips product, dashing across the field right up to a person and then demanding his share of corn chips or potato chips.

"Oh yeah, I'm going to get rich," Bott said.

If she has a horse as charismatic as Mr. Ed the sky's the limit.

With Colt Chlarson sidelined in a sling because of his broken collar bone, the saddle bronc event offered opportunity for other riders to seize points. James Greeson missed the first 10 days of Cody Nite Rodeo, but from the moment he showed up he was a factor. Greeson, 22, finished in a fourth-place tie at the College National Finals Rodeo in 2013 for Sam Houston State and when he put up an 83-point score in a saddle bronc ride he opened some eyes right away in Cody.

Muscular, but lean, Greeson played baseball and football when he was younger in Okeechobee, Florida. Even though father Lynn was a bull rider, Greeson's parents weren't crazy about his rodeo habit until he earned a scholarship to Trinity University in San Antonio before switching to Sam Houston.

"They weren't all for it at first, but they liked it better when I got a scholarship," Greeson said.

Greeson's 83 was recorded after being off horses for a month, so he was feeling pretty heady about making the splash in Cody.

"It's been a while," he said. "I had a lot of fire."

Part of the reason for Greeson's layoff was not having money for entry fees. He was one of those young cowboys who carried a saddle slung over his shoulder, wore his hat on his head and jeans on his legs, and didn't have much more luggage.

"I've been riding on what I've been winning," Greeson said.

He began winning in Cody, which wasn't going to buy him first-class air fares, but would at least give him eatin' money and keep him in the saddle.

"You've really got to want to do it," Greeson said of the saddle bronc mindset. "You can't just say, 'Hey, I'm a rodeo cowboy' and get on. It's about staying focused and positive. It's an art. It starts with heart. You've got to do your part and the horse has to do its part – just buck. I really admire those horses with spirit, an animal like that which has so much power."

Man against beast for eight seconds can be a thrill or it can be heart-breaking. Staying on until the buzzer sounds is what it's all about. As a man who has hit home runs and scored touchdowns, Greeson said staying on a saddle bronc to the end beats all of them.

"There's no feeling like it," he said. "It's the excitement and the thrill."

★★★

BILL GARLOW

Of all the places in the wide world to be a member of the Buffalo Bill Cody clan, Cody, Wyoming is where it's at. The city is named for Buffalo Bill. The Buffalo Bill Center of the West, the extraordinary museum that focuses on Buffalo Bill and other aspects of the West, is located only a football field away from downtown. Buffalo Bill's picture is on a sign at the visitors association. His name adorns hotels. The Irma Hotel still stands and thrives.

The Buffalo Bill Center for the West is a showpiece tourist attraction in Cody and displays exhibits of many highlights of Buffalo Bill's life, including his famed appearance with his Wild West in England before Queen Victoria (photo by Lew Freedman).

At age 72, so does hotelier and business man Bill Garlow, Buffalo Bill's great-grandson. While expressing an interest in western history, the doings at the Buffalo Bill Center, and items of historical relevance to his great-grandfather, Garlow doesn't care much for rodeo.

"Cody is a cowboy town," Garlow said in his Cody office. "Rodeo is part of the culture. But I'm not even a rodeo fan. It's not a big deal to me. I'm interested in western history, and I've read about Buffalo Bill Cody. I know enough."

Garlow's grandmother was Buffalo Bill's daughter Irma. She married Frederick H. Garlow of Iowa – her second husband – in 1908. Irma, the namesake of the famous Cody hotel built in 1902 by her father, had three children. One of them was William Cody Garlow, who later in life changed his name to William Cody and whose memorial headstone is at Old Trail Town in Cody. Bill Garlow is his son.

Many books have been written about Buffalo Bill. Posters advertising his Wild West performances have been duplicated and are easily obtainable at inexpensive prices. Some pricier genuine stuff can be purchased at auctions and on e-bay, but Garlow doesn't own much Buffalo Bill memorabilia dating to the old scout's life between 1846 and 1917.

"The Garlow side inherited most of the stuff," Bill Garlow said. But his father and uncles sold most of it. "I don't have much left."

What Garlow does have is his heritage and the Cody family tree has been dissected, studied, and detailed back to 1698. The International Cody Family Association has an online presence and there are periodic reunions, including one that was held in Cody in 2012.

Garlow believes there are about 70 living descendents of Buffalo Bill, with about 30 living in England. A dozen relatives came from England to Cody a few years ago while others traveled from Washington and California.

"We're kind of spread around," Garlow said.

Garlow was born in Texas in 1942, but came to Cody as a child. He left again and became a certified public accountant in Dallas. When he tired of the heat and humidity of Texas he moved back to Cody because of family connections.

Buffalo Bill was so famous during his lifetime that it is sometimes hard to believe in this hectic, overwrought American society of high tech and crazed traffic jams. "He was probably the best-known American for a few years," Garlow said. "And the most photographed."

Most Americans probably underestimate the overseas interest in Old West history, gunfighters, cowboys and Buffalo Bill. While most of them are legends of the past, Buffalo Bill separated himself from the herd by actually traveling to foreign lands. Those long-forgotten trips in the United States, except by museum curators, are remembered well in Europe.

It may be difficult for Americans born after World War II to believe, especially after the mid-1960s when TV westerns faltered in the top-10 viewing ratings, but Buffalo Bill Cody remains a large presence in some of the places he visited.

"Buffalo Bill is probably better known in Europe than he is in the United States," Garlow said.

That is a statement that is echoed by Bruce Eldredge, the executive director and CEO of the Buffalo Bill Center, and Steve Friesen, the director of the Buffalo Bill Museum at Cody's Golden, Colorado gravesite. They have witnessed the Buffalo Bill affection and connection first-hand on their own trips to Europe.

Being a Buffalo Bill descendent does have its perks. Being the great-grandson of Buffalo Bill Cody has put Garlow on the road for adventure more than once.

"I've had some interesting trips because of it," he said.

Garlow has traveled to Dublin, Ireland for a Buffalo Bill Center of the West meeting. He has traveled to Scotland for a Buffalo Bill Symposium. He went to France for a film festival because he was a Buffalo Bill descendent. He attended a Buffalo Bill exhibit in England. England may have stronger ties to Buffalo Bill than other European lands because Buffalo Bill spent more time there.

"He was there so long," Garlow said.

Cody toured Europe eight times, four times between 1887 and 1892 and four times between 1902 and 1906.

England's King Edward VII requested a private performance of the Wild West when Cody first hit the continent and had so much fun that he set up a command performance for Queen Victoria in connection with the Golden Jubilee celebration of her time on the throne. A good time was again had by all and another Wild West exhibition was performed for Queen Victoria's royal guests. Cody met kings and queens, princes and princesses from all over Europe who by all accounts were spellbound by the western cast of cowboys, Indians, horses and buffalo.

London, Birmingham and Manchester were among the Wild West stops in England and it was estimated that more than 2.5 million people saw 300 performances. In 1892 Cody brought the Wild West back, conducted another command performance for Queen Victoria, and spent six months in London. Cody was in England for so long and toured Great Britain so much he practically qualified for citizenship.

One of the stories stemming from Cody's visitations to England is that Queen Victoria made the grand gesture of shipping a fabulous cherrywood bar to him as a gift that was installed at the Irma Hotel and remains there to be admired. Some researchers dispute the origins of the bar, even if that makes a good story, but the hotel's website does make the claim that the bar came from Queen Victoria.

England was fun for both Buffalo Bill Cody and Bill Garlow, but Garlow said one of the most surprising and fascinating overseas endeavors he was invited to led him to participate on a German TV show that was sort of a "What's My Line?" panel of descendents of famous people. Besides Buffalo Bill, Garlow was aware of subjects being related to Richard III and Ethiopia's Halie Sellassie. Panelists had the chance to ask 10 questions to narrow down their guesses as to who Garlow's famous ancestor was.

"They got it right," he said.

One thing Buffalo Bill was famous for, and was an aspect of his physical stature that helped make him so photogenic, was his long, flowing locks. Lesser known was that late in life Buffalo Bill was bald and wore a wig to keep up appearances for the millions that easily identified him.

As it so happens, Bill Garlow is bald, and he does not wear a wig.

★★★

STREAKS

Wyatt Bartels was just finishing high school and he was starting to ride bulls for real in rodeos around his Guthrie, Oklahoma home as well as on the road and at Cody Nite Rodeo.

When he won his third straight bull riding competition in Cody with a mark of 79, it was official that he was on a hot streak. When Bartels pulled out the abacus he realized he had won $3,000 in a month. That's not much for most professional athletes, or the top rodeo guys, but for a young rodeo journeyman that was doing pretty well.

"It feels great when you get on a good run," Bartels said. "It brings your confidence through the roof. I just came up here to have fun."

Bartels said he telephoned his parents in Oklahoma every night after competitions to relay the play-by-play action. It wasn't as if this was strange to them. His father Jaye rode bulls. When Bartels was a little boy he found a picture of his father riding a bull that was tucked into a photo album and it intrigued him. He pretty much confiscated the photo.

"I just carried the thing around with me," he said.

Bartels first climbed on a calf when he was four and then progressed to steers. The big bulls were a natural progression. Bartels qualified for the National High School Finals Rodeo in 2014 and that took him to Rock Springs, Wyoming. He extended his stay in the state by entering Cody Nite Rodeo.

"It's a lot of hard work and dedication," Bartels said. "You need good balance. You have to keep your feet down and your head down and your eyes on the bull's shoulders. You have to ride them jump for jump. You go at it 110 percent, but you can't ride them all."

This was a sound way to think because although Bartels rode them all for a while inevitably his hot streak was extinguished. The bulls began throwing him with the same regularity as he had ridden them before. It happens.

It was difficult to categorize the streak of Blake Miller, a 17-year-old from Texas. He began the season with a concussion, knocked out of rides almost immediately. Cold streak. While he was healing he began working as a bull fighter, helping Zack Flatt and Justin Josey. Then he made a return to sitting on bulls instead of dodging them and produced a 74 score. Hot streak. It wasn't long before he was back to bull fighting, though.

Poor Wyatt Lehman was on a cold streak as definitive as Bartels' hot streak. There was no doubt that Lehman possessed a lot of try. The average human being would take a gander at the pent-up energy in the bulls as they stood in their little jail-pens about to be released, kicking the sides of the fencing, snot pouring out of their noses, and their faces seemingly scrunched up with hatred – and run the other way. But Lehman came back every night, fighting back as the bulls heaved and snorted and chucked him in the air. After another attempt with no time, announcer Kade Rogge said, "Nobody tries harder than that kid."

The old guys in the tie-down roping were trying pretty hard. Coleman White may have carried that AARP card in his wallet, but others possessed birth certificates in the neighborhood of the big 5-0, too. Daryl Lamb, an Australian by birth, living in Texas as a cowboy, worked the arena grounds by day caring for livestock and worked the grounds by night as one of the main pickup men. Lamb still found time to enter tie-down roping even though periodically he would say his 50 years were catching up to his body.

Daryl Lamb, an Australian now living in Texas, completes a tie-down roping effort — Lamb won the all-around cowboy title for the Cody Nite Rodeo 2014 (photo by Lew Freedman).

Lamb was at least young at heart when he posted his second win June 13 with a 10.5-second roping and takedown.

Brandon the Music Man pressed buttons quickly and played tunes appropriate to the action to entertain the crowd when something happened. Breakaway roper Sara Arthur seemed to have a calf roped, but the rope fell harmlessly away. Brandon immediately played Lesley Gore's "I'll Cry If I Want To."

James Greeson was on a hotter streak than Bartels, but every once in a while a horse came along that not even he could handle. Riding a bronc named Darth (as in Darth Vader from "Star Wars") Greeson was going after his eight seconds but abruptly grabbed the rope with two hands to prevent an unwelcome face plant into a fence.

"About six seconds into that ride he saved his life," is the way Kade Rogge put it.

It is always better to pull back in order to ride again rather than be sent to the hospital. Cowboys are much more acquainted with emergency rooms than they would like to be. So on the rare occasion when an action of their own can prevent potentially serious injury, they choose the move to alter fate.

This is especially true in Cody Nite Rodeo where all a cowboy must do to ride again is wait-till-tomorrow, rather than wait-till-next-year at a bigger annual event.

Greeson would have been hard-pressed to win the rodeo on Darth that night since Kaleb Asay was in town and rode Hurricane so well he scored 86 points. The Asay family of nearby Powell breeds fine cowboys to contend with the finest of bred livestock. Kaleb, 25, is a saddle bronc man and he had just returned to the neighborhood from a rodeo in Sisters, Oregon.

Dad Mike was a rodeo guy too, and brother Kanin is a pro bull riding star, the winner of the 2007 and 2012 XTreme Bulls Tour championships. Kaleb Asay was not fibbing when he said he has been involved in rodeo his whole life.

"When we were babies we were on horses in a papoose (on his mother's back)," he said. "That was when I was too young to walk."

Kanin gravitated towards bulls, and Kaleb leaned towards bucking horses.

"It's always amazed me as a really neat event," Kaleb Asay said. "It was always on my mind because it wasn't easy. You've got to get on a bucking horse every day. You have to have super fast hand-eye coordination." Super fast as in...he snapped his fingers.

Asay sounded as fatalistic as any cowboy when he both shrugged off the serious injuries he has incurred and the likelihood that a horse will take out his anger on a cowboy.

"I broke my back a couple of times," Asay said with the calm inflection of someone commenting on a pleasant picnic. "I had to take most of last year off. You're going to get knocked around a bit and bruised up. That's part of the beauty of it. It takes a special person to take that risk."

As Kaleb passed through Cody to get some riding in his brother Kanin was on his way to town, too. Once Cody Nite Rodeo beginners, Kanin Asay and Dusty Tuckness, who is from Meeteetse, pretty much on the opposite side of Cody from Powell, have chosen to honor their roots with an annual bull riding and bull fighting festival each June.

★★★

TUCKNESS & ASAY CLASSIC

There was rodeo in Cody on June 14, but it was not Cody Nite Rodeo. Dusty Tuckness and Kasin Asay, two local boys who made good, had taken over the arena to provide Xtreme Bulls competition for bull riders and bull fighters only. Horses can stay home for a day.

The duo, both about 28, grew up together, and they have been rodeo buds all along. They liked the idea of giving something back to the community and rodeo is their method of communication and entertainment, so it had to be rodeo-related.

"It was just destined to happen," Asay said.

The bull riders were members of the usual Cody Nite crowd. Cleve Spang was on Bull Devil and when he was thrown he landed awkwardly, giving the bull a chance to wipe him out. Zack Flatt dashed in-between and distracted the bull.

"That man just saved a life," Rogge said.

Wyatt Bartels was on Meatball and was thrown fast. Skeet Chadwick drew Gravedigger, and Rogge made sure to alert clown Andy Burrelle that this was an appropriately named bull. "There's one of your nasty bull names," Rogge said.

Clowns are often referred to as "the man in the can." That's because they have their own reinforced protective barrels to jump into if a mad bull attacks. Rather than pierce flesh bulls blast the barrel, flip it over, and perhaps roll it. Burrelle saw one bull coming, ducked down and suffered a drive-by bashing. The bull hit the can so hard it rolled into a fence.

Burrelle calls his barrel a "clowndominum" and in its own way it does for him what the suit does for Iron Man. The barrel is made of aluminum and has layers of high density foam, fiberglass and rubber.

"You want the outside to be padded so it takes all of that force," Burrelle said. "I've probably got $3,000 in that. The bulls end up getting their teeth rattled, and they wonder why. It's not bad at all for me inside."

Junior steer riders were included in the action and Lukaksey Morris, one of the Cody Nite regulars, turned in a stellar 81-

Lukasey Morris of Oklahoma, who turned 12 during the season, was one of the top junior steer riders all season (photo by Lew Freedman).

point ride, although the 12-year-old was limping when he came off the dirt.

"Do you mean to tell me that you can't whip your kid in Walmart, and they can do this?" Burrelle said.

"It's the last legal form of child abuse," Rogge said.

There were some iffy landings amongst thrown bull riders. Clayton Ahlrgren was thrown, but landed straight up on his feet. He may have jarred his back. Blake Miller drew Samson, but not for long.

It didn't matter too much what the young riders did. In the end, Kanin Asay got on a bull and showed how it is done on the circuit. Winner of nearly a million dollars in rodeo prize money Asay was rounding into top form and just wanted to ride. He rode the bull called Have Mercy, and Asay showed it none, scoring 88 points to win his own event.

"It was more of a practice thing for me," Asay said. "It's been a little bit slow for me this season. I need to get on more bulls."

Probably a bigger attraction – a rare thing to be said in rodeo – than the bull riding was the bull fighting. In their jobs bull fighters are attired like clowns, but are as important to cowboys' health as the EMTs standing by, and sometimes more so because they prevent injuries rather than treat them.

Occasionally there are contests of skill just for bull fighters to show off their ability to elude bulls, distract bulls, or trick bulls simply through guile and quick feet. It's pretty much man against bull, not in an effort to stay on the bull's back for eight seconds, but in a match of wits and dexterity. The goal is to out-think and out-run a bull. This is called freestyle bull fighting. The only life you are trying to save is your own.

Tuckness invited an all-star cast of bull fighters who for the most part had the words "bullfight champ" and "world champion" and a cross-section of other honors on their resumes. They were a bunch of clowns that were sort of the Navy Seals of rodeo, able to stay alive in challenging conditions.

Amongst the biggest luminaries were Evan Allard, the 2010 world champion, Logan Blaisdale, winner of several contests, and Tony Scott, another regular winner of fancy titles. Also in the field were Justin Josey and Zack Flatt, the Cody Nite bull fighters. Tuckness, who a few months later won his record fifth Bullfighter of the Year Award, did not compete.

Flatt's record was thinner than most: Wichita Falls Bullfight Champ and Ardmore Bullfights Top 5. Josey's resume was thinner than a piece of paper slipped under a door. For the visitors they were probably looked upon as courtesy entries. For Cody fans, they were familiar names (if not familiar faces given their clown makeup).

Before his turn in the competition, Flatt sat alone, earphones on, eyes closed, almost meditating. This time it was not about preventing damage to a body, it was about distinguishing himself.

Nearby, two emergency medical technicians stood next to the fencing and chatted. "Hope nothing happens and we can just watch," one of them said.

When a bull was loosed into the shortened and rounded arena, bringing the animals even more up-close and personal, Flatt was ready, staring at it, then coaxing it to c'mon, come after him. But the bull must have been in protest trot form for not being paid union wage. Rather than participate in a showdown with Zack, who was right there trying to tease it into clobbering him, the bull ran in circles, paused to inspect Andy Burrelle's bright yellow barrel, and began head butting it. Zack? Who's he?

Judges decided that since the bull didn't even try Zack would get a do-over a little later on the card.

The bull fighters were in top form. They stared down the foe, side-stepped horns, performed ballet-like twists avoiding charges. Logan Blaisdale scored an 82, but nearly ended up with an ambulance ride to the hospital. A bull's charge caught him with a horn and it was a loud "Ooh," scary moment. During the 40 seconds leading up to the whistle Blaisdale was hit and tossed and hit again. Things looked grim. Surely Blaisdale was down for the count, or maybe worse.

"Logan took a hooking," Kade Rogge told the crowd. One rodeo sponsor is Wyoming Whiskey and a bottle was given away each night during Cody Nite Rodeo to a competitor who had hard luck or showed sportsmanship in the face of adversity. Blaisdale seemed to fit the bill. "Pour it in the wound and gulp it," Rogge instructed him.

Justin Josey was in the ring ready for anything. Or at least he thought he was. He drew a particularly nasty bull that chased him right over a fence – it was a pretty good vertical leap for Josey to save his hide. Pickup man Harold Adema rode up to distract the bull, so Josey could climb back inside the fencing.

"I don't want to get frequent flyer miles like Justin Josey," said Andy the Clown. "Here comes Harold to the rescue. He looks like the Marlboro man."

Zack got his do-over and was magnificent, just about as artistic as a Spanish matador, and more athletic. He leapt over his bull as it came at him, and Flatt dodged close calls over and over again, eluding danger. He was extremely light on his feet, springing off his toes. Flatt was rewarded with a score of 86 points and that sent him into the finals.

Blaisdale rebounded from his near-death experience and the finals came down to what kind of show he and Zack could put on in 40 seconds. Flatt's stamina and endurance workouts paid off. He ran for all 40 seconds, leading the bull, reacting to the bull, and avoiding the bull with last-second twists and turns. He scored 89 points, the second most he had ever recorded. But so did Blaisdale. There was no run-off. The tie gave each man a piece of the title. But becoming co-champion of the Tuckness/Asay Classic was a huge get for Flatt. It was a big-league crown and for someone on the cusp of earning his PRCA card a credit that could be life-changing. He was ecstatic.

"It feels great, real great," said the happy Flatt afterwards. "I put a lot into it. I've been working my butt off for that."

For the rest of the summer season when Flatt was introduced to the Cody Nite Rodeo fans – tipping his hat each time – the announcer mentioned his newly earned title. The spectators might not have understood the significance of him winning the Tuckness/Kasay Classic, but Flatt certainly did. Deep inside now he knew that he was one of the big boys. When opportunity beckoned he had seized it.

★★★

BACK TO REGULAR RODEO

Although they would never admit it, a one-day break from Cody Nite Rodeo competition may have helped regulars refresh mentally and help heal bruises. June 15 was a good night for those rodeo guys and gals who were staples of the show, ready to deflect challenges from one-and-done cowboys and cowgirls just passing by.

Except for the bull riders. The bulls were probably even more emboldened by their night as stars on the marquee. It was 11 up and 11 down in the bull riding. Cleve Spang, who had been in the Tuckness/Kasay Classic, was ditched by Shooter and the pickup men had a hell of a tour of the world before they could bring Shooter back to the pen.

Shooter hated a man on his back, but he seemed indifferent to being roped.

"He looks like a pit bull on dental floss," Andy the Clown said.

Bucking animals not only must put up with cowboys, they have what is called a flank rope tied around their middle. While the rope does not hurt, it annoys, and the animals are pleased when a pickup man pulls the rope free. Sometimes that calms down finicky buckers.

Coleman White — Mr. AARP — won the tie-down roping at 11.9 seconds. Pam Vanek won the breakaway roping in 3.2 seconds, although she had to be mindful of Shanni Shipley's performance. Shipley posted a time of 2.9 seconds, but broke the timing barrier a smidgeon too early and was penalized 10 seconds, wiping out her success. Still, that was as fast as anyone had gone all year

On a night when no barrel racer incurred a penalty or turned in a singularly brilliant run, all eight competitors, running clean, finished the course between 17.77 seconds and 18.96. It was a rare night of racing for Cydney Tate, one of the organizers' daughters, who recorded an 18.33. Tate had been ill in the off-season and did not compete as often as her younger sister Hadley, who notched an 18.50. Anna Allshouse, piling up the points, won with the low time.

James Greeson won the saddle bronc again, riding Volunteer. For a moment when the gate swung open Volunteer just stood still. He had been nervous in the pen, but now when he was free to run and buck, initially he did nothing. But after stalling out for a second like a slow-to-turn-over automobile engine, Volunteer remembered why he was there and bucked like mad trying to eject Greeson. Volunteer couldn't do it and Greeson scored 79 points for the victory.

"Something clicks and then they go," Greeson said of Volunteer's stock-still start. "Yes, sir, that was a good horse."

Andy Mumm, the bareback boss, was rocking and rolling on Twister, a horse that seemed to bounce across the arena. For a moment it seemed Twister was going to bound across the width of the arena and simply heave Mumm over the opposite fence. But the horse was a step or two shy of that and Mumm scored 75 points. It was a solid ride on a worthy bronc, but there was just one problem. Again there were no other riders entered. Where were the bareback riders?

"No money for me," Mumm said of the virtually non-existent field. "I got two kids recruited to enter tomorrow night. They're high schoolers from Idaho. It makes it funner for me. You get old and crippled in bareback. None of the kids want to do it."

It was less work for pickup men like Harold, though they didn't mind full fields. Adema was one of the hardest working men at the rodeo. Much like Daryl Lamb he worked a full day shift, feeding up to 35 horses. Then he worked nights as a pickup man, helping riders dismount from horses and bulls and rounding up that livestock and herding the animals back to their corrals. On most nights, he, like Lamb, also signed up for tie-down roping.

"I love picking up," Adema said, sitting in the trailer he lived in on the grounds during the season. "But I've trained

Some of the hardest working men in rodeo are the pickup men, who help cowboys off mounts and then herd the livestock back to the pens. Harold Adema (front) and Daryl Lamb did much of the heavy lifting (photo by Lew Freedman).

horses since I was 18 years old." At 53, Adema had a little of that craggy-faced cowboy look going for him, with blue eyes. His uniform was more or less a long-sleeved, one-color shirt, boots and jeans and a hat that he always wore in public. "I don't take my spurs off either."

Adema lists his home as Riverton, Wyoming, two hours from Cody, but spends much of the winter in Arizona. Over the years Adema has spent considerable time in Minnesota, North Dakota and Texas, too. A while back Adema rode bareback horses in high school rodeo and competed in rodeo for Dickinson State in North Dakota. At one time he had 75 mares, but now keeps eight in Wyoming and seven in Minnesota.

Adema takes a lot of teasing from the announcer and the clown, but he is so focused on the animals running loose and roping them that he doesn't hear it all.

"The cowboys think we're there for them," Adema said. "More important than that is handling the stock, getting the flank rope off to calm the horses down. We're there for the safety of the horses and the cowboys."

Once a horse ran free without its rider, Adema and the other pickup men, Lamb, Luke Newsom, or Matt Scott, teamed to soothe its nerves and lead it back to food and water. They rode up alongside the wilder horse, sometimes on each side at the same time. When the ride ended Adema wanted to be in close proximity.

"I want to get up next to them and have the horse buddy up to my horse," Adema said. "The cowboy is supposed to reach out to us and then slide off. Bareback riders jam their hand in with the rope and they can get hung up pretty easily and be dragged pretty badly."

That's why it was important to soothe the bucking animal by crowding it with other horses.

"It's herd instinct," Adema said. "We call it mothering up."

The bucking broncos still have a wildness gene in them, but some get used to the routine and are anxious to return to the pens. Some are new to the scene and get spooked by the crowd and a bit panicked once they are rider free. Once, Adema recalled a horse trying to jump into a fence. It had never seen so many people before.

"He was just a wild horse," Adema said. "It takes a long time to make a good bucking horse and five minutes to ruin it." Some smart horses never get used to being roped, but recognize when it's coming and they "don't like it too well."

The pickup men's horses can out-run bulls, but the rider must carefully steer them clear of any kind of dust-up because an angry bull will gladly gash a horse. If they are all headed into a corner the rider will accelerate to keep his horse out of harm's way.

"Once, when a bull got into the neighbor's cows my bay horse took a hooking in a pasture," Adema said. "That bull came at me and got me in a corner and lifted my horse, but he was fine. He took care of me and saved my life. It was a horse called Stretch."

The 2014 season was Adema's second full-time year at Cody Nite Rodeo. When he was younger he liked to be on the road for rodeo all of the time. Not as much now, so it suited him to settle into a place where the rodeos came to him every night.

"We've got all kinds of people from all kinds of countries," Adema said of the Cody fan.

Adema knows the clown and announcer make jokes at his expense. He is usually too busy to do more than smile, but once in a while he gets in a lick for the abused pickup men.

"Andy Burrelle's my buddy, but last year I roped his barrel and started dragging it with him in it. It got a lot of dirt in it."

Just a little payback.

★★★

HUMANS TOP BULLS

On a rainy night with the wind blowing so hard it was a wonder that all of the cowboys' hats did not make their own way downtown, more riders got the better of the bulls. The show must go on in bad weather, but maybe the bulls didn't feel like bucking so hard. No matter, scores counted.

Wyatt Lehman happily took his score of 64 from the eight-second ride. Jeremy Jacobs conquered Gravedigger, even if his score was only 69. Gravedigger didn't buck as much as usual. Skeet Chadwick rode clean for 75 points. But Wyatt Bartels beat them all with 77 points after a day off.

"I got my money's worth," Bartels said. "I'm happy it was a good ride."

For a change the cowboys played the bulls just about even.

It rained early and stopped. It rained in the middle of the rodeo and stopped. It rained later in the rodeo and stopped. Then it rained again. Four times. Good thing the grandstands had a roof, but even so wind blew some of the wetness sideways.

James Greeson won his third straight saddle bronc ride with a 76. "It's always nice," he said of victories. "It wasn't as good as some of the other ones, but how can you not be happy?"

In a kind of intermission, in the midst of Cody Nite Rodeo each night there was a Calf Scramble. This game was open to children 12 and under. They came pouring out of the stands into the arena, some days a couple of hundred strong, and were lined up by the clown. At the far end of the arena, where the ropers emerge to chase calves, two calves with red ribbons tied to their tails, were set loose. The kids charged after them to try and pluck the ribbons from the calves' tails.

"They call this Wyoming day care," Kade Rogge told spectators.

It only took a couple of minutes before the kids ran down the ribbons and won prizes like a free horseback ride or free ice cream.

Pam Vanek and Eric Fleming, the engaged couple from Montana, were on hand for the team roping. Scheduled to marry in July, the music welcoming them was the Dixie Cups' "Going to the Chapel."

Kooper and Bryce Boot teamed up. Kooper was the header and she snared it. Bryce missed the legs.

"Your sister is going to beat you up and take your lunch money," Rogge said.

Bill Parker, a veteran Montana cowboy, and his partner Jace Crabb, won the team roping in 7.2 seconds, a first-rate time. They were contenders every night they showed up.

The wetter it was the less friendly the dirt was to barrel racers and some entries scratched for fear of injuring their horses. Anna Allshouse gave it gusto. Head down on the sprint to the finish line, blonde hair blowing out the back of her hat, she whipped her rope back and forth as the sound man played "Shake It Up Baby." Her time was 17.72 seconds.

This night she got beat by Raelyn Gould of nearby Meeteetse. Gould's races were deceptive. It did not appear as if her horse was going as fast as some of the others, but her excellent horsemanship helped her guide it tightly around the red, white and blue barrels and when she crossed the finish line she was invariably near the top of the list. Her 17.52 won the rodeo.

Bull rider Jake Adkins was in the house. He was aching to ride, but doctors disagreed with his thought process. Adkins had a severely strained left arm and was told to keep it away from rodeo for up to three weeks and to stay away from his construction job, too. It was a double whammy for Adkins.

"I can't do that," he said, itching to get back to both endeavors, though he was considering a different event which would not immediately tear up his arm again.

Normally a bull rider, Skeet Chadwick gave bronc busting a try (photo by Lew Freedman).

No one was happier about covering a bull and obtaining his 75-point score than Skeet Chadwick, who had been taking some bruisings. He had even diverted his attention to saddle bronc riding for a night.

"That was my first one," Chadwick said.

But Skeet's heart was in bull riding. He took a mid-June evening night off from competition for two very important tasks. He did his laundry and then he returned to the doctor to have those five stitches out that had been decorating his forehead. He was a new man.

"I covered a bull and now I've got to keep it going," he said of his 75-point effort. "It's getting worse. I've got bull riding fever."

Apparently the knock on the forehead did nothing to knock sense into Skeet, but then neither had the occasions of being thrown around the lot done any convincing either.

A second straight night of cool temperatures, high winds, and yucky rain made the scene less-than-hospitable. Wyoming is known for its winds and Cody is right at home with that stereotype. The weather also made for a muddy track for the riders and that was not ideal.

Tony Martoglio was back as the clown and said, "This is exactly how I remember it 35 years ago." It was a fairly sardonic observation.

Cody Culver, another of the budget-conscious cowboys living at the far end of the grounds parking lot almost saw some serious damage done to him when flipped by a bull. Tony the Clown went to his aid, Culver favoring his right leg as he leaned on Tony's arm.

But Culver's mind was more on the monsoon affecting his campsite than on his health. "I got flooded," he said. "Everything that was allegedly waterproof got wet, including the bedding."

Daryl Lamb put together an excellent tie-down roping performance at 11.3 seconds, but was hit with a 10-second penalty, so Bryce Bott won with an 11.4.

Tony the Clown, whose only appearances of the season had been early on doing duets with Sid McFarland, was now chief clown. In one of his riffs, which was barely comprehensible, (and no doubt purposely so), Tony claimed to be related to Buffalo Bill Cody through his grandmother's sister's neighbor who cooked for Bill, or something like that.

Martoglio had a superb shooting act. He enlisted Justin Josey as a volunteer to hold up a balloon as Tony shot at it with a pistol and exploded it (or made it look that way).

"Are you scared Justin?" Tony asked. Justin just nodded. Tony took a behind-the-back shot. Bang, the balloon popped. Tony took a between-the-legs shot. Bang, the balloon popped. Tony fired and told everyone the bullet was bouncing off a pole in the grandstand and off the fence and all of that stuff, much like the basketball commercial that Larry Bird and Magic Johnson filmed long ago that called for ricochets. Eventually another balloon popped.

The young bull fighter was getting into more and more show business angles at rodeo all of the time.

"I like some of them," Josey said. He said he was confident he was not going to be shot.

Tony the Clown was a stout man, just past 60, and perhaps not as loose-limbed as he once was. In his story-telling he made it sound as if he had been one hellacious bull rider at one time – up to a point.

"I used to ride bulls," Tony said. "I kicked him on the right. I kicked him on the left. Then I kicked him on the back side."

Playing straight man, Rogge asked, "What happened?"

"Then they opened the gate," Tony said. "It was terrible."

It was pretty terrible that night, as well. The famous Howard Cosell boxing call from the George Foreman-Joe Frazier heavyweight championship bout of years ago came to mind. Wyatt Lehman was tossed. Wyatt Bartels was tossed. Jake Gebhardt was heaved. Curry Fielder, who was emerging as one of the most consistent riders, not only got thrown, but limped off the arena floor.

Fielder sat down behind the holding pens and took off a boot. "It was my ankle," he said. "As soon as I got my boot off it felt better. I'm OK."

Unless they require hospitalization, bull riders always say they are OK, regardless of what damage has been done to their bodies.

Rodeo is the most unforgiving sport. Any bronc rider or bull rider who doesn't recognize he is playing Russian roulette with his health, present-day and for the future, is in denial.

★★★

INJURIES COME WITH THE TERRITORY

Cody Culver limped off. Curry Fiedler limped off. Wyatt Lehman limped off. That was just part of one night's casualty list at Cody Nite Rodeo.

If you are going to rodeo, you are going to get hurt. The odds are much higher of injury when a cowboy rides a 2,000-pound bull or a 1,200-pound bucking horse, but ropers do not escape free and clear. Sometimes fingers get tangled in ropes and ripped open. Sometimes breakaway riders fall off their horses. Once in a while a barrel racing horse will throw a young lady.

Except for ducking pitches that fly at their head at 100 mph, baseball players (outside of pitchers whose arms practically fall off once a season) mostly cope with sprains, strains and some muscle tears. Basketball players pull muscles and sprain ankles. Hockey players do get their share of concussions, lost teeth and other injuries. Football is the most extremely physical of the four major team sports in the United States as the two sides run into each other on almost every play.

The incidence of serious injury is obvious to the casual football fan. Several times a game a referee may signal a timeout so a player can be helped off the field. Concussions are common. Broken bones occur with regularity. Muscles and ligaments give out. This all despite wearing sophisticated body armor that covers what would otherwise be exposed and susceptible areas. Equipment helps, but it is hardly foolproof.

It was the observation of a medical professional at the National Finals Rodeo that rodeo contestants are injured 10 times more often than football players. Although that estimate was offered more than a decade ago, there is no reason to believe things have changed.

In 2013, a University of Calgary researcher in Canada issued a report indicating that what fans see is what cowboys get. Dr. Keith Markey studied injuries and noted that the head, the face, chest, ribs, shoulders, elbows, thighs, knees and ankles are all routinely injured. Some cowboys did note that they hurt their backs while staying on a horse or bull because they are bounced around so much.

It is carnage out there on the rodeo grounds. Most cowboys don't like to admit that they are hurt. The old shake-it-off syndrome is strongly ingrained. Nonetheless, Yellowstone Sports Medicine has personnel standing by every minute Cody Nite Rodeo is going on, and that includes slack performances of late entries late at night after fans leave. The docs cannot leave.

The reasons an ambulance is not on the grounds the entire time is because West Park Hospital is only about a mile away and most injuries can be cared for on the premises. If not, an injured party can be transported to the hospital within minutes. Only serious injuries of a life-threatening or immobilizing nature require summoning an ambulance. Despite all of the physical damage visited upon rodeo competitors the call does not go out often.

For a 25-year period the Professional Rodeo Cowboys Association documented and studied injuries that occurred in pro rodeos all over the country. A 2013 report indicated the numbers were eye-opening, but probably not terribly surprising to people who follow the sport.

The PRCA noted 12,654 injuries with 96 percent of them occurring in bull riding (50 percent), bareback riding (23 percent), saddle bronc riding (15 percent) and steer wrestling (8 percent). Even if it has a regular spot on the program nationwide in pro rodeos, steer wrestling is not contested at Cody Nite Rodeo. The other four percent of injuries occurred in other events such as barrel racing and roping contests, clearly much safer.

Although the spread was not nearly as pronounced the most frequent injuries occurred to the head and face, back and neck, knees and shoulders, in that order. Many of the neck injuries were categorized as whiplash. If a 30 mph car crash can produce that problem then it is easy to see how being thrown back and forth on the back of a horse or bull can also account for the same issue.

In late June, Cody Ohl, a six-time world champion rodeo roper and all-around champ suffered a serious injury in a fluke accident that kept him from traveling to the early-July Cody Stampede. He was actually riding a horse herding cattle, not in a rodeo event. A heifer stabbed him in the side with a horn, shattering a rib into 17 pieces, with one piece piercing his lung.

It wasn't even a rodeo injury, though Ohl is no stranger to those. At the National Finals Rodeo in Las Vegas in 2001, in a legendary performance that has gone down in rodeo lore, Ohl was trying to hold onto his lead and win a world title in tie-down roping.

Ohl, then 28, had a big lead going into the ninth round, but when he dismounted after throwing the rope over the calf's head his right knee gave out. Ohl crawled to the calf, cut the end of the rope and sought to tie it off to acquire a time, no matter how slow as the calf dragged him through the dirt. In obvious pain, Ohl finished off the event in 40.9 seconds, and then fell over on his back grimacing.

Commentators described the effort as "pure grit." Ohl received a standing ovation at the Thomas & Mack Arena and then was carried off the grounds. He tore anterior cruciate and medial collateral ligaments. Mention of athletic courage is frequently overblown, but this was one example in the flesh, at the same time illustrating the kind of commitment a cowboy sometimes required.

At Cody Nite Rodeo a cowboy may take a fall or have his arm stepped on by a horse or bull and then be assisted off the dirt. A medical professional will check him out and perhaps apply ice in a large bag taped onto the sore area. A recommendation will be made that further attention be paid via a trip to the emergency room. Not all cowboys heed the advice. Either they believe they can shrug the injury off and it will improve with a night's rest, or they don't have medical insurance to cover treatment.

It's fair to say that if a cowboy returns to Cody Nite Rodeo one day after being injured, and has a body part encased in a cast or a sling, he was really hurt, not just banged up.

"Injuries are nightly to a certain degree," said West Park Emergency Medical Services director Kevin Neff. "Once a week we have a fracture. Cowboys are mostly poor. They don't have money or insurance. To a large extent they want to be taped up and go out again. They refuse (ambulance) transportation because it is not covered by insurance. Pretty much unless someone is unconscious they refuse transportation. They have a right to as long as they are of sound mind."

The definition of sound mind in rodeo may differ from the definition of sound mind in society at large.

Cody Nite Rodeo is every night during the summer, and Neff said some person probably needs hospital treatment every night, too, whether they seek it or not.

"There are soft tissue injuries like sprains," Neff said. "But there are also blunt force traumas when they get hit by a bull. It's rare not to have someone every night."

Bronc riders and bull riders have added more protective gear in recent years. Vests that don't show under shirts are routine and can help protect a thrown rider from being gored, although they do seem flimsy. Similarly, especially amongst the younger generation of up-and-comers, helmet use for bull riders is more commonplace.

The plastic shell helmets with cages in front to protect the face were ridiculed at first. But that has been true of just about every single sports equipment innovation designed to protect athletes since the early 20th century. Even the inventor of the shin guard for catchers in the early 1900s was made fun of, as were the first converts to wearing hard-shell baseball helmets. Hockey goalies used to play with no head gear at all. Football players initially competed bare-headed. That was followed by wearing soft leather helmets and then helmets with no facemasks.

Modeling the latest in safety technology, bull rider Billy Cobbler watches the action and waits his turn (photo by Lew Freedman).

The improved pieces of equipment all proved their worth. Neff believes, though, that the new flak jacket vests and helmets, while a step up, don't always do the job.

"Even that's not enough," he said.

A bad bruise is shrugged off by a cowboy for sure. A muscle strain almost certainly. A stretched ligament might be. A torn ligament or broken bone, probably not.

"I doubt that 20 percent of the cowboys that get hurt are even seen by a physician," Neff said. "They don't make money. They are barely covering their feed bills and fuel. Plus, you've heard the phrase, 'Cowboy up?' A lot of those guys subscribe to that. They think it's not manly to rub it (an injury)."

Neff said the doctors know that cowboys don't want to be ordered to lay off because if they don't ride they don't get paid. That's not an issue for members of a team in a major professional sports league. Those athletes not only have insurance, they have hot and cold running trainers and doctors at courtside.

"It's a brutal sport," Neff said of rodeo.

More physically demanding and damaging than football?

"Oh, absolutely," he said. "Much worse."

★★★

CODY NITE RODEO = HABIT FORMING

Every time Kade Rogge introduced Kooper Bott to fans when her breakaway roping turn came up, he made it sound as if she had just returned from Lourdes in order to compete.

Although there was no talk about apparitions of the Virgin Mary, Rogge did make it sound as if Bott was a miracle on horseback. She had entered the arena on crutches and – Behold! – threw them aside to ride. To further gild the lily, he also told everyone that Bott had just "gone under the knife" and implied that she had hitch-hiked from the operating table to Cody Nite Rodeo. That was not quite true.

"Well, I did have stitches," Bott said.

On this night, Bott went out and scored a 3.7 in the breakaway, quite good by anyone's standard. Also, a few weeks into the season the crutches were stashed away in a garage or basement and never accompanied her to the grounds again.

James Greeson's three-night winning streak had been interrupted, but he came back to win a fourth time in five nights with a 77-point score. His arm was pumping like a slot machine as he rode the animal for eight seconds. Afterwards, he was teased. Did he think the horses were getting scared of him? Greeson laughed and said, "I don't think so."

Caleb Nichols had a worse time of it in the same event and took a beating. He caught a hoof in the leg while still nursing a cut on his nose from being thrown forward on a different ride. "He got me a little bit. I hit myself, it was my fault," he said of the first damage.

Nichols, 23, from Priest River, Idaho, was traveling with a friend and had just stopped in Cody for a brief visit on their tour of western rodeos. "I started off good picking up checks everywhere," he said. "I'm going to Canada and then maybe come back here for a week. I've had too much fun. I get too much partying in when I come to Cody." The next day he was off to Ardmore, Montana.

Nichols was an example of the transient cowboy who might pause in Cody for a week and then move on for a change of scenery. Isn't that how all of the drifters did it in those old westerns, never parking their horse or sleeping in one place for too long?

James Greeson had another clean ride, but for once it was only good for second place. Corey Terry, a new arrival from Brownwood, Texas, got the win with 70 points.

In the bulls, Wyatt Lehman drew Tombstone, who lay down in his pen before the gate opened. Jeremy Jacobs had better luck with his bull and was in top form with 80 points.

The bull Nunn Betta staged a private sit-in after dumping Lane O'Neal. With no interest in returning to the corral, the bull decided to see the sights, check out the crowd, and stretch his legs by circling the arena. The first pickup man's rope barely slowed him down. The second pickup man's rope pissed him off. So stubborn Nunn Betta sat down in the middle of the arena and prevented the action from continuing. The bull just flat out didn't want to leave.

Although this was expanding his job description by a little, Zack Flatt tried to help by dashing up to the bull and touching it. He could have pulled the tail, but was reluctant.

"When they were trying to drag him out, it choked him down," Flatt said. "It takes a minute for him to get his breath and gather his chickens. I didn't want to get his tail. He might have kicked out. It's not often that you will see that."

However, earlier on the same night pickup men Harold Adema and Daryl Lamb had a heck of a time rounding up a horse named Speckled Boy. Just like the bull he didn't want to go home. At one point the two men had three ropes on Speckled Boy trying to coax him off the playing field. Speckled Boy must have enjoyed the time in the limelight. For once, it was no exaggeration by Rogge to refer to the pickup duo as cowboy pickup trucks. They had to dig in with four-wheel drive

Blake Miller, from Betton, Texas, came to Cody to ride bulls, but was converted to bull fighter by his early-in-the-rodeo concussion. "Being a bull rider helps being a bull fighter," said Miller, who was developing some moves. "I started when I was five riding on sheep." Twelve years later he was pretty much following in the footsteps of his father Terry, who rode bareback horses. "I tried that one time. It's more painful than bulls. I got on my first and last time. It jerks your arm and your head."

It was probably whiplash soreness, whether Miller called it that or not.

Miller may be young, but he has already had his share of bull riding injuries, from the concussion two days into the Cody season to a pulled arm muscle and getting stepped on and scraped by a hoof on his ankle. He does not pretend to be free of fear of the one-ton beasts.

"It helps to be scared of them," he said.

Jake Adkins was out there watching. The sling he had been wearing was retired, and he said he was on prescription steroid medication. He could move his arm, but it still hurt. He also defiantly repeated his claim that, "I'm not going to be out two weeks." Two weeks was closing in, though.

As Cody Nite Rodeo wound down the night of June 19, Rogge issued an announcement. He reminded fans to buy their tickets to the Cody Stampede. The big rodeo was less than two weeks away.

It was not clear if it was a useful notification or not. The one-time rodeo fan passing through Cody as a byproduct of a Yellowstone stop was almost surely not going to be in the neighborhood in early July. But it was a good reminder for the locals that it was time to shell out or they would miss the pros when they came to town for Independence Day.

★★★

AL SCHULTZ – THE STAMPEDE

The 2014 president of the Cody Stampede board of directors was Al Schultz, 67, a lifelong team roper. He has gray hair and a stocky build, with powerful arms. There was a lot of roping in those biceps, going back to when he was eight years old.

When it comes to old-time Cody, the Schultz family pretty much goes back to the beginning. Buffalo Bill Cody and his friends founded the town in 1895, and the first Schultz, Al's grandfather, showed up in 1896. The family has ranched, rodeoed and done whatever came naturally ever since. Al likes to say that his father was born on the dining room table (still in use in the family home), and he ate his last meal at the same table 90 years later.

Schultz took up team roping as a teen, graduated from Cody High School and attended college in nearby Powell where he competed for the school team. He rode bulls as a younger man and then went back to roping again. He has earned all of the gray hairs on his head, and they have permeated his mustache, too. Schultz wears glasses, and he seems to smile most of the time. Maybe it's the team roping that keeps his heart beating. Not many athletes can keep up in the game they love until they are senior citizens.

"I stuck with it all my life," Schultz said.

He and his first wife Judy, who passed away from cancer after 45 years of marriage, had three daughters: Cherain, Kitty and Misty. Cherain runs the office for the Cody Stampede. Misty works at Cody Nite Rodeo. Kitty also passed away from cancer.

Schultz, who married for a second time on New Year's Eve 2014, acknowledged that having such rodeo longevity has caused its share of injuries. They are inevitable, as every cowboy knows. The week before his first wedding he broke a leg. Schultz said he had a veterinarian cut the cast off for the ceremony. It wasn't as if Judy didn't know what she was getting into. She had team roped and was once the Lander (Wyoming) Pioneer Queen. Even the honeymoon involved rodeo, hazing for a friend.

"Rodeo is very appealing to young men," Schultz said. "There's some ego. I've been competing for 55 years. I still get a thrill when I am back there in the box. I go blank. I don't hear anything that's going on."

Depending how busy he is, Schultz still enters Cody Nite Rodeo events during the summer and ropes in tandem with Cherain at times. Other times he hooks up with son-in-law Mark Aragaon.

Schultz and Aragon, who was 50 at the time, shocked Cody and the rodeo universe in December of 2014 when they won their division at the World Series of Team Roping in Las Vegas. They split a $240,000 prize and collected 30-pound bronze sculpture trophies, glittering belt buckles and other prizes. Schultz didn't stop beaming for ages.

The Cody Stampede, one of the richest rodeos over the July 4 week, offers steer wrestling, an event not contested at Cody Nite Rodeo (photo by Lew Freedman).

Even though Cody Nite Rodeo is contested under much dimmer lights than those in Vegas, Schultz always gets a kick out of entering with Cherain.

"I think it's a high point of a father's dream to participate with his child," he said. "It's a treat. When I make a run with Cherain, I look over at my daughter. The pride is unspeakable. I imagine it is the same for the parent of a baseball player."

The Stampede is the general supervisor of Cody Nite Rodeo, but not the daily operator. Especially in June as the days count down to the start of the annual Stampede rodeo, there is simply not enough time in the day to ride herd over Nite Rodeo, compete and still make sure the big-name rodeo competitors coming to town walk away with fat wallets and a good impression of how the Stampede is run.

"Our sole purpose is community enhancement," Schultz said. "From an economic standpoint it's to put heads in beds. The community support for the Nite Rodeo and the Stampede is phenomenal."

Whether it is Cody Nite Rodeo all summer long or Stampede time, Schultz pretty much runs an open house. His ranch is a way-station for ropers. He has 200 acres for cattle and also operates an environmental cleanup company. Ropers come for the Schultz hospitality.

"They have all stopped at my place along the way," he said. "This is sort of a hotel for ropers. That's kind of the cowboy way. They're kind of all my kids."

The Stampede purse is about $400,000, making it a major stop during the Fourth of July week of Cowboy Christmas. Entry fees go into the pot. Board-raised money contributions run around $20,000 per event, and the Wyoming tourism board chips in $20,000. In 2014 the rodeo was scheduled for July 1-4. A key reason why the Stampede is so successful is its status as a one-header rodeo, which means they don't have to accumulate scores over a several-day period; they can compete for just one score. So a cowboy can blow into Cody, compete in his event on a Thursday and then take off for another rodeo. Roughly 600 contestants come to Cody during the four-day event.

Although some big names come and go quickly, attendance is strongest on the holiday and the day before. Fans fill the grounds to 50 or 60 percent capacity the first day. The crowd is closer to 75 percent the second day, and the third day is usually a sellout or near sellout. July 4 is standing-room only.

Sitting around talking rodeo in his workshop, Schultz was actually wearing a Cody Nite Rodeo baseball cap. But soon he would be switching hats. The Stampede was swiftly approaching.

"It's a very special week," Schultz said. "The town fills up. I shut my business down for a week before the rodeo and for two days after."

★★★

RIDERS OF THE PURPLE SAGE

Zane Grey would have liked the guys at Cody Nite Rodeo.

The great western writer lived into the 20th century and spent as much of his time big-game fishing as he did writing cowboy copy. One of his western novels was called *Wyoming*.

Born in a town founded by his family, Zanesville, Ohio, in 1872, Grey was much more at home in the West and on the ocean. His books definitely indicated an appreciation for roughing it. He was a brilliant fisherman. Grey is credited with catching the first 1,000-pound fish, a marlin. In an age before air travel, he somehow got himself to far corners of the earth to fish (and then write about it for popular magazines). Grey, who attended the University of Pennsylvania on a baseball scholarship, also wrote baseball books for boys. Above all he is most identified as being a western writer, although here's betting he enjoyed the outdoors writing the most.

Funny thing, a century later he could still do the fishing (with much shorter trips to Tahiti, Australia and New Zealand, where he had previously spent months at a time just in transit) and still write about baseball, but he might have had to look harder for authentic cowboys at the rodeo.

Wyoming is a bit on the romantic and sentimental side. Maybe Grey liked his main character so much because he saw himself in him. The hero of the book went West as a tenderfoot. He fell in love but had to fight for his gal against a mean and ornery bad guy. In a classic western plot, the good ranchers had to defend their cattle herds against rustlers.

Grey's first magazine article was published when he was 30, and after reading Owen Wister's classic *The Virginian*, he set out to write popular westerns. It took some time to gain publishing approval, but *Riders of the Purple Sage*, his best-seller, was first printed in 1912. It remains in print today. Grey wrote more than 90 books and many, many of his western stories were filmed for movies and television. His works are considered to be some of the most influential in the shaping of opinions about the Old West, alongside those of Wister, the sculptures and paintings of Charles Russell and Frederic Remington and the Wild West shows of Buffalo Bill Cody.

Grey probably would have like Corey Terry, the 31-year-old, slow-talking cowboy from Texas, who has spent years in rodeo and came to Cody in mid-June to stay for the rest of the season.

"I've got to get the rust off," Terry said as he eased into the saddle bronc competition.

Another newcomer was Ty Miller, a 17-year-old from Pennsylvania whose life aspiration is to become a rodeo announcer. Kade Rogge planned to hit the road after the Stampede and Miller was his designated replacement. It was going to be learning-on-the-job for young Miller, and it was a real coup that he had landed the opportunity.

Whoever showed up, and whatever the event, the most consistent competitor night in and night out was Andy Mumm in bareback. He won the June 20 event with a 72 score on a horse called Lightning that behaved as if its name was no accident.

"That was power from that horse," Mumm said. "As soon as that chute gate opened he got pissed off. You could hear him bellowing." Mumm had difficulty freeing his hand from the holding rope and said he just may have seen this horse too often since he started riding it in 2013.

The saddle bronc riders as a group were getting thrown left and right.

"If you think it's easy, we take entries every day," Rogge said.

One guy who stayed on was James Greeson, notching another win with a 78-point ride on the unfriendly Darth. Darth came out of the starting blocks like Usain Bolt and nearly ran right over the tall fence on the other side of the arena. Such a leap over six feet of slats seemed impossible, but veterans say that a couple of times a year a worked-up horse clears the fence as if it is a high jump bar. That probably scatters the spectators.

In the bulls, Skeet Chadwick walked off favoring his right side. What were the odds?

Zack Flatt, Justin Josey and Blake Miller were painted up at the ready doing the bull fighter thing, but one bull went full

Ready to help. Bull fighters Zach Flatt (left) and Justin Josey (from behind) are poised to step and distract a bull in their direction if a rider is thrown (photo by Lew Freedman).

blast after clown Tony Martoglia. Rogge shouted, "Tony! Tony! Tony!" as a warning. Tony ran for the fence. Whew. "Oh, my god, that was scary," he said. "There are three bull fighters out here and he chases me."

Martoglio was born in Cody and, with a few gaps had totaled 35 years as a rodeo clown. He said the Cody Nite Rodeo season used to run from Memorial Day through Labor Day, stretching things to about 100 days.

"For years I did the whole season," he said. "How hard is it to be funny 100 days straight? Oh, my gosh." He has had other jobs as a firefighter and construction worker, but he has been a clown the most.

"How can I not have fun?" Martoglio said. "Even in bad weather."

One of Tony's popular acts involved a boomerang hat. He flipped the hat straight out in front of him and it made a half-circle and returned. Usually, someone else stood out on the dirt with him and threw his hat, which always failed to return to them.

"People love that boomerang hat," Tony said, "because they can't figure it out." It was not as if he was going to reveal any secrets about the how either. Magicians do not tell.

Tony's scare did not keep the competition from continuing, and Curry Fielder, starting to make a mark, won the bull riding with 73 points, his second victory of the week.

Bull rider Cody Culver, 19, was born in Casper, but moved around Wyoming because his father was a ranch hand. His dad, Matt, also rode rodeo saddle broncs. Culver had some interest in riding bucking horses but more interest in riding bulls. As a youth he rode sheep, calves and then steers.

"I just looked up to my dad and thought that was the way I needed to be," Culver said. "I thought he was the coolest guy around. I've always ridden bulls. That's what I was best at."

But the season hadn't been going very well for Culver and he dabbled in saddle bronc riding.

"I got to fighting bulls in my head," Culver said. "I was doubting myself before I got on. Who knows, I might get good at saddle bronc riding and never ride another bull. You can always get hurt in both of them."

Cowboys thrown are depressed cowboys. Cowboys who hit eight seconds on the clock are elated.

"Riding bulls is kind of a blast," Culver said. "It goes by so fast, but it's so wild and crazy it's like you're riding a tornado. It can seem like a really long time. You have so much concentration because you're trying so hard. You're gritting your teeth. Your adrenalin's going. Everything's tense. You're either riding them too much or you're not riding them enough. You've got to get on lots of them. You have to get in a rhythm."

Culver was waiting for that rhythm to reach out and grab him.

★★★

SHANE STEEVES

If rodeo in general is no country for old men because their bodies are broken and battered by riding bulls and bucking horses, there is one exception. Long after the riders have retired, gone into the raising of livestock or found a new profession altogether, the ropers go on.

Al Schultz was 67 during the 2014 Cody Nite Rodeo season. Coleman White was 53. Daryl Lamb was 50. Harold Adema was 53. Shave Steeves was a younger brother by comparison, being only 46.

A tie-down roper who grew up in Montana, but has lived in Stephenville, Texas, a kind of rodeo haven, since 1997, Steeves had whitening hair, blue eyes and a football player's body, a bit stocky, with a weight-lifter's arms.

"Not everybody understands tie-down roping," Steeves said. "They say, 'Oh, you and your partner rope.' Nooo."

Steeves trains horses in Texas for most of the year and has trained them a lot. He was trying to avoid retirement from roping, even though by most standards of the rodeo world he is an old-timer. Cody was an escape for him.

"I can't get enough of this town," said Steeves, and it keeps him in the rodeo game. "It's hard to give it up. It's every day, but there's not a lot of money involved. You put down $25 to win $200. The only thing you're really paying for is your food and hay. I thought I'd come and try it last year. We older guys can stay in it and be competitive."

Shane Steeves of Stephenville, Texas, puts the finishing touch on tying three calf legs together in a Cody Nite Rodeo tie down roping competition (photo by Lew Freedman).

On a good day Steeves posted a 10-plus-second time, and on the right day that can win the round. Other nights he might score in the 11-second range and come in second or third. On off nights, which everyone has, he'll miss his throw and it will be over before he even gets to tackle the calf. But Steeves is still a player. He can contend on a given night and score points, maybe get a shot at a monthly belt buckle and make the finals.

Steeves grew up around horses. He used them in hunting and in transportation. Rodeo was all he wanted to do. He had no life backup plan. In the 1990s Steeves toured, entering rodeos in Reno, Cheyenne, Alberta, Canada and Whitehorse in the Yukon Territory. In 2003 Steeves won an NRA (National Rodeo Association) timed event championship and received as his prize the spiffiest of saddles. He still uses it today, although he hates to run it in sloppy weather.

"I keep it out of the mud," he said.

Steeves said he has spent his entire life as a journeyman in rodeo or training horses, living the life he craved. He knows how rare it is to still be in competitive rodeo at his age. Not everyone lasts so long.

"That's the lucky part," Steeves said. "I'm still doing it. It's all I know. If you put 30 years into something, no matter what the career, you just can't give it up. There's a difference between being a weekend warrior and selling your soul. I'm one of the two percent of guys who has never lived in the box, 9-to-5. I go do my thing. It's all on me."

Drinking coffee in the Rawhide, a downtown Cody shop that sells caffeinated beverages and baked goods, Steeves sounded philosophical. He is fascinated by Cody. He soaks up the Buffalo Bill Cody connection, the Rodeo Capital of the World theme, the Old Trail Town, the gunfighters show. Cody to Steeves is one of the last western towns out there.

"It takes me back," he said. "Rodeo is the history of the West. That's all that's left other than going to see a movie."

In some ways Steeves is living a movie plot. The aging cowboy hanging on, trying to make do, to wring every minute out of the sport he gave his heart to long ago. He returned to that theme of weekend warriors, of American men and their real-life jobs where they punch clocks, settle down in the suburbs and raise families. He prefers to raise horses.

"Not everybody can be a horse trainer," Steeves said. He might ride 10 or 12 horses in a day and that's his work day. A millionaire ex-client told Steeves once, "If I could quit it all and do what you guys do for six months, I'd do it."

There are probably a lot of cowboy wannabes like that tucked away in corners of American society, inspired by cowboy TV shows that everyone loved when they were kids. Those men drifted into the business world, sitting behind desks, prisoners in offices and they made it big by most definitions. But something remains in their souls that tugs at them, that reminds them that someplace inside they would prefer to roam free on the open range, just sitting in the saddle, alone with their horse under the sky.

That is a romantic vision of the cowboy and that mystique, that image, still holds appeal today. So yes, it can be possible for a millionaire businessman to be jealous of the freedom he sees in Steeves' lifestyle. Steeves made his choice long ago that he would rather ride those horses then be trailed through life by a beeping telephone.

He doesn't know how much longer his body will let him rodeo, even if it is merely throwing a rope and tackling one calf a night for a 10-second performance.

"Long-term rodeo has taken its toll," Steeves said. "I go day-by-day. To stay in there and battle it out every night, that's a good feat. I'll go home to Texas and tell my friends the stories. Besides, there are horses waiting to be trained."

There will always be horses to be trained. A man can do that into his 60s, for sure, even if his roping arm gives out and he no longer has the strength to tip a cow. That day hasn't arrived for Steeves yet, but he knows it lurks just over the horizon.

★★★

TWENTY-ONE RODEOS IN

After three weeks of nightly Cody Nite Rodeo Andy Mumm was the undisputed star of the show. He put up his 12th victory of the season in 21 days, not only dominating bareback riding, but performing better than anyone in any event.

It wasn't hard to be ahead of any particular bull rider. Those 2,000-pound behemoths with the dexterous hips, the powerful kick and the bad attitude beat the crap out of the cowboys many nights.

On one night the bulls finished 13-0, 13 cowboys up, 13 cowboys thrown. Cody Nite didn't need bull fighters so much as it did first responders. Wyatt Lehman may have suffered a first – he hiked out of the arena limping on both sides.

Billy Cobbler, 19, one of twin brothers competing, walked off grimacing, but his biggest achievement following his bull ride was that he was walking at all. When Cobbler was hurled off his bull he tumbled in front of it and nearly got creamed.

A bit stunned after hitting the ground, Cobbler didn't know where the bull was, and he wasn't thinking clearly yet. The bull turned back toward the chute and bucked wildly.

"I didn't even know he was behind me," said Cobbler, a member of the rodeo team at Northwest College in Powell. "I

Hanging on for dear life isn't always a good idea (photo by Lew Freedman).

felt the horn hook around me. Then he gave me a kiss and I scooted out of the way."

Close call, for sure.

Bull rider Clint Strawser was in the area behind the gates with his left wrist taped and his left knee wrapped.

"I'm not going to the hospital for this," he said.

Maybe not, but he wasn't going to ride at full strength, either.

Shane Steeves won the tie-down roping go-around in 11.8 seconds. One thing about Cody Nite Rodeo that can be an advantage or disadvantage is a growing familiarly with the livestock. There aren't enough bulls, horses, or calves to draw different ones every single rodeo night. Once in a while Maury Tate changed the pool of calves to a new pen's worth. This was one of those nights and Steeves said it worked out well for him.

"I drew a good calf," he said. "My horse got off well. He's just a huge amount of horsepower. I had a little oops. The rope caught on the horn of the saddle and jerked. It stopped me for a second." Or given the way events were timed, maybe a tenth of a second or two.

James Greeson pulled out his eighth win of the season with a 78-point ride on a night when the others were gunning for him. Three other saddle bronc riders posted scores and Greeson won by a single point.

"I'm not going to change anything, and I'm not going to take a day off," Greeson said.

Why would he? You don't fool with a hot streak whether you are playing cards in a Vegas casino, or as famously explained in *Bull Durham*, playing baseball.

Although Kade Rogge had not yet departed, Ty Miller got some air time. Rogge mentored him for a few days while they overlapped in Cody. Miller had a good opener for the crowd.

"For the next two hours I'm gonna be your best friend in rodeo," he said.

Brandon Milburn usually spoke for others with his tunes. When contestants were slow readying to ride out of the roping chute he played, "Any Day Now." Miller chimed in: "That's harsh," he said.

Any time he was on the start list, it was beginning to seem as if Curry Fielder from Battle Mountain, Nevada, was the man to beat in bull riding. At 26 he was more seasoned than riders just out of high school. Fielder stayed on his bull's back while most of the rest of riders were thrown — the overall rider success percentage stayed low — and his 74 points won it.

"That's how it goes a lot," Fielder said. "There are a lot of young kids out there."

Fielder scored enough to win, but not to satisfy him.

"I didn't feel I rode very well," he said, "but it always feels better when you win."

Ty Miller tried to drum up some support for the bulls, although they hardly seemed to need a cheering section. "What do you think of these bulls? Miller said. "They're athletes." However, it seemed the audience sympathy was with the humans that were hurled through the air.

The new clown in town was Matt Tarr, 30, who was also from the town. He not only had Cody ties, he got his start at Cody Nite Rodeo. Tarr claims he has had a rope in his hands from the age of three or four. He was a bull fighter for about seven years, but turned to clowning almost accidentally.

Tarr dressed as a clown for the first time at the Crow Fair Rodeo at Crow Agency, Montana on the Crow Reservation. Bull fighter Dusty Tuckness, the Meeteetse guy who shares promotion of the Tuckness/Asay Classic, asked Tarr to help out.

Tarr told Maury Tate that it might be fun to try it again.

"Maury said, 'Here, try,' and handed me a microphone," Tarr said.

Over the previous two years Tarr had been working toward acquiring his pro card. He drove more than 8,000 miles, usually with his wife Stacie and their baby son who was starting to mature into a toddler.

One of the popular clowns who entertained part of the summer was Matt Tarr of Cody, who is also a roping expert (photo by Lew Freedman).

Stacie said she didn't find it hard to picture her husband as a clown. "He's always funny," she said. "He makes me laugh."

Tarr often makes most of Cody laugh. He has a strong attachment to Cody Nite Rodeo.

"This place has made me what I am," Tarr said.

Every clown has different specialties. Sid McFarland had his rocket and his hokey jokes. Tony Martoglio had his boomerang hat and his pistol shooting. Matt Tarr incorporated fancy roping into his act. He could step in and out of the rope as it looped above his head. He could make butterfly circles. He could treat the rope like a Hula-Hoop.

Tarr told the fans that he took his two-year-old to McDonald's and ordered a happy meal.

"They gave me an Obama Happy Meal," he said. "It comes with chicken McNuggets, fries, and the promise of a toy."

In conservative Wyoming, Tarr roped 'em in with that joke.

★★★

BILL PARKER

When you gaze at Bill Parker's lined face under his hat and watch him enter the rodeo grounds with his erect bearing, you form the impression that even if you saw him walking on the platform of the New York City subway you would identify him as a cowboy.

At 60, Parker has spent a lot of time as a cowboy and as a rodeo competitor, but he also has one of the most unusual resumes around. When he was one of the top ropers in the country, the Billings, Montana native was a regular at the National Finals Rodeo in team roping and tie-down roping.

Then he retired at 36. What neither Parker nor anyone else expected was that he would come out of retirement at age 53. How many athletes lay off from their sport for 17 years and then make a comeback? The list of names could be written on a file card and stuffed into a thimble.

Is he as good at team roping as he was in his prime? No. Is he good enough to win on any given night at Cody Nite Rodeo with his regular partner Jace Crabb, or on an off chance with his nephew Delon Parker? You bet. And it happened regularly whenever Parker threw his name onto the entry list. The only reason he didn't compete every night was because he was also busy training horses at the nearby Northwest College Trapper Arena, home of that school's rodeo team, on the outskirts of Cody.

"We rope all day and train horses, and then we give them rodeo experience," Parker said. "It doesn't get old."

Neither does he apparently.

A Montana guy who competed for Dawson Community College in Glendive, Parker said he was 12 years old when he first came to Cody Nite Rodeo. He has rodeoed in Cody for generations of livestock contractors.

"I think it is just absolutely amazing that it has not changed one bit," Parker said.

Actually, it has changed a tiny bit. Once the rodeo ran from 8:30 p.m. to midnight, but now it is packaged to go from 8 to 10 p.m. Before there were up to 20 teams in team roping and other events, but now the fields are limited and the remainder go in slack after the crowd leaves the building. The fundamental purpose of Cody Nite Rodeo has not changed, though, according to Parker.

"This is the best training ground for a guy who wants to rodeo," he said.

As a younger man Parker was one of the dominant figures on the Montana Pro Rodeo Circuit and set several standards at the Montana Fair Rodeo. But Parker began easing into retirement in 1989. For four years he competed less frequently and then hung up his rope in 1993, turning to horse sales. He continued to work with horses, but wanted to try some new things. That changed in 2010 when nephew Delon, whom he had mentored, started having success.

"I made a real cowboy out of my nephew," Parker said.

Rodeo competitors thought they had seen the last of Parker. He did not spend years thinking about making a comeback. Just all of a sudden he decided he wanted to try it. When he informed his wife Jann, she said what a lot of people thought: "You're crazy."

"I thought I was probably done," he said. "I think a lot of people were surprised." Then they saw him on rodeo grounds again with a rope in his hands and exclaimed, "You're back!"

However, Parker's comeback did not go smoothly at first. He had a heart attack in 2010, doctors inserted two stents, and he underwent vigorous rehabilitation. Some might say that there was a message in there for the old man, but if so he ignored it.

OK, he figured, I'm as good as new. Until the next injury. Parker broke an ankle in 2011 when his horse gave out beneath him on sandy ground. It was a slow-motion fall, with Parker able to see everything as it occurred, but unable to arrest his tumble or prevent himself from getting hurt.

"I knew he was falling and I knew he was going to break my leg and there was nothing I could do about it," Parker said. "My body just would not let me get away from him."

Stubbornness solidifying, even then Parker had no intention of retiring again. He had known injuries as any veteran cowboy would.

"I've had two knee replacements," Parker said. "It had gotten to the point where I couldn't get on a horse. And if I got on one, I couldn't get off. I couldn't ride." Well, that circumstance was out of the question, so Parker had surgery.

As in every other sport, rodeo continued to evolve while Parker was away from the game. Whether it is football, basketball, baseball or rodeo, there are always equipment modifications and the caliber of play continues to improve. Athletes are better conditioned than ever. Seventeen years away is an eternity.

"It was almost a completely different sport when I came back," Parker said. "The times were a lot faster. There was way better equipment, especially the ropes, in diameter and weight. They go where you put them. Now there are more good ropers."

Parker was older than anyone else in the Cody Nite Rodeo team roping fields, but he held his own with partner Crabb, who was 33.

"Jace is an extremely good roper and he's a talented horseman," Parker said.

They were tough to beat as a team in Cody Nite Rodeo, winning often, perhaps two out of the approximately three times a week they entered. Roping is an event where contestants thrive on practice, putting in time, making repetitive throws.

"Everybody thinks they can ride a horse," Parker said. "You have to have good hand-eye coordination and a willingness to work long hours day after day after day. We rope every day. Really the horsemanship is a huge part of it. There are fewer guys these days who ride good."

For as long as Parker has been a rodeo cowboy and a horse training cowboy he has sensed that the cowboy mystique still runs strong.

"The history of this sport is very important," Parker said. "I don't know if the kids know the rodeo history as they did in my era. But I'm in horse selling and we sell horses to people with disposable income who want to be cowboys. They want to be part of what I do. People still want to be part of the western way of life."

★★★

A MONTH IN

As the days of June dwindled and the Cody Stampede drew closer, the Cody Nite Rodeo was abused by the weather.

When it rained Maury Tate was under intense pressure to dry out the grounds for the night's performance. It wasn't always possible. He could haul in dirt, grade the arena floor, but in the absence of a brontosaurus-sized mop, he could not make all of the water evaporate.

Rodeo went on as scheduled, but there was a puddle so large to the right of the chutes where calves broke for tie-down roping that it ran the risk of being reclassified as a lake. On the other side of the arena was a puddle that could have been reclassified as a pond. Going left or right the new variable was to avoid drowning.

No one had it worse that night than tie-down roper Coleman White. Sure enough, his calf exploded out of the gate and ran right through the largest puddle. White caught the calf at the edge of the puddle and had to wade through the water after it was roped to flip it. His black hat flew off and got soaked. The entire scenario was a muddy mess.

Grimacing afterwards, White looked at the Cody Nite belt buckle he won in 2013 and it gave him heart that mucking through the slop might prove worthwhile in accumulating points towards winning another one.

"I've got to swap it out," he said.

Upstairs in the announcer's chair, Ty Miller was dry and he could offer up dry wit. "This calf roping is pretty salty," he said.

You had to look fast to see if White shot him a murderous glance. Being unable to tackle the calf made White a candidate for a spot on America's Funniest Home Videos. "I was doing all I could," White said. "If I could have caught him I would have thrown him in the water."

As events continued, James Greeson tried to ignore the yucky terrain, but the horse named Hurricane must have felt it gave him an advantage. Greeson was tossed head over heels off his bronc and failed to escape without a need to do a laundry. Ryan Bestol claimed the triumph with 82 points.

In bull riding Wyatt Lehman wore white tape over one of his boots. He was limping, as he had been for a couple of days, favoring the left side because of a groin strain.

But the next night, June 27, the unthinkable, or at least the very unusual, happened. Cody Nite Rodeo was called off. Even worse, by 8 p.m. the sky was clear. It had rained hard overnight and stopped. Maury Tate trucked in fresh dirt and groomed the arena in plenty of time for the night's event. Only then the skies opened again, drenching everything all over again, virtually turning the entire arena into an ocean.

"It was this deep," Tate said of the worst quagmire, holding his hand a foot-and-a-half high.

At 7:40 p.m. when the grounds ordinarily bustled and the parking lot filled, the rodeo arena was empty.

Justin Josey, sans makeup, emerged from his bunkhouse hideaway with a towel draped over his shoulder, on his way to the men's showers. "I don't know what to do," Josey said. "I'm doing what I usually do after a rodeo."

The Tates, rodeo workers, and some competitors, dined at the Irma Hotel and then some of the gang went bowling. "It was the first time I've been bowling in my life," Josey said later.

Ron Lewis, who worked the back gate several nights a week, felt he had to take the hit for the rainout.

"I figured it was my fault because I planted seeds and pasture grasses," Lewis said. "But I didn't ask for that much rain.

The weather cancellation marked only the third time in 10 years that Cody Nite Rodeo had been called off on the Tates' watch.

Cody Nite Rodeo was back in business one night later. Mongo was at his usual perch. Blake Miller, in bull fighter regalia, helped customers on and off the bull's broad back. In-between, Miller scratched Mongo behind his ears.

"He likes that," Miller said.

Clown Matt Tarr decided if that everyone was going to get wet and down and dirty he might as well join in. During one of his acts, Tarr dove into the water. He called it "clown surfing." The rash act that soaked his clothing with half a rodeo to go came into his mind as a brash thought about five minutes before the rodeo began. This was why he did not have a change of clothes with him. Tarr retreated into the medical office, stripped down, and tried to dry his baggy overalls out, at least a little bit.

Who does your laundry, Matt?

"I do now," he said.

Nobody, but nobody despised the muddy, water-soaked course more than the barrel racers. Making their sharp turns around the three barrels required some short-notice braking and if their horse couldn't plant comfortably the riders really didn't want to be out there.

"It's just not worth it," said Jennifer Lewis, one of the top barrel racers. "Your horse is worth more than a $25 rodeo." Lewis and her husband live on 80 acres of land in Meeteetse and it takes her about 45 minutes to drive to the rodeo grounds. By day she works for a dermatologist.

It may seem like a decent ride hauling a horse that distance several nights a week, but if someone wants to hold a professional job with office hours and still rodeo Cody Nite Rodeo is as convenient as it gets.

"Why would you go anywhere else when you have a $25 rodeo in your backyard," Lewis said. "You can win $180-to-$200. You can't beat that."

Lewis said she was on horseback from the time she was a little girl, but was about 12 when she became interested in barrel racing. Her father bought her a how-to book.

"We taught ourselves," she said. "My first horse cost $800. I had a 4H horse. I liked it from the start. I was going to Cody Nite Rodeo as a kid."

Barrel racing is a tougher discipline than some people think, Lewis said. Horses must be superbly trained. In the beginning some skittish horses are afraid of the barrels appearing on the

Meeteetse cowgirl Jennifer Lewis was one of the hottest barrel racers over the summer and was a season-long contender (photo by Jason Koperski).

course right in front of them. Overcoming any fear is the first obstacle to be weaned out of a horse.

"There are a couple of aspects to it," Lewis said. "You've got to put in your time. Your horse and you have to be in shape. It's a hard 17-to-18 seconds. One tenth of a second is do or die. The mental game is a lot of it. You have to prepare yourself to win. It can all be a humbling experience. You develop a relationship with your horse. If you don't have that mental bond, you can't win."

Lewis brought two mares to the arena each night, but her top horse is named Gator. When Lewis first obtained Gator, the horse bit people. Now, as a five-year-old Gator knows what to do. Lewis may call her rodeo life a hobby, but in 2013 she was the Cody Nite Rodeo year-end champion.

In barrel racing Pam Vanek looked sharp, but then clipped a barrel. "That definitely wasn't in her game plan," Ty Miller told the fans.

Carly Schaff clocked 16.90 in the barrel racing, a rare sub-17 time. She blew away the field. The other top riders weren't even close that night.

Ryan Bestol, 28, from Hyannis, Nebraska, was passing through Cody on his way to Cheyenne Frontier Days, picked off a saddle bronc win, but also had some hard luck.

"This is my first time here," Bestol said. "That horse bucked me right out of there. There are some that buck like a son-of-a-gun."

As the bull riding began, Miller announced, "The toughest sport on dirt." Every bull rider but Billy Cobbler was thrown. Cobbler won with a 71-point ride on one of his first bulls following recovery from a broken arm.

"It feels good to get one covered," Cobbler said.

The Cody Nite regulars were planning their week off. During the Cody Stampede most of them intended to try their luck at other small rodeos since they were not invited to the big show with an all-star cast of America's best. They hoped to exploit their Cody Nite experience and cash in elsewhere.

Cobbler said he didn't know where he would be on July 4 because his twin brother Rob made the schedule. "Lincoln, Montana," Cobbler said. "I think."

Andy Mumm won his 15th bareback ride of the season and definitely hoped that his Cody Nite seasoning would pay off as he hopped from rodeo to rodeo over Cowboy Christmas.

One guy whose Cody tenure was coming to an end was Naudy Esposito. He didn't compete often because he worked with livestock. His job would take him on the road with the animals for the rest of the summer, though he hoped to make a cameo back in Cody at the end of the season.

Esposito, 34, was born in Villaclar, Cuba, and made his home in the U.S. in the aptly named Freedom, Oklahoma. He had just won the bareback ride at a Lovell, Wyoming rodeo for the second year in a row. How was he going to celebrate?

"I'm going to have a beer and go to sleep," Esposito said.

The points were tabulated for June and buckle winners – interim champs – were determined.

Mumm won the bareback buckle; White, the tie-down event; Greeson, the saddle bronc category. Delon Parker was the top team roping header, and Jimmy Morris led the heelers. Anna Allshouse paced the barrel racers. Kooper Bott, crutches or not, won the breakaway title. Jeremy Jacobs captured the bulls belt buckle. Pam Vanek was all-around cowgirl, and Daryl Lamb all-around cowboy.

★★★

CAROLINE LOCKHART

Although Buffalo Bill Cody and Caroline Lockhart overlapped in Cody, Wyoming for many years, they were only acquaintances, not friends.

Caroline Lockhart, who knew Buffalo Bill Cody, was an author of western novels, the first president of the Cody Stampede in 1920, and then the editor of the Cody Enterprise, *the newspaper Buffalo Bill started in 1899.*

Yet Lockhart, who was born in 1871 in Eagle Point Township, Illinois, was the second best-known citizen of the community that Buffalo Bill founded. Originally a prominent journalist in Boston and Philadelphia, Lockhart became a prominent and appreciated author of western novels after moving to Wyoming.

Her home was a mansion in the early 1900s. It remains alive as the Carolina Lockhart Inn after being moved two miles from downtown to an area not far from the Cody rodeo grounds. It is a rooming house these days, though for years served as a bed and breakfast.

After Buffalo Bill died in 1917 and the first rodeo was held in his honor in 1919,

Caroline Lockhart played a major role in jump-starting the Cody Stampede. Several of the important people of the community met at Lockhart's home and — after suitable lengthy conversation around the dining room table — they established the Stampede and selected a board of directors. Lockhart became the Stampede's first president.

In the 1920s, Lockhart owned the *Cody Enterprise*, the newspaper which Buffalo Bill founded in 1899. In the dining room of the Caroline Lockhart Inn hangs a panoramic photograph taken in downtown Cody that includes Lockhart and Buffalo Bill (and many others).

Cindy Allen, who has owned the Lockhart Inn for three decades and once hosted B&B guests while wearing Victorian dress with her hair up like a Gibson girl, has ensured that Lockhart's memory is well-preserved in the house.

"We would turn on Caruso and dance to it," Allen said.

Allen, a real estate agent, did not know anything about Lockhart until she bought the house. There are definitely elements of Caroline through-out the home. Tenant rooms are named after Caroline, her pet, characters in her novels and the like. Photos of Lockhart are sprinkled around the house and replica book covers hang on walls. Several biographies have been written about Lockhart, who never married or had children, but did have numerous boyfriends.

Lockhart was a lively figure by any account and she delighted in outraging the prim and proper.

"There were poker parties with Buffalo Bill and lots of dancing," Allen said.

At various times Lockhart had a pet bobcat, which she called Wampus Cat, a boa constrictor, a bear and an eagle.

Just about the first thing that anyone who lives in Cody says if one mentions residing at the Caroline Lockhart Inn is, "I've always heard that it's haunted."

Allen doesn't duck the ghost stories. Once, Allen was sitting in the Caroline room unpacking boxes and said aloud, "I wonder how Caroline Lockhart would feel about me wallpapering the wall blue." The door to the room flew open and hit Allen in the back. The wallpaper in that room remains yellow with small floral designs of white and pink.

Allen raised her family in the house, and another time her children were playing the piano and heard the swish, swish of taffeta, the clink, clink of crystal, and the smell of lilacs.

Still another time Allen was looking out a doorway and saw a woman with her hands out, palms against a wall. She had gray hair and was wearing a 1910ish dress. "I opened and shut my eyes three times, one, two, gone," Allen said.

On one occasion, a guest complained about the maid service. "They told me, 'Your housekeeper is not to move my toiletries behind the bathroom door,'" Allen said. Nobody had.

One male guest actually asked Allen if the house was haunted. "Last night I woke up to a woman in my room holding towels," Allen repeated. "This man pulled the sheets up over his head. My response was, 'She likes you.'"

It wasn't very clear what the group of football players staying at the Lockhart Inn thought when the lights in their room suddenly came on and the water started running. So did they — their stay was cut short.

Finally, Allen finished her litany of ghost stories with the tale of a guest who saw a woman standing in the Wampus Room. Later he saw a woman holding a whiskey bottle and a shot glass. "That was the last time he stayed with me," Allen said.

Allen has become quite fond of Caroline Lockhart the legend, who died in 1962. "I adore this woman," Allen said. "I sure love her spirit."

Although Lockhart was from the Boston area she was heavily involved in horse shows, so she was well-prepared for riding in Wyoming. She owned a ranch on the outskirts of Cody. Ironically, when employed by the *Boston Post* Lockhart interviewed Buffalo Bill Cody and saw his Wild West show. Cody liked the story Lockhart wrote so much that he presented Lockhart with a horse. It is possible Lockhart's experience with Buffalo Bill influenced her move West.

In many ways Lockhart was a liberated woman way ahead of her time and her time spent as a staff writer at newspapers in Boston and Philadelphia (writing for the *Bulletin*) over 15 years made her seem like a wild-eyed radical in Cody when she arrived in 1904. One way that Lockhart gained a reputation as a journalist when there were few women in the profession

The Caroline Lockhart Inn is a rooming house converted from the mansion where the author once wrote her novels. It is said to be haunted (photo by Lew Freedman).

was by undertaking daring first-person assignments, including donning scuba gear and diving into Boston Harbor.

Lockhart touched upon the scandalous, posing topless for a photograph. She also made some enemies by basing fictional characters in her novels on real people living in town – they were only thinly disguised.

Several biographies were written about Lockhart's. In one, *Caroline Lockhart: Life and Legacy*, she was quoted as saying, "All fiction is a good story based on fact." Tell that to the people of Cody who were ticked off by the evil lead character in the book, *The Lady Doc*. Lockhart and the real-life model for the bad lady of the story were enemies, though many local citizens thought highly of the woman.

It is probably a bit strong to read too much into descriptions included in fiction, but Lockhart may well have been including her thoughts about Cody people when she wrote in *The Lady Doc* about a meeting. "There were no covert glances of dislike or envy, nor shrugs of disdain, no whispered innuendoes. The social lines which breed these things did not exist. Every man considered his neighbor and his neighbor's wife as good as himself and his genuine liking was in his frank glance, his hearty tones, his beaming, friendly smile. Men and women looked at each other clear-eyed and straight."

If that did reflect Lockhart's personal feelings about Cody, no wonder she made it her home.

Some of Lockhart's other western novels were *Me, Smith, The Dude Wrangler* and *The Man from the Bitter Roots*.

In 1918, at 47, Lockhart took a leave of absence from Cody to write columns for the *Denver Post* and they could be acerbic. At the end of World War I Lockhart suggested Kaiser Wilhelm II of Germany be shipped to Cody as punishment for war crimes, saying, "My home town would take care of him all right." Included were several harsh proposals for giving the Kaiser what she felt he deserved.

Lockhart's last novel, *Old West and New*, was published in 1933. It has been suggested that one character, Charles Summers, was modeled after Buffalo Bill. In the book, Summers says that progress has accounted for "law and order, substantial citizens, churches, better schools." An old cowhand dislikes the image and responds, "I've seen enough of the East to thank God there's a West."

Lockhart couldn't stay away and returned to Cody from Denver. Eventually she ceased writing altogether and lived her final years quietly compared to the early, more adventurous period of her life.

In 1960, two years before Lockhart passed away, she rode in a lead vehicle in the Cody Stampede parade, 40 years after she served as president of the first one.

Although most of the ghost stories pertaining to Caroline Lockhart seemed somewhat ho-hum, there is a particularly juicy one. It goes like this: Sometimes, if a resident opens the door of a room at 2 a.m. he can see Buffalo Bill Cody and Caroline Lockhart dancing together in the living room.

That's about as good as it gets for Cody, Wyoming royalty of the past. Close friends or not, they probably did hoof it together a time or two in long ago days and the image is a precious one to retain. Why wouldn't anyone like to think that such early stalwarts of Cody were still looking down upon the community with smiles on their faces?

July

THE CODY STAMPEDE BEGINS

The rodeo that started it all in Cody in honor of Buffalo Bill began in 1920 and brings most of the best cowboys in the United States to Wyoming over the first few days of July while providing the area's biggest week-long extravaganza of entertainment.

Stampede Week included events July 1, 2, 3, and 4, but the build-up began June 30 as some of the big names in non-competitive endeavors drifted into town to promote the show. The Cody Stampede is renowned in the rodeo world for its $400,000 Cowboy Christmas payout and its format.

The Stampede is attractive for cowboys' Fourth of July week because it is a one-and-done competition, a "one-header" as it is said. A cowboy can blow into town, compete for good money for one day, and the next day be on the road to another rodeo for another ride.

"We always try to make it to Cody," said Trevor Brazile, who in 2014 at age 37 would win his 20th world championship. "It may take a plane to get you there, but you do what you have to do to be able to ride for that amount of money in just a one-head rodeo."

In the rodeo world, where so many competitors are just scraping by and the only way to make money is to perform at the highest level, Brazile is one of the haves. In December of 2013 at the National Finals Rodeo he passed the $5 million mark in earnings.

Certain team sports pay their athletes annually far more in guaranteed, long-term contracts than the $5 million that Brazile has taken a life-time to accumulate. Brazile also owns the single-season record for winnings with $507,921 earned. By comparison, the minimum salary for a Major League Baseball player in 2014 was $507,336. That includes the last man on the 25-man roster. During the 2013-14 National Basketball Association season the minimum player salary was

$490,180. The National Football League rookie salary minimum salary was $420,000 with a minimum of $495,000 for a one-year player.

Professional sports leagues have collective bargaining. In rodeo every individual has to account for his own travel money and entry fees and that's why a rodeo where the payout might be $13,000-plus in an event is worth busting your hump via the planes Brazile mentioned, or even stagecoaches.

Dusty Tuckness, the bull fighter of the year from Meeteetse, Andy Burrelle, who had been acting as the Cody Nite Rodeo clown in recent days, and Justin Rumford, who got his start as a rodeo clown at Cody Nite Rodeo, sat at a table outdoors in downtown Cody next to the Irma Hotel signing autographs on the last day of June as an attention-getter for rodeo fans and tourists.

Burrelle, from Ardmore, Oklahoma, was without makeup. He said it is a funny thing to be a clown performing in front of thousands of people with face painted and then walk down the street with no makeup and not be recognized. That very thing had happened to him earlier in the day when he bumped into Cody Stampede President Al Schultz. Schultz thanked him for coming to Cody. Burrelle said something akin to, "Al, you've known me for two years."

Rumford, 33 and the father of triplets, did not aspire to be a rodeo clown, even though by the end of 2014 he would be named the Professional Rodeo Cowboys Association clown-of-the-year for the third time. (There is something about Rumford and those threes.)

Rumford was working Cody Nite Rodeo one day when a clown scheduled to perform failed to appear. "I worked for Maury (Tate), and one of the guys didn't show up," Rumford said. "Maury said, 'You're funny.' I said, 'Maury, I hate clowns.'" Next thing Rumford knew a one-night clown gig turned into a career.

The June 30 kickoff to the Stampede featured the Cody/Yellowstone Xtreme Bulls competition. It was bulls-only that night. Forty of the best bull riders in the country were invited, including all 15 of the finalists from the preceding December's National Finals Rodeo.

Making a guest appearance – on foot and in voice, not riding — was Donnie Gay the eight-time world champion bull rider from Texas. Gay, who had turned 60, owns the mark for the most titles and is a popular television announcer.

He ran onto the rodeo grounds, waved and shouted, "Are you all ready for a little bull riding tonight?" About 3,000 fans yelled back that they definitely were.

If Cody Nite Rodeo is the long season, the Stampede is a traveling show come to town, bringing buzz and a ramped-up flavor. A big, fancy, electronic scoreboard and video board was erected at one end of the area, technology capable of instant replay. The only time the smaller, opposite-end-of-the-arena scoreboard which reported the tallies at Cody Nite Rodeo was in use was for some advertising.

Festivities were introduced by a song highlighted by lyrics, "It's time to cowboy up."

The master of ceremonies was Kade Rogge, whose announcing obligation carried him through the Stampede before heading out on the circuit. Bruce Springsteen's "Born In The USA" played. A huge American flag was displayed as the video board screen went red, white and blue striped.

In tune with the patriotic theme of the week Rogge spoke of faith and freedom and said, "It starts with pride. It starts with heritage." He may have meant being a rodeo cowboy. He may have meant being an American. Or he may have been wrapping the two together in a tight bundle. When he introduced the bull fighters, Rogge told the crowd they were the bravest men in the world.

Gay, whose regular rodeo commentating partner is Dan Miller of Cody, the singer who is the front man for a music revue that performs downtown for four months each year, added his authority to Rogge's.

"The bull can't read your resume," Gay said. "Otherwise, I'd still be riding."

Bull riders got two chances. Their combined score was how the winner was determined. Gay gazed at the list of bulls the dozen finalists were being challenged by and thought one bull's name sounded meek. But, he added, names didn't matter. "This bull has not been ridden, but there ain't one that can't be rode."

Ty Wallace, a top rider, drew a bull that came out of the gate and spun in circles. When he flew off the bull turned on him and Gay shouted, "Look out! Look out!" Bull fighters dashed in to earn their money. "It's not so much the horns, but you've got to keep those bulls from stepping on you," Gay said.

Wallace ended up in a tie for second place with reigning world champion J.W. Harris. Harris, from Mullin, Texas, posted a score of 90.5 in the second round aboard Pretty Boy.

Brett Stall, 25, from Detroit Lakes, Minnesota, managed to stay safe and edge them out. He totaled 176 points for his two rides. Stall waved his hat to the fans after his second ride. That is one time it was appropriate for a cowboy to remove his chapeau.

Stall grinned as he collected his championship belt buckle and $13,203. "It worked out," he said.

Stall was not one of the Xtreme Bulls favorites. He was an NFR qualifier in 2012, but injuries slowed him in 2013. Coming into Cody Stall was ranked 19th for 2014. His second ride on Kojak produced 89.5 points.

"This is one of the biggest wins of my career," Stall said.

Cowboys on the pro circuit are keenly away of Cody's rodeo reputation. Stall said the fans know their stuff. "This town, with the Nite Rodeo and all, they get behind us," he said. "It's just a great rodeo."

Stall's itinerary was typical of a traveling cowboy during Cowboy Christmas. He was in Cody Monday night for Xtreme bulls, was off to Livingston, Montana and Red Lodge, Montana for other rodeos and then planned to circle back to be part of the Stampede's bull riding Thursday.

His car was gassed up.

★★★

STAMPEDE JULY 1-JULY 2

At many rodeos, Cody Nite Rodeo included, more competitors wish to enter than can easily be accommodated in the field in front of the crowd without the rodeo lasting an unwieldy amount of time.

The spillover entries, on a first-come, first-serve basis at Cody Nite Rodeo, and by seeding at a large rodeo like the Cody Stampede, transplant into a segment of competition called "slack." At Cody Nite Rodeo this means the entrants compete late in the evening after the crowd leaves. At the Cody Stampede that meant the overflow entries competed early in the day.

Beginning at 8 a.m. on the first day of the Stampede a few dozen barrel racers showed up in the morning sun to compete in front of fewer than 50 spectators. The most enthusiastic spectator was Stampede board president Al Schultz. Whether they were competitors in the limelight or not Schultz wanted everything to be just right for the ladies. He personally drove a small tractor to smooth the ground near each of the three barrels as one after another the riders roared out of the chutes. They received no applause, but they were in the rodeo.

After each rider, Cody Nite Rodeo workers (and competitors) Naudy Esposito and Wyatt Lehman made sure the barrels stood straight in the sand and were placed just so. Riders from Dewey, Arizona; Pavillion, Wyoming; Kissimmee, Florida; Bromide, Oklahoma; Eldora, Iowa; and Carmine, Texas, received first-class service as slack barrel racing went on for hours and the temperature inched towards 90 degrees.

Schultz didn't care where the riders were from, what their names were, or what kind of times they clocked. But this was his rodeo, and he wanted to make sure everyone had a fair chance. Schultz may have been 67 at the time, but he seemed to have the energy of a 27-year-old.

During the Stampede Schultz was on the grounds so much it would have been best if he brought a cot with him for naps rather than pretending to sleep at home. There were other responsibilities outside of the arena, too. Later Schultz admitted he probably slept about two-and-a-half hours a night during the Stampede.

Pageantry is part of the game in big time rodeo. The Stampede's first day of competition opened with a Marine Mounted Color Guard carrying the flag — and every day thereafter. That faith and freedom thing ran strong.

The rodeo grounds were transformed. The back parking lot for competitors was so jammed that horse trailers had to be parked on adjacent grassy land.

Cowboys were coming. Cowboys were going. Some competitors passed through Cody so quickly that they had to be confused where they lay their heads down for a half-night's sleep.

Some competitors from Xtreme Bulls were ready for another go in the Stampede bull riding, including world champion J.W. Harris. In fact, Harris was one of a small number of big-name rodeo guys targeting Cody for family fun time. The Harris family visited nearby Yellowstone National Park before daddy went to work.

"I like coming to Cody and bringing the family here because there is so much to do," Harris said. "It's a cool place to hang out."

And to ride. Harris got his second-place tie in Xtreme bulls and left town headed to other rodeos with a 90-point ride and the lead after day one in the 95th annual Stampede.

Jesse Wright of Milford, Utah, and his brother Jake, were entered in the saddle bronc riding. Jesse's horse Big Wig came tearing out of the gate, bucked, turned and tried every trick known to broncs, but couldn't throw him. Wright scored 82 points and within minutes was packed and ready to roll out of Cody to another rodeo.

Jesse was hauling his weighty gear on his back, weighing 49 pounds. He said he had seen the horse before at another rodeo and thought it would be a good one. "I thought, 'Man, that's a nice horse,'" Wright said.

Wright said he was on his way to a rodeo in Casper, Wyoming and within the next several days was good to go in rodeos in Greeley, Colorado, Springdale, Arkansas, and in Portland, Oregon. But he always makes time for the Cody Stampede.

"This is one of the highest paying rodeos every year," Wright said. "It's known for its atmosphere and the crowd."

Not that Wright had time to mingle. He barely had time to sit down and take off his chaps.

"I've got three rodeos to go," he said. "I started riding bulls and then got scared. It's easier to hold onto a bull than a horse, but it takes a toll on your body."

Wright couldn't linger any longer. He walked at full speed out the back gate to the parking lot. A few more steps and he disappeared into the sunset.

Just about the only riders sticking around very long were the Ehcapa Bareback Riders, part of the entertainment, performing nightly. Formed in 1956 in Nampa, Idaho, the group of Native American horseback riders dressed in Native garb and performed coordinated horse riding between events. The group, whose performers range in age from eight to 19, has been affiliated with the PRCA for a quarter of a century. The riders use no saddles or bridles while performing. In order to inform the horse what the rider wants the message is transmitted through either voice command or subtle pressure from the legs.

It was sunny, with some breeze, an almost perfect night for rodeo July 2. This was a breast cancer awareness night, and the Cheyenne Dandies, on loan from Cheyenne Frontier Days, all wore pink shirts as they performed. Of course, The Cowgirl Up Rodeo Drill Team of Cody was involved. Even

During the annual Cody Stampede the Ehcapa Bareback Riders provided daily entertainment (photo by Lew Freedman).

guys on the Cody Stampede board wore pink shirts. A slogan flashed on the video board: "Tough enough to wear pink."

One steer wrestler put up an excellent 4.3-second score, but was smacked with a 10-second penalty. "You watched dollars fall out of his pockets," Kade Rogge announced.

A team roper named Nathan McWorter listed a hometown of Telephone, Texas. It made people wonder if the town's name should be updated to Cell Phone, Texas.

One cowboy definitely tough enough to wear pink was the legendary Fred Whitfield, a Hall of Famer from Texas. Born in Houston in 1967, Whitfield owns eight world championship tie-down roping belt buckles. Not many cowboys have a resume or a background quite like Whitfield's.

He is the rare African-American star rodeo competitor, and at 47 he had seen it all — including discrimination on the rodeo circuit. These days when Whitfield is spotted on rodeo grounds he is not only greeted warmly, the man nicknamed "Moon" is viewed as rodeo royalty. Recently, he wrote a book called *Gold Buckles Don't Lie,* an autobiography that tells of his hardships and triumphs.

Over the years Whitfield has qualified for the National Finals Rodeo 20 times and won more than $3.1 million in rodeo. When Rogge introduced Whitfield to the crowd for his turn in tie-down roping the applause was huge. Whitfield touched the back of his cowboy hat to make sure it was on firmly, and then exploded out of the gate chasing his calf. Whitfield was a little slow on his rope toss — 9.6 seconds, a good time, but not a great one. He finished in fourth place behind leader Catfish Brown of Collinsville, Texas, whose ride was timed in 8.1 seconds.

In his book, Whitfield said he grew up poor in Cypress, Texas, coming from "worse than nothing." There was violence in the household. He gained rodeo help along the way from friends, many of them white, particularly patron and pal Roy Moffitt. When he was 16 Whitfield beat a crowd of top ropers in Giddings, Texas in the first round of a rodeo to get noticed. It was an impressive breakout, but not necessarily a surprise to Whitfield, who won a peewee rodeo at 9. Whitfield long had been passionate about roping and at times practiced roping his five siblings.

Also as a kid Whitfield won so often on a borrowed horse that he said other parents conspired to implement new rules forcing him out of rodeos so he wouldn't keep beating their children. Sometimes when Whitfield showed up for a rodeo and showed up the other competitors he heard someone call out "Nigger." That kind of ugly language followed Whitfield for years, but eventually disappeared from opponents' vocabularies after Whitfield beat them and beat the whole world.

Whitfield was not the first black cowboy, nor was he the first top-notch African-American cowboy. Bill Pickett, born in 1870, and also from Texas, was a ranch hand and a rodeo man who invented bull dogging.

Bull rider Myrtis Dightman, another African-American from Texas, is sometimes called the Jackie Robinson of modern rodeo. He broke several barriers for black cowboys and twice finished as high as third in the PRCA standings. Whitfield later became friends with Dightman, whose prime was the 1960s and 1970s. Still, Whitfield said, "As far as having black heroes that rodeoed, there was a select few."

In some ways Roy Moffit was Whitfield's hero. He was his best friend and sponsor. On the night when Whitfield won his first world title, Moffitt, keenly aware of the disadvantages Whitfield had endured could not hold back tears.

Whitfield has been a rodeo star for a long time now. Ironically, after he became a high profile cowboy, one of Whitfield's friends told him that he had an advantage being African-American because fans could easily recognize him. That thought probably did not cross Whitfield's mind earlier when he was regularly being insulted.

Once in the 1990s, Whitfield stopped by Cody and participated in Cody Nite Rodeo briefly. His stays in Cody for the Stampede have been quick ones, but in 2014 Whitfield estimated he had entered the Stampede "at least 20 times. Why wouldn't you? It's the money for a one-header rodeo. I like to come to Cody. I have friends from Jackson Hole."

Riding a 15-year-old horse named Jewels in the 2014 Stampede, Whitfield thought he had a shot at a better time. "That calf didn't want to get up," he said. "I would have had a chance to get him in eight (seconds)."

A pensive looking Fred Whitfield at the Cody Stampede. The eight-time world champion tie-down roper from Texas, is a member of the Rodeo Hall of Fame (photo by Lew Freedman).

Whitfield still kept up the pace of a young cowboy, moving on from Cody and heading to Livingston, Casper, and Calgary. "There's still a lot of fun to be had," Whitfield said.

Certainly, this Stampede was hardly the best performance of Whitfield's career, and perhaps at his age he may not win another world title. When you have collected eight world championships and the call for induction into the Pro Rodeo Hall of Fame came a decade earlier, there is not much left to prove. But there is absolutely no rule against continuing to have fun. Whitfield's is a truly unique rodeo story, but it is also a universally affecting American success story.

★★★

STAMPEDE JULY 3-4

When Trevor Brazile's turn came for the tie-down team roping with partner Travis Graves, it was almost as if he was a one-man show. Actually, it could be said that Brazile has been a one-man show in rodeo for a long time.

Born in 1976 in Amarillo, Texas, Brazile has been the biggest name in rodeo for most of the last generation. He has captured 20 world championships in tie-down roping, team roping, steer roping, and as an all-around cowboy.

When Kade Rogge introduced Brazile he began his brief commentary with, "The living legend. Any Trevor Brazile fans in the house tonight?"

Brazile wore a white hat and a black shirt, but his horse was tough enough to wear pink, dressed in pink socks.

Easy going and friendly, Brazile seems to have a little bit more polish about him than many rough-edged cowboys of the range. Brazile often travels with family, including wife Shada, son Treston and daughter Style, and in 2013 they hunkered down in the Cody area for a couple of days and took in Yellowstone National Park.

In 2014, Brazile was on the fly. He arrived in Cody on the day of his team roping and tie-down roping and planned to leave Cody at 8:30 a.m. the next morning, heading to other rodeos in Livingston and Calgary. On this trip, Brazile went in with seven other cowboys to rent a plane in order to hit this trio of rodeos. Well-off cowboys can invest in these ventures while scuffling cowboys drive all night. The well-off cowboy also can afford more than one horse trailer and hire a driver to deliver his horse to the next rodeo while he allows his muscles to rest on an airplane.

Brazile never competed in Cody Nite Rodeo, but has always heard talk on the circuit. One thing that has amused him over the years is hearing how some big-name cowboy just pops in at the Nite Rodeo. "You never know who will show up at Cody Nite," he said.

Just maybe one day it will be Trevor Brazile. In any case, Brazile always makes it to the Cody Stampede. "The money's too good to pass up," Brazile said. "I make it a regular part of the swing every year."

The 2014 Stampede was not the best performance of Brazile's summer. He and Graves, from Day, Oklahoma, clocked an 11-second time in the team roping, good only for fourth place. Then in the tie-down Brazile was again not quite good enough to place high.

After two days, Randall Carlisle of Baton Rouge, Louisiana, led the way with a 7.7-second time. Tuf Cooper, one of the best in the world, from Decatur, Texas, was locked in a tie for second at 7.8 seconds.

After he cooled off his horse in a corral behind the chutes, Brazile bluntly analyzed his showing. "Terrible," he summarized. "I just didn't do my job tonight."

When Brazile was younger he played basketball and ran track, but he never suffered a sport identity crisis.

"I always knew what I was going to do," he said.

That involved throwing a rope and cruising around the country entering rodeos.

Not many cowboys can afford to take their young families with them, but Brazile has managed the trick of being on the road and still being in rodeo. Style, 4 years old at the time, just likes going anywhere and "she has fun whatever she is doing," Brazile said.

Treston, 6, seemed to have an affinity for throwing another type of rope. He loves to fish. Brazile sometimes uses Treston as his personal roping dummy, throwing a rope over his head. Wouldn't you know it — the little boy has been starting to think he knows more about roping than dad?

"The six-year old is starting to critique my roping," Brazile said.

Actually, that night Brazile critiqued his own roping. But hooking up with your children right after a competition loss it takes the sting out of the down-in-the-dumps feeling. Besides, in two decades of rodeoing the bad days on the dirt have been out-numbered by far by good days. The list of the championships Brazile has won is too long to be tattooed on his arm. The artist would need to borrow the other arm and maybe a leg also.

Some Cody Nite regulars appeared on the grounds they knew so well, also passing through between rodeos. Wyatt Bartels had driven to the western part of Wyoming, Saratoga, a five-and-a-half hour drive, for a rodeo, and won $700 on a bull with a 78-point score.

"It wasn't a bad day," Bartels said.

The next day he was off to Steamboat Springs, Colorado for another rodeo. Unlike Brazile, Bartels would be driving.

Al Schultz was putting miles on his little tractor again, smoothing and grading the dirt around the barrels to ensure first-class racing conditions. He drove the machine as devotedly as if he was bringing in a crop, which in a way he was. There was mud on the periphery of the fencing, so the grounds needed care: only the best for the best, in Schultz's mind.

There were so many members of the Wright family from Milford, Utah competing in the Stampede – with Jake and Jessie having come and gone – that it was no surprise when another clan member, Rusty, gained some crowd support, even though Cody Wright (78 points) and Spencer Wright (77) out-scored him in the saddle bronc riding.

Rusty Wright, son of Cody and cousin to Spencer, Jake and Jessie, was aboard a snortin', in-a-bad-mood bronc named Jacob when the gate flew open and Wright flew in the air. This horse bucked madly and it nearly tossed Wright over a fence, something that might well have rearranged his spine. When Wright's hard-earned score of 67 was announced, fans booed. They thought he deserved better for his grief.

Rogge chimed in: "You know the judges are staying at the Antler Inn in rooms 14 through 16."

There may have been a bunch of Wrights in the saddle bronc riding, but none was the leader after three days. Jesse Wright's first-day ride of 82 was hanging tough for second place, but he ended up fourth overall. By the time the places were sorted out he was at another rodeo in a galaxy far, far away.

At the end of the season, the four Wright brothers became as famous in rodeo as those plane-inventing Wright brothers from Kitty Hawk, North Carolina. Members of a family of 13 children — six girls and seven boys (the youngest ones are on the way up and plan to ride professionally, too) — Jesse, Cody, Jake and Spencer all qualified for the National Finals Rodeo in Las Vegas in the same event. Cody won the title in 2008 and 2010.

Spencer, the youngest of the competing brothers at 23, won the world championship, with Jake placing third, Jesse fourth and Cody ninth. Cody dislocated his left shoulder in the seventh of the 10 rounds, could not go in the eighth and ninth rounds, and did not record a score in the 10th round.

"I'm speechless," Spencer Wright said of his victory.

This was the first time in history that four brothers qualified for the National Finals in the same year and all four finished in the top nine. It was almost as if they had worked out the kinks at the Cody Stampede in July.

The Cody rodeo grounds were tightly packed with 6,000 fans for the Stampede's Fourth of July show, culminating the 95th Stampede.

Barrel racers gave Al Schultz good feedback on how smooth the dirt was. Schultz was on alert for crisis management throughout the rodeo, but to the public eye there were no real crises, so he must have done his job well.

"Everything fell into place," Schultz said. "It was a great year. The barrel racers loved the ground."

A half-hour before the 83-degree afternoon start on July 4, some cowboys ran through the back gate carrying saddles and other gear. They had just tumbled out of a small plane – shades of the circus clown car – after flying in from the rodeo in Greeley. It was 4:30 p.m. and one of them shouted that his event began in an hour.

One of the half-dozen cowboys who had to compete and run was Cort Scheer, 28, of Elsmere, Nebraska, in his sixth Cody Stampede. "The crowd's great," he said. "I wouldn't miss it."

He might miss his plane, though. The gang that had just landed was scheduled to take off again at 6:30 p.m. and land for another rodeo at 7:30 p.m. No more time to talk, Scheer said.

Probably the happiest winner of the week was Steven Peebles of Redmond, Oregon, who capped the final day with an 88-point bareback ride on Smack Daddy to win $10,540 and the championship belt buckle.

Peebles, 25, was injured the day before arriving in Cody. Competing in Oakley, Utah he bashed his face against a horse's head and needed medical treatment before departure. He had a black eye, a bloodshot eye, six stitches, and was lucky to be able to see when Smack Daddy sprinted out of the gate.

"It could have been worse," Peebles said of the original injury with a typical shrug-it-off cowboy comment. "But I wasn't going to take time off to let my head heal. The horse came out of the gate and he reared back and hit me in the face. It was a really good horse. Good horses make you compete at your best."

Peebles, who said he has probably competed in the Stampede six years, never hesitated to follow through on his commitment in Cody. He was hurting and had trouble focusing on the sights right in front of him, but he was a happy dude.

"This is a huge win," Peebles said. "It's right up there, for sure. This is darned sure one I'll remember for the rest of my life."

★★★

CODY NITE RODEO IS BACK

One of the first orders of business upon the resumption of Cody Nite Rodeo after the Cody Stampede hiatus was awarding belt buckles to the June champions.

Although some of the competitors were under 20, most of the winners were still good enough to have a collection of other buckles, the main trophies of rodeo.

"I have a lot of buckles," said Kooper Bott as she collected another for her June performance in breakaway roping. "I have no idea how many."

Bott did not lose her touch during the short break, winning the July 5 return rodeo with a 3.6-second toss.

Some competitors roamed the Rockies, visiting other rodeos while the Stampede took control of the grounds, and some took stay-cations. Bryce Bott said he practiced his roping. Curry Fieldler said he "just hung out."

Shane Steeves competed in the tie-down roping in Ten Sleep, Wyoming on July 4 and wasn't yet sure how he made out. "I was sitting second when I left," Steeves said.

Andy Mumm, the bareback leader, added another buckle to his trophy shelf and was a busy guy during the break. In two days at Ten Sleep he won a round and took second place. At Roundup, Montana, Mumm scored a 79 and won.

"I'm still on one shelf," he said of his trophy case, "but it's a long shelf."

Mumm had also recently won a buckle in Lovell, Wyoming.

"It's in the mail," said Mumm, who was snacking on peanut M&Ms and iced tea. "Hopefully. I figured out that for 36 seconds of work I made a thousand bucks the last two days."

Mumm rode Alabama for 76 points to mark his return to Cody and add a few more bucks to his bank account.

Diane DeLorenzo made herself known in the barrel racing with a time of 17.69 seconds, just edging regular Jennifer Lewis' 17.78. Hundredths of seconds do count in barrel racing.

Bull rider Skeet Chadwick had taken off from Cody on July 4 and entered a rodeo in Jackson Hole, a few hours away. Chadwick had been studying himself on film religiously to see what he might be doing wrong atop the bulls.

"The video camera is the best thing ever invented," he said. "It really is."

At Jackson he scored a 72-point ride and won $200. Illustrating how little Cody Nite cowboys make, especially when they are in the beginning stages, Chadwick described that ride as if he had won a million: "I covered, and I won a big pot of money."

Chadwick drew a bull named Magic Moment for his Cody Nite return, but did not cover that one. Neither did almost anyone else. Twelve out of 13 riders were heaved off by their bulls, but Tylor Bird, who totaled 84 points, was a very pleased winner.

"I'm broke, and I got a check," said the 30-year-old Powell cowboy. "I rode that bull before," he said of Show Girl, "and the first time he hooked the crap out of me. He stepped on me again tonight."

Yet despite the danger and the apparent vendetta of this particular bull, Bird had already tried bucking horses and preferred bull riding.

"Horses scared me," Bird said. "Horses in the chute shake and go crazy. Don't get me wrong. Bulls scare me, too. But horses are a lot more skittish. You want a bull to kick high and spin fast, but some bulls can be the nicest animals in the world. Some you can pet." Perhaps he was thinking of Mongo.

The more he spoke, the more Bird revealed his somewhat schizo relationship with bulls.

"Livestock are a lot smarter than people think," Bird said. "They know what their job is. But bulls, afterwards some want to hook you. We wouldn't ride bulls if it wasn't hard."

McKenzie Fair, on Big Dreamin', was nearly hooked. Fair went down and the bull seemed deadly interested in pursuit. Bull fighter Zack Flatt dashed in to save the day. Still Fair limped out of the grounds.

James Greeson was back for July 6. He had a profitable visit to the Ten Sleep rodeo the day before. Greeson took Ten Sleep by storm just the way he had been scoring big in Cody. In Ten Sleep one ride gave him 75 points and the championship.

"They gave me a nice buckle, $600 and a bottle of whiskey," Greeson said. "It was a good day."

Even though Greeson said the horses were good, and he trumped the competition, it was not a perfect day. He rolled up his jeans pants leg above his right ankle and showed off a long and wide bruise of fabulous color. Calling it rainbow bright didn't do the bruise justice.

"It's pretty sore," Greeson said. "I jumped off a horse. I'll see how it feels tonight. I've got a brace for it."

Greeson did not score that night, and he disappeared from Cody Nite Rodeo for a while after that. Perhaps he was prudently waiting until his skin returned to its natural coloration.

Lewis, who had not been thrilled with her June barrel showing, triumphed for the first time in July in 17.81.

Kade Rogge turned the microphone over to young Ty Miller who was about to cram a couple of years worth of rodeo announcing experience into less than two months. He was also about to learn that anything an announcer said was fair game for the clown. Andy Burrelle let him know that immediately after Miller told the fans he was from Pennsylvania despite a verbal twang.

"How did a guy from Pennsylvania get a Texas accent?" Burrelle instantly zinged him.

"I have no idea, my friend," Miller replied.

In his mind, Miller spoke rodeo, not southern.

The bulls were back in top form, teasing and taunting the cowboys. Quickly, the bull score went to 3-0. Then adding insult to injury, a bull named Boogie Woogie charged Burrelle in his yellow can, marking the first time in weeks that a bull had taken off after a clown: Burrelle's clowndominium saved him.

Jake Adkins, so optimistic about an early return from his arm injury, still was in no condition to ride bulls. His indignant pledge of not sitting out for two weeks to recover had long ago faded. Now doctors were telling him that he probably needed surgery.

So the summer would not go to waste Adkins toyed with the idea of roping. But a new obstacle was as gloomy as his arm woe. Adkins had had to put down his horse, so if he even tried roping, he would have to borrow a horse.

Strangely, another bull went after Andy Burrelle that night. But for one brief shining moment, the humans overcame the bulls. Curry Fielder turned in a triumphant ride, scoring 86 points, to win the round.

"He faked right and spun to the left," Fielder said of the bull sounding as if he was trying to defend an NBA guard attempting to drive to the hoop. "He was a good bull. Man, everyone was falling off."

Fielder spent his entire day working construction, which wasn't exactly resting up for the ride, but his wide smile indicated he felt fine.

"This is fun," he said.

Carol Bachman thought so, too. Unlike the young novice riders taking their baby steps in rodeo and dreaming of bright lights of Las Vegas in their future, Bachman did not begin rodeo until she was 40. She is actually the same age as Coleman White, 53, but the announcers did not tease Bachman about her age or being a member of AARP. If that happened she would probably rope and drag the MC through the dusty streets just like the scenes in one of those old western movies.

Bachman does not look her age, anyway. Most likely rodeo agrees with her after growing up south of Dayton, Ohio and working at an ad agency during her younger years. She moved to Arizona to work at a dude ranch and discovered, like Billy Crystal in the movie *City Slickers* (but without Jack Palance), that she just loved riding horses.

Carol Bachman ropes a streaking calf in the women's breakaway roping competition (photo by Lew Freedman).

"I was just entranced by it," she said.

Now Bachman splits her time between Wyoming in the summer and Arizona in the winter. While a lot of the dude-ranch customers are Americans, many are Europeans.

"It's a different vacation for them," she said. "It's the West. It's the mystique of the American cowboy."

The transition from ad agency to cowgirl took some work. When Bachman decided to try breakaway roping she knew she would go head-to-head with women half her age that had more experience. Before Bachman competed she spent four months practicing on a dummy.

"You've got to give it five, six, seven days a week of practice," Bachman said. Even on Cody Nite Rodeo days she often rose early and practiced in the morning.

The results started to show. As the season wore on Bachman got better. At the July 6 rodeo, her clocking was 4.3 seconds. Bachman had become an everyday contender against the young women. It helped that she was gaining confidence in her horse, Stewart, whom she'd had for only three months. It was an eight-year-old that had never been a rodeo horse before, but she felt they were beginning to become pals. Rider and horse gained trust in each other and learned how to rope together, too.

"We're just starting to form a bond," Bachman said. "I know I'm roping against girls who have grown up with a rope in their hands."

Just maybe some of Bachman's general life experience would help when the pressure was on.

★★★

THE REGULARS DO THEIR STUFF

After the traveling cowboys departed for other rodeos, many of the same everyday contestants did the same thing in July they had been doing in June. In some cases that was winning. In some cases that was contending. In other cases it was simply trying.

Andy Mumm won the bareback competition again July 7. Mumm had no answer for why only a few guys showed up to take him on. Mostly, it hardly mattered who else gave it a shot, the Irishman from Powell ended up on top most nights. This night he won with a 72-point score on a horse named Moofasa that couldn't throw him.

In western Canada, the Calgary Stampede, one of the biggest, grandest and most important rodeos, was underway. Mumm said that is his dream rodeo. He always hoped to check it out, but pledged not to go unless he qualified for it.

"I always wanted to go to the Calgary Stampede," Mumm said. "But I won't go unless I am a competitor."

He was young enough, determined enough, and good enough to believe it was a real possibility.

Matt Tarr was back on clown duty. He turned 30 on this day but did not take a day off to be himself. He had no wild and crazy plans in mind to celebrate either. In fact it sounded as if he had peace of mind.

"I'm just going to have fun," said Tarr, a comment that seemed appropriate for a clown. "I've got everything I want, and not many people can say that."

A new regular appeared. K.C. Jones, who grew up in Ralston, just up the road between Cody and Powell, and a professional rodeo cowboy since 1990, settled in for a lengthy stay. Jones teamed with Willy Gould in team roping, and they immediately made an impact, winning or contending. They took the nightly prize July 7 in 7.7 seconds. Jones, currently of Burlington, Wyoming, had recently won a $50,000 prize at the Houston Livestock Show and Rodeo.

Jones' specialty was timed events, team roping, tie-down roping, and the like. Each year in Guthrie, Oklahoma, there is a Timed Event Championship and Jones excelled, regularly winning championships there.

At the moment Jones was on his way to Cheyenne Frontier Days and stopped in Cody to tune up. Jones and Gould and Bill Parker and Jace Crabb engaged in some stirring duels.

"One of the best in the business on the front side," announcer Ty Miller told the spectators when Jones' turn came up. Jones and Crabb were very fast, posting a time of 6.5 seconds, but were slapped with a penalty and that killed their chances this night.

Riding solo a couple of nights later, Jones pulled off a tie-down roping win in 11.2 seconds. But on another night Jones tossed his rope at a calf and stunningly the rope exploded in half. The good, old, sturdy lasso simply disintegrated.

"I don't believe I've ever seen that," Tarr said.

Miller had a similar reaction. "That was pretty insane."

As in any sport, no matter how long a fan watches something can happen that he has never seen before and might not see again.

New face Ethan Hecht could be described as a long, tall drink of water since he is 6-foot-4 and slender. Hecht scored 74 points in the bareback ride.

"That's the mark to beat," Miller said.

Hecht, who topped Mumm, also doubles as a bull rider, but although he entered both events several times he rarely posted scores in both events in the same rodeo.

The breakaway roping seemed to heat up with the July weather. Cindy Lee and Sierra Spratt recorded wicked fast times of 2.9 seconds and Misty Mills notched a 3.0-second time that would ordinarily win the night.

The barrel racing was close. Anna Allshouse, the 12-year-old equal of any other woman, topped a rugged field with a 17.79-second victory, edging Jennifer Lewis and Laramie Terry. Lewis came up two-hundredths of a second short.

Wyoming Whiskey, a rodeo sponsor, kept awarding those consolation prize bottles of whiskey. It was up to the clown to decide which rider suffered the most from a bruising ride and that night Ty Purcell collected the bottle.

"For the wildest, most painful buck-off," Matt the Clown said. "I think he just earned it."

Not so surprisingly, it was a tough night all-around on bulls. The lights were shut off at the arena after the bulls strutted away with a 10-0 record.

On some nights it seemed as if the livestock took lessons from each other. How else to explain spinning horses and spinning bulls left and right on the same night? Jordan Couch drew a horse that tossed and kicked and kept turning left. Matt the Clown said, "Its blinker is stuck."

Curry Fielder caught a bull that took him around in circles. He stayed on, scored 74 points, and threw his arms in the air with pleasure when he made the eight seconds.

The bulls almost seemed as if they were on peyote. Bull fighter Justin Josey ran one bull in circles after it repeatedly pawed the dirt, kicking up a dust storm. One bull head-butted a fence right in front of it.

"Those bulls," Tarr said, "were a little younger and a little wilder."

The bulls were not much saner the next night. Tyler Sterner got his hand hooked in the rigging and the bull fighters worked desperately to free him before he was seriously injured. They also fought the weather — a strong wind coming off of nearby Cedar Mountain — and some light rain.

Corey Terry had a moment on his saddle bronc that made him wonder. It appeared as if the horse might be switching from rodeo to equestrian without telling anyone given the way it charged the opposite fence. Terry rode him for 70 points anyway.

"I just go with it," Terry said. "I've seen them jump fences." He was supposed to be riding a horse, not a kangaroo. "The horses know their surroundings. I've had them turn so hard they hit the fence. You are not supposed to grab the fence. That's a big no-no. You get scraped."

Hecht, 21, is a University of Wyoming student. He vacillated back and forth between bucking horses and bucking bulls for his major. At one point he chose bulls based on them being "easier on my body." But he couldn't commit at Cody Nite Rodeo, entering both bronc riding and bull riding.

"I'll probably mix it up," Hecht said. "I have to keep riding saddle broncs until I get one covered. In bull riding you've got to really charge to the front. In bareback, you've got to lay back. In saddle bronc riding, "it's the classic event. You can be 45 and still be doing it. They're all hard on your body in the long run. In bareback you'll end up with a chronic injury. With bulls, you'll have an injury some time."

No one can accuse Hecht of being blind to the risks.

The wind roared, regular behavior out of the blue in Wyoming. It was bad-luck night for the women in barrel racing. The wind chose to flare up to perhaps 40 mph directly into their faces as they completed the run to the finish line. The home stretch turned into a dust storm area. Bull fighter Zack Flatt, who also helped make sure the barrels were properly placed said, "I'm surprised we haven't had a barrel blow over."

Head down, driving her horse, Jennifer Lewis sprinted for the finish-line and pulled off the win in the shadow of a start area where giant flag poles seemed on the verge of bending in half and breaking.

"Oh, my gosh, that was some wind," Lewis said. "It didn't bother me too much while I was riding. It wasn't really ideal, but it was OK. That was not pleasant, but I'll take it. If I had goggles I would have worn them."

The next morning Lewis was still picking grit out of her contact lenses.

★★★

MAYOR KNOWS RODEO BIG DEAL

It was just about halfway through the summer rodeo season and Mayor Nancy Tia Brown, Cody's first female mayor, was talking about how Cody remains a western town and how Buffalo Bill Cody still influences lives in the city named after him. Brown has lived in Cody since 1982 and was serving a mayoral term due to expire in 2016, when she planned to retire from the office.

"I think people in their heart – including myself – think Cody is a western town," Brown said. "Cody and Cody people are very proud of their historical connection. The Yellowstone National Park connection is huge, but Cody stands on its own. The Buffalo Bill Center of the West is definitely an anchor. But Cody is a western town in the sense of having western hospitality where your word is your bond and the handshake is your word."

The West is still prominent in Cody in several ways. Old Trail Town sprang up out of nothing except the passion of the late Bob Edgar.

"That was a very genuine effort on one man's part to recreate a piece of history," Brown said. "That speaks to the western spirit in Cody." Bob Edgar, she noted, was buried in his cowboy hat.

Many residents, and certainly tourists, lap up Cody's western heritage with a definite nostalgia, and maybe Brown is the only one who says so, but when she thinks about Buffalo Bill's legacy, his securing of the water rights leading to the construction of the Buffalo Bill Dam, impressed her most.

Not that Brown overlooks rodeo's importance. Cody Nite Rodeo and the Cody Stampede are critical aspects of Cody's identity and are gold mines for the economy. "That's (Rodeo Capital of the World) become a tag line for that part of our community," Brown said. "It's a nice element of who we are. Some if it comes as an outgrowth of Buffalo Bill."

As does so much of Cody.

On the night in mid-July when bull rider Tyler Donnelly was flipped by a bull, he couldn't get out of the way fast enough and Zack Flatt and Justin Josey couldn't intercede quickly enough. Before he rose to flee Donnelly got stepped on. A

2,000-pound bull dug a little piece of his hide from his formerly whole body.

Donnelly struggled to the sideline a bit woozy. "I've got a pain in the front of my head," he said.

It didn't go away immediately either. Donnelly only watched Cody Nite Rodeo the next night. His seat was closer to the action than fans in the grandstand, but he had no more to do with the outcome than they did. He did say he was feeling much better, though. Hooray for Ibuprofen.

Of all rodeo events probably the most benign in terms of likely injury is breakaway roping. But it still has its moments. Veteran roper Codi Gines was galloping along and roping one night, the rope tangled in her hand as she threw and she nearly tore off a finger. Maury Tate had to cut her wedding ring off. As if that wasn't bad enough, Gines then broke the same hand.

Gines had to sit out some rodeos, but still hoped to score enough points to qualify for the end-of-season finals. It was not going to be easy. On the nights she could go she had to play hurt.

The Cobbler twins were both around. Billy rode bulls and Robbie rode bareback. Billy had been hurt worse than his brother.

"I got dumped on my head once," he said. "I once had a concussion that knocked me out. I woke up in the hospital."

Skeet Chadwick survived his bull ride a little bit better than that, but was tossed all over the neighborhood and again limped off the dirt. Behind the gates he lay down on his back, chaps still on, flat on the dirt outside the view of fans. It was a sure sign of a weary, hurting body.

It was Cody Culver's night to shine in bull riding. Culver took some beatings early in the season, but now had things clicking. Whether it was the study of video, more experience, or just getting the hang of it, Culver became an every-night contender. When he scored a 79 on an eight-second ride Culver pumped a hand in the air in celebration and practically vibrated with glee.

"That's the first one I got in a while," Culver said. "I was happy I didn't give up on myself. Despite this success Culver's right hip hurt, and the night before a bull stepped on his left foot.

Also riding consistency well was Curry Fielder and he decided to take a weekend break from Cody Nite Rodeo to try some bigger rodeos in Montana.

"I'm going to see if I can win some real money," Fiedler said.

There was a full moon on July 14 and the way the livestock behaved, especially in saddle bronc, it was difficult to imagine the celestial occurrence didn't affect them. One horse flipped completely over on its back, kicking its legs in the air like a toddler throwing a tantrum. The horse crashed to the ground on rider Tim Ditrich, and Ditrich needed medical treatment. Corey Terry, riding the same batch of finicky horses, addressed the rude behavior laconically. "They were just babies," Terry said of the young group of horses. "You touch one in the wrong place and it sets them off."

Culver had pledged to take the night off. So did Chadwick. But Tate called upon the old reliables to fill out a short field, and they competed. Chadwick said, "I was about to eat a hot dog" when pressed into the bull riding as if it was just any old night.

Jeff Gideon was also summoned. The phone rang from Tate when Gideon was about to nap since he faced an hours-long drive for an oil-field job in Colorado. He too showed up out of loyalty to Cody Nite Rodeo. Was it worth it to come knowing he was going to have little shuteye before work?

"Sometimes it feels that way and sometimes it don't," Gideon said.

Neither Gideon nor Chadwick covered his bull. Culver, riding his streak and a bull named Titanic, did make the eight seconds and scored 72 points, though he did not win. Good rides or not, the trip did help the show.

Hanging on the wall in Mayor Brown's office was a little poster offering a reward. But the picture did not feature a wanted outlaw. Instead it offered a reward for anyone wanting to do business in Cody. The face on the poster belonged to Buffalo Bill. Nearly a century after his death Buffalo Bill was still recruiting people for his home town.

He would have gotten a kick out of Cody Nite Rodeo, for sure, and the sight of all those young bull riders and horseback competitors riding in the town he helped build would have warmed his heart.

★★★

DAN MILLER AND LARAMIE COLLINS

For 120 nights a year between May and September, Dan Miller does his part to keep the Old West alive in Cody with his Dan Miller Cowboy Revue.

Miller owns the Cody Theatre where he and his musical group play. While he loves rodeo, he has great difficulty ever seeing any Cody Nite Rodeo competitions because his show starts at 8 p.m., the exact same time as the rodeo every night.

Miller is originally from Indiana and his broad shoulders hint at his personal history as a former linebacker at Hanover College, an NCAA Division III school. Miller, who has also promoted various musical shows in Cody in other parts of the year, had dreams of turning Cody into "a small Branson," though it doesn't seem likely that will pan out. Before settling in Cody, Miller traveled everywhere to sing. Some of his trips took him to Los Angeles, and he performed in Alaska.

The Cody Theatre holds 800 people and Miller draws about 300 people a night. A lot of his crowd is older and those fans want to hear the classics and old favorite tunes. Miller knows the words to them all and knows the history of the songs. Sometimes he livens up his introductions with jokes only slighter newer than those performed by clown Sid McFarland.

"I thought there was a need here for entertainment," said Miller, who has two daughters, one a featured part of the act.

A typical Miller show includes songs like "They Call the Wind Mariah," "Cool Water," first sung by the Sons of the Pioneers, Roy Rogers' old group, and Gene Autry's "Back in the Saddle Again." Those are definitely oldies, but goodies.

In Cody, Miller is pretty much known as a music man for his summer show and for his promotional efforts. He said when he walks down the street local residents often thank him for "all you do for Cody."

But Miller has another audience completely divorced from the tourists that visit the theatre and the Cody residents that attend concerts. For 30 years he and former bull riding champion Donnie Gay have been the voices of televised rodeo summaries under the umbrella of "This Week In Rodeo." The show has aired on TNN and it has been on The Wrangler Network.

"I love it," Miller said. "I love the independence of rodeo. Rodeo is the biggest link to the Old West. There are still some big ranches in Wyoming, but rodeo is bigger."

Miller said he has worked to build a summer clientele and a big connection for him is tour buses that bring in visitors from everywhere.

"We play for a lot of Europeans," Miller said. "They're interested in the classics. Word of mouth is huge. People say, 'Are you going to Cody? You need to…' The Cody Theatre is located across Sheridan Avenue from the Irma Hotel in downtown. "The perception of Cody is that we stem from Buffalo Bill."

Buffalo Bill is still everywhere in Cody and does seem to still be part of everything.

For a guy who is so in touch with PRCA rodeo around the country and who has handled rodeo broadcasts since 1985, Miller is really shut out of the goings on a couple of miles down the street at Cody Nite Rodeo. A tourist with two free nights to spend in Cody can hit the rodeo one night and Miller the next, but Miller has to be on stage every night.

While Miller performed downtown, Laramie Collins performed uptown. In the true spirit of Cody Nite Rodeo, a past star, Collins, 23, of Alpine, Texas, (and brother of Molly Jo) reappeared in mid-July after three years of capturing the All-Around Cowboy trophy. Why was he back in Cody?

"I'm on vacation," Collins said.

His was a different type of vacation than those older tourists were taking.

Vacation? So what else would Collins do but spend a week competing at Cody Nite Rodeo? Collins just couldn't stay away after spending those three whole summers in Cody. With a thick, flowing mustache, a mischievous look in his eye, and hair that gets unruly after a ride, Collins resembled an Old West desperado. It would not be hard to envision him playing the Johnny Ringo role filled by Michael Biehn in the movie *Tombstone*. He'd probably love it, too. The funny thing was that announcer Ty Miller called Collins' 'stash a 'Doc Holliday mustache." Apparently everyone thought Collins was ready for a career in western movies, though rodeo riding is more in the forefront of his mind.

Laramie Collins, the Cody Nite Rodeo all-around cowboy champion for 2013, only competed for a week in 2014, traveling the circuit instead (photo by Lew Freedman).

"There's nowhere else you can go and where you can say that you got on 90 broncs in a row," Collins said. "You can get on every night. Nobody can tell me that's impossible. You will not find a better place to train."

Collins, whose lifetime high score on a saddle bronc is 92 points, said the Collins family was always a rodeo family, so it's no surprise that he and Molly Jo took up the sport.

"My father wanted me to be an all-around cowboy," Collins said. "God gave me this ability, and I'm going to use it to the fullest amount. I didn't really want to ride broncs, but my father wanted me to ride broncs. It was not fun at first, but I didn't want to piss off my dad. I didn't think I could do it."

It turns out that Collins can ride just about anything.

"With a bull you've got a hand on the rope and you've got the legs on the side," he said. "In the bronc riding you have to move your feet, lift the reins and lean back. It's hard to do that many things. It has to be reaction. You don't have time to think."

Collins expected to spend the summer touring the rodeo circuit, but early in 2014 he broke his left arm when a bronc fell on him. So in July he was just rounding into shape and needed as many mounts as he could get in saddle bronc riding, bull riding, and team roping in one week.

It didn't take long for Collins to run across danger once more in the saddle bronc competition. After just one ride in Cody he was busy icing down his arm. It seemed possible he would be laid up, defeating the purpose of his vacation. But no, he entered the rodeo the next day.

"It takes more than that to sit out," Collins said.

No doubt, as Collins entered the saddle bronc riding, bull riding and team roping all in one evening. Someone joked, "You're taking advantage of your time in Cody, huh?"

"Yes, sir, I am," Collins replied. But he withdrew from the roping.

Soon enough Collins was off to other rodeos. He had accomplished all he could in three full seasons at Cody Nite Rodeo, and it was time for him to keep on moving on and up.

★★★

SILLY CLOWNS AND SERIOUS RIDERS

There was a new clown in town.

Johnny Douglas from Texas was the new painted face, at least for a short while. You definitely couldn't tell the clowns without a scorecard, but it only mattered to the rodeo regulars, fans and participants, since they watched Cody Nite in and Cody Nite out.

Nikki Tate said the rapid change of clowns over the summer was as much for the organizers as for anyone else, because if they heard the same jokes every night for 90 straight days they might go nuts.

However, wouldn't you know it but Douglas immediately picked up on Coleman White's age, as if he had been listening to the other clowns all along. "Wow, you said he was 53?" Douglas asked after a first-rate White tie-down roping showing of 9.7 seconds.

Legend Mills, an Arkansas cowboy, turned in many top marks in tie-down roping (photo by Lew Freedman).

Circumspect as always about Carol Bachman of the same age, announcer Ty Miller told the crowd, "I ain't gonna say her age, but she's a veteran of the sport."

There was a new force to reckon with in tie-down and team roping. Legend Mills, 21, son of Misty Mills of the breakaway competition, needed some rodeo action and nowhere could beat Cody for obtaining a lot of rides in a short period of time. Mills, from Arkansas, had been in a car wreck which slowed him down. He had broken his left leg earlier too.

"I'm just getting back into it," the younger Mills said. "They have it every night, and I can get back into the rhythm."

Mills usually partnered with Jimmy Morris, his mother's life partner, and they were a good team, even if Morris was twice his age at 42. Mills' best results came quickly in the tie-down category, and it was apparent right away that if he was in the mix he could win on any night.

Curry Fielder returned from his little getaway to rodeos in Newport and Red Lodge, Montana. Testing himself against fresh competition and fresh bulls paid off. He won $500 for riding a bull that had never been ridden before.

Fielder faced an unusual challenge when he returned to Cody Nite Rodeo when the bull he was on ran over the clown barrel with him aboard. Fielder somehow stayed aboard and earned a score of 71 points. He probably should have received extra credit for demonstrating that power of concentration.

While Chris McCombs was on a bull named Brown Bomber the bull crashed right over a dummy clown nicknamed Justin Bieber. "I guess he doesn't have Bieber Fever," Johnny the Clown said.

The big news was the return from the injured list of sidelined cowboys. Colt Chlarson, his broken collar bone healed, made a triumphant return. On his first ride after the enforced lay-off Chlarson rode his saddle bronc for 78 points and a victory. He high-fived pal Skeet Chadwick.

"What a way to come back!" Chadwick said.

During his recovery period Chlarson returned to New Mexico as his bones knitted and where he was mostly bored. "It was five weeks of lying around," Chlarson said. This ride was a nice reward. "I darned near got bucked off. It feels awesome. It was a good score on a good horse and it was the best I've felt (since the injury)."

Chlarson's return was good for Cody Nite Rodeo, too. He added flash to the event and made the field deeper.

So did Tim Ditrich, also on the verge of getting back in the saddle again. A rodeo competitor for Cal Poly State-San Luis Obispo, Ditrich suffered a rather embarrassing injury. He was smiling now, but not so a few days earlier when a horse stepped on him below the belt.

"I was kicked in a bad area," Ditrich said. "I'm supposed to get the stitches out tomorrow and then I can come back when I feel it won't affect me."

That kick could have affected him for life. Somewhat cruelly and mysteriously, from then on when he competed Ditrich was introduced to spectators by Miller saying, "We call him 'Stitches.'" No explanation was given, something Ditrich had to be thankful for, but without the background the comment didn't make sense to fans.

Anna Allshouse was still out there in the barrel racing, winning regularly and contending always.

"She's 12 years old!" Miller proclaimed. "The future of rodeo." No one argued with that assessment.

Bill Parker and Jace Crabb were as sharp as ever, blowing away the team roping field in 5.5 seconds. However, they were done for a month, moving on to other rodeos, but mostly to take care of some horse-sale business.

Chlarson was back in business as if his missed injury time hadn't existed, winning again and tipping his black hat with the feather in it to the crowd. Always outgoing, Chlarson seemed to ratchet up his showmanship.

One of Misty Mills' characteristics as she broke out of the gate on her horse was her cowboy hat fly off. Misty never lost her head, but she almost always lost her hat. It was reminiscent of the days when Willie Mays' baseball cap seemed to whip off his head at will for effect when he ran the bases or sought to field a fly ball. The status of Mills' hat was inconsequential as she scored a 3.0 in breakaway.

But then her ride was quickly overshadowed by Shanni Shipley. Shipley broke out of the gate swiftly, drew a bead on her calf instantly, and perfectly lassoed it in the stunning time of 1.9 seconds.

"That is one of the fastest runs you will ever see!" Miller gushed.

He was right. A time of 1.9 seconds in breakaway roping is roughly the equivalent of lightning striking. The average fan might never see a sub-2.0-second breakaway time in a lifetime of rodeo watching and this was the only sub-2.0 all season at Cody Nite Rodeo.

Shipley, 24, of Pine Creek, Texas, was ecstatic. Shipley said she felt she had been in a two-year slump and was just coming out of it. At one point, some years earlier, Shipley owned a world-record time of 1.76 seconds, set in Pueblo, Colorado.

This ride was essentially the perfect storm of breakaway roping.

"It felt good," Shipley said. "You don't see it very often. You've just got to get a good start."

One bull rider oozing confidence after a series of good rides was Cody Culver. When he scored 84 points and dismounted Culver tossed his helmet into the air. His body language told the rest of the story.

There was a new bull fighter in town. Seventeen-year-old Willie McCombs, a friend of Justin Josey's from Oklahoma, wanted to try it. He was dressed for the part, seemed light on his feet and did well to hide any nerves, though clown Matt Tarr did not let him off easy.

"I want everyone to know that this is Willie's second night fighting bulls, and he's ready to throw up," Tarr said.

That may well have been so. McCombs said he was going to stick around until school began, but he disappeared soon after.

Chlarson climbed on his assigned horse behind the gate and was ready to bounce. The gate was flung open and the horse just stood there. Tarr shouted, "Hey, Colt, put your quarter in." The gate was shut, Chlarson readied himself all over again, and this time the horse came out bucking.

Back to that no scorecard, no ID thing. The team roping event included seven entries with the last name of Garlick. The family that ropes together stays together. Lance and Jason were a team. James and Levi were a team. Bill and Troy were a team. The odd relative out from this Cody Nite Rodeo family reunion was Austin Garlick, who teamed with Harold Adema, on break from his pickup man duties. The Garlick-Adema duo won the whole thing in 11.4 seconds.

Itching to rodeo, Jake Adkins was still hampered by the sore arm that had wrecked his season. But after much internal debate, Adkins talked himself into giving team roping a Cody Nite Rodeo try. First, he needed to borrow a horse. Then he felt he needed a suitable cowboy shirt since his T-shirts and plain shirts wouldn't do.

Cowboy Shane Steeves said even the borrowed shirt didn't cut it. Adkins appeared wearing something on the gaudy side. Steeves took one glance at Adkins' shirt and proclaimed it bad karma.

"He shouldn't be wearing leopard skin design on a black shirt," Steeves said. "It's not manly enough."

Well, if cowboys are tough enough to wear pink then maybe they are tough enough to wear leopard. Probably not many spectators noticed the leopard shirt, anyway, because their eyes were glued to Adkins hurtling through the air.

Adkins rode out of the gate pursuing a calf, but before he could lasso the little doggie his horse stopped of its own accord. Adkins sailed out of the saddle and over the horse's head. The horse seemed to realize Adkins wasn't the gal who was his usual rider and took umbrage.

"That horse kicked up and I wasn't ready for it," Adkins said. "If I had my horse I wouldn't have fallen off."

As embarrassing as that little maneuver was Adkins came back a night later on the same horse and trying to rope.

"I'm trying to learn," he said. "The horse was a lot better tonight."

Even the best ropers have tough nights. Sometimes the calf refuses to be caught and it zig-zags with such verve a rope bounces harmlessly off its head or side. Coleman White had two such nights in a row, leaving him disgusted with his roping.

"I'd try to hang myself," White said, suggesting an alternative use for his rope, "but I'd probably miss."

★★★

JIMMY MORRIS

Usually up working for Cody Nite Rodeo by 6 a.m., Jimmy Morris' long days of summer are completely built around rodeo.

That makes sense since his entire life has been built around rodeo. Morris, 42, was once a champion bull rider. His girlfriend Misty Mills is a breakaway roper. His son Lukasey, 12, competes in junior steer riding.

Morris is also a tangential part of the story of one of rodeo's most legendary figures, although not everyone knows the connection.

Mornings when he rises Morris takes bucking horses and bulls for a 20-mile ride to pasture. On a given day he may also do a brand inspection for some livestock being loaned out by the Mo Betta Rodeo Company to another rodeo. Then he sorts out the stock for the Cody Nite Rodeo performance of that night. During the rodeo Morris often acts as an official, slipping into a Wrangler vest. When he can squeeze it in – as often as possible – Morris enters the team roping as a heeler. Lately, his partner has been Legend Mills, but Morris will be paired with anyone available if it means getting into the field.

The event requires teamwork and cohesion, so it is a disadvantage to head out onto the dirt with a different partner each time. Somehow, and he was proud of it, Morris made it work well enough in June to obtain the monthly championship belt buckle.

"Oh yeah, I sweated for the June belt buckle," Morris said as he sat in his on-the-grounds living trailer during a rare day-time breather. "Shoot, in the month I had eight or nine different partners."

Morris has always bled rodeo. He grew up in the tiny town of Atoka, Oklahoma in the southeastern corner of the state, the same area where Maury Tate hails from and still lives.

"I was four years old when I got on my first steer," Morris said. "I didn't ride him very far. I've known Maury for years. I made my living riding bulls. Lukasey rides pretty good now."

Morris also gained familiarity with a rope from a very early age, something which has been useful to him much later. He was probably three or four when he first twirled a rope, Morris said, although he didn't envision his long-term rodeo future tied to a lasso. Eventually, as they do for every rider, the bulls caught up to Morris. They pummeled his body sufficiently – left shoulder surgery that needed six months to heal, torn bicep – so that Morris recognized the bulls were getting the best of him.

After Morris waved goodbye to bulls for good he began competing in team roping. Making a major switch in specialties was difficult. It's rare when an athlete that has excelled at one thing can adapt successfully when change is forced on him by advancing age or injury. Morris wrestles with trying to be as good at team roping as he was at bull riding.

"I'm the kind of person who hates to suck," Morris said. "I'm not a very good loser."

So it's not that surprising that Morris has won as much as $11,000 roping at one time.

It was bull riding, though, that really got Morris' juices flowing. An uncle was a bull rider and that helped steer him into that realm. Morris was a star bull rider in high school and he competed as a member of the Professional Rodeo Cowboys Association throughout the 1990s and then competed for the Professional Bull Riders when it started up.

Jimmy Morris, a former champion bull rider in his 40s, worked as an official most nights, but took time out to enter team roping too (photo by Lew Freedman).

As a youth, Morris' mentor was Lane Frost, one of the most iconic and tragic figures in rodeo history. Although Frost was born in Colorado and spent most of the first 14 years of his life in Utah, Frost's family lived in Lane, Oklahoma, 11 miles from Atoka where Morris grew up. Frost was born in 1963 and was already making his legendary mark on the pro rodeo circuit when Morris was still in school, but they did both attend Atoka High.

"I rode practice bulls at his parents' house," Morris said. "Lane would help me out."

Frost was tutored in bull riding by former world champion and Hall of Fame competitor Freckles Brown and won the 1981 National High School Rodeo title, and then joined the pro circuit in 1982. Frost passed along knowledge to Morris, the first similarly talented high school bull rider to come along after him from their small corner of Oklahoma.

In 1987, Frost won the PRCA bull riding championship, his long-time goal fulfilled. Youthful, handsome, charitable and personable, Frost was a popular front man for the sport and seemed destined to have a long and successful rodeo career. However, on July 30, 1989, at Cheyenne Frontier Days, riding a bull named "Takin' Care of Business," Frost was thrown. As the bull turned, a horn hooked Frost in the side, breaking some ribs.

Knowing he was hurt, Frost rose and tried to run to the sidelines, but he fell and the ribs punctured a lung and his heart. The heart injury was fatal. Frost died before his 26th birthday.

In subsequent years, a protective vest developed partially as a result of Frost's death, and one worn under cowboys' shirts, has become standard-issue safety equipment in rodeo.

The movie *8 Seconds*, released in 1994 and starring Luke Perry, is the story of Frost's life. Several country songs mention Frost by name or implication. The most haunting, moving and riveting song referring to Frost is Aaron Watson's "July in Cheyenne." Watson sang the tune against a backdrop video of Frost riding and smiling. In part the lyrics go, "A little part of every heart of every rodeo fan died there in the rain in the mud in July in Cheyenne."

On some nights, leading up to the start of Cody Nite Rodeo, sound man Brandon Milburn played "July in Cheyenne" for the fans streaming into the grandstands.

In 1990, Frost was inducted into the Pro Rodeo Hall of Fame in Colorado Springs, Colorado. Numerous tributes were afforded Frost in 2014, commemorating his life and career 25 years after his death. A display was erected at the National Cowboy & Western Heritage Museum in Oklahoma City taking note of the anniversary. Also, Cheyenne Frontier Days observed the quarter-century anniversary of Frost's death at the 2014 rodeo, an event his parents participated in.

As Frost was being killed during the bull riding in 1989, the protégé from Oklahoma was scoring the then-biggest victory of his life. Jimmy Morris became the second person from Atoka High to win the National High School Rodeo Finals.

Morris does not generally come across as a sentimental man, but there was a catch in his voice when he talked of the link between Frost's last ride and his own big ride in Pueblo, Colorado.

"I won the national high school title on the same day he got killed," Morris said.

It was 30 minutes after he began celebrating his title that Morris, then 17, learned Frost had died in the sport they both loved. Morris' reaction to a newspaperman was powerful. "It just crushed me," he said. "I went from being the happiest man in the world to the most unhappy. I didn't have a clue what I was doing until I met him. Now I kind of feel like I'm doing this for Lane."

Frost, who was buried next to his own mentor, Freckles Brown, was the conduit of generational bull riding knowledge funneled to Morris. Morris turned pro after his high school triumph and competed all over the country in big rodeos.

"Four years to the day after Lane was killed I won the bull riding at Cheyenne," Morris said. "From high school until my mid-20s I got on bulls five days a week. There's never been a more humbling sport in the world than bull riding."

Yet despite that belief he has not discouraged his son Lukasey from choosing the event. He revels in watching the youngster learn how to master steers – which he did with regularity – and spending the summer in Cody together where he can be involved in rodeo every night without the wearying physical travel of his own youth.

"It's one of the coolest things to watch him (Lukasey)," Morris said. "To be here and not have to travel around the world is great. I get to spend time with my kid and still be a cowboy. I am absolutely loving it. I'm having a blast at the rodeo."

★★★

HOLDING IT ALL TOGETHER THROUGH SOME TOUGH DAYS

Even Andy Mumm, the dominant bareback rider, had off days, although his off days didn't include being thrown from his horse.

After winning just about every bareback competition he entered, Mumm hit a weak streak when he kept being disqualified for missing his mark or improper placement of his feet. He even struck out on his 26th birthday.

"It's all in my head," Mumm said. "I'm taking a couple of nights off to fix it."

Coleman White was in his own slump in the tie-down roping and getting a headache from being reminded of his AARP membership and his age. He missed another calf.

"Do you know how old that guy is?" Ty Miller said.

Fortunately for White, Tony Martoglio was back as the clown, and he was 60 years old.

"He's just a pup," Martoglio said.

Once in a while, Maury Tate substituted ranch bronc riding for saddle bronc riding. The main difference was the gear riders used. In the ranch bronc event cowboys had to use working saddles instead of standard PRCA saddles.

Colt Chlarson thrived on the ranch broncs, scoring 78 points to win a Cody Nite Rodeo nightly title. Chlarson lifted his black hat off and waved it to the cheering crowd and then blew kisses to the fans.

"I heard the crowd go wild when I blew the kisses," Chlarson said.

A showboating cowboy, Colt Chlarson waves his hat on a successful ride in ranch bronc riding, a rarely contested event (photo by Lew Freedman).

Chlarson planned to take the night off because he hurt his foot on a previous ride, but changed his mind at the last minute. "I have fun every time I nod my head on a bronc," he said.

Jake Adkins was still trying to adjust from bull riding to tie-down roping and he discovered that the two events affected his body differently.

"I'm hurting in different places," Adkins said, noticing that his left index finger was bleeding. "My butt and pelvis hurt. My ass hurts. But I'll try it again. Why not?"

Apparently, Adkins did not realize that he had just listed reasons for why not.

Skeet Chadwick was struggling on bulls again, repeatedly drawing ornery animals that brushed him off. He was trying to regain the form that enabled him to win money elsewhere over July 4.

"That cover did me some good," Chadwick said. "It got my confidence back up."

But he kept draw spinners in Cody that damaged his psyche all over again, even if Chadwick's nature seemed difficult to dent.

Ethan Hecht had been switching back and forth between horses and bulls. He finally drew a bull named Mama's Boy that spun like a top but helped him gain a first-rate score of 84 points.

"It's been bugging me," Hecht said. "I was getting close. It's the first one I got a score on. It gets in your head a little bit. I've got to keep going from here."

In a way that's the theme of Dave Eubank, a preacher who each summer for the last three years had stopped in Cody for a week. Eubank, born in Texas as the son of missionaries, spends most of his year in Burma with his family doing missionary work.

However, for two months a year he brings his wife Karen, daughter Suu, and son Pete back to the United States to make sure the kids get some semblance of American life in their background. Eubank, 53, is actually an Alaska resident now, a place where he has hunted and climbed 20,320-foot Mount McKinley.

The Eubanks love Cody Nite Rodeo, the spectacle of it, the realism of it and the fun of being part of it. Suu (named for Burma's Nobel peace prize-winning Aung San Suu Kyi) entered the junior barrel racing for several nights, and Pete, just eight, tried the junior steers once.

"This is one of the great things in the world," Eubank said as he watched rodeo from the grandstand. "This is a highlight."

As a religious man what Eubank couldn't get over was how the night's events not only kicked off with the National

Anthem, but with a prayer for the cowboys. He was amazed anybody started an event with public prayer anymore.

"They pray out loud in 2014 America," Eubank marveled.

Rodeo nights passed swiftly and then the Eubanks were off by vehicle to Montana, Seattle, and Alaska before returning to Burma.

Over a two-day period near the end of July it seemed as if the entry lists were jumbled in a computer. Colt Chlarson was listed in the bull riding, and Skeet Chadwick was listed in the saddle bronc riding. Chlarson challenged some of the bull riders to compete in his event and they retaliated by entering him in bull riding. Chlarson probably had more bull experience than they had horse experience, however.

"I don't crave it," Chlarson said of bull riding. "I think I am two out of 11 lifetime on bulls. This is payback from the other guys."

It was quickly shown that Chadwick might be better off with bulls than horses when astonishingly his horse Snap erupted from the gate, dashed straight across the width of the arena and heaved Chadwick over the fence. Despite the crash landing, Chadwick jumped up, climbed back over the fence and dusted himself off. That was the end of Skeet and bucking horses.

Chlarson's horse Hatchetville tried to mimic Snap, but Chlarson stayed on for eight seconds and waved his hat to the fans again. The horse led him in a loop parallel to the opposite fence where Chadwick had been thrown, and Chlarson took the risk of dismounting by grabbing the fence. He escaped injury, blew kisses to the crowd again as he dangled from the fence, and walked off.

Almost as if winning a dare, Chadwick broke out of his bull riding slump and scored 76 points for second place. Playing to the crowd as well, Chadwick twirled his hat into the air. There was never any doubt, though, about whether the bulls would come out ahead for the night. They always led the cowboys and often gave them a scare.

"They're not Teddy bears," Ty Miller reminded folks.

Although they were not the numbers he was looking for, Ethan Hecht finally pulled off his goal of a same-night double ride, scoring 68 points in bareback riding and 69 points in bull riding. The scores were fairly low, but Hecht survived eight seconds on each animal. Unfortunately, survived was the operative word. His bull slashed his leg, drawing blood.

"It's a pretty good gash," Hecht said of the beast's payback.

Maybe it was just the law of averages, but as July pulled to a close, wrapping up a second month of Cody Nite Rodeo, the grounds seemed to resemble an emergency room as much as a sporting site. Scars were visible, blood flowed and legs couldn't hold the weight resting on them. If this was football, baseball or basketball guys would hit the disabled list at a startling rate. But this was rodeo and these guys pretended nothing hurt.

Pickup man Harold Adema couldn't hide his bruises. Although he did acquire stitches from riding a horse, his accident did not occur during rodeo. He was in a pasture with livestock and experienced a close encounter with a rattlesnake. The rattlesnake made a move. The horse reared up and its head hit Adema in the face. Adema's cheek was bruised, as was the area around his eye. How many stitches did it take to close the cuts?

"I didn't count," Adema said.

Skeet Chadwick suffered a similar injury, albeit on a bull in the arena. The bull bucked. Chadwick's feet popped up. He then was jerked forward and hit his face on the bull's horn, bruising his left cheekbone and collecting a black eye.

"I remember nodding my head, and the lights went out in the arena," Chadwick said.

A couple of days later Chadwick was riding a bull named Revelation when he had one himself. He let go as he began to slip off. "I was going to hang on to the side," Chadwick said. "But I was kind of scared. I've been hit in the head enough lately."

Tim Ditrich, who already earned the unflattering nickname "Stitches" from a previous mishap, had more tough luck on a bucking horse. After being thrown he lay flat on his back on the ground and then accepted on-site medical treatment

Tim Ditrich rode well all summer when he could stay healthy, a development that ended his campaign before the finals (photo by Lew Freedman).

resulting in him walking around with a bag of ice pressed to his head.

"I don't remember very much," Ditrich said. "I've had concussions before."

In-between occasions of his body being bashed Ditrich rode terrifically.

There are mishaps and there are injuries and every once in a while there is equipment failure. Those who witnessed K.C. Jones' rope breaking never thought that they would see such a thing again in competition. Only then it happened again. This time to Legend Mills, who saw his rope snap as he attempted to lasso a calf. The rope broke and a strand flew backwards and hit him in the face.

Cowboys are reluctant to show pain and they are not supposed to show disappointment either. It's called not losing face. But that doesn't mean they don't feel it when something is amiss.

Ken Sabbath, in Cody from Wilmette, Illinois, and entering tie-down roping on a horse lent by Coleman White, said he fondly recalls the summer of 2008 when he competed just about every night. This year, at 49, his body was feeling the strain of everyday competition and it was becoming more difficult to consistently rope well.

That meant Sabbath had to cope with more misses. He offered a piece of advice for handling adversity in the arena – keep the emotions inside and then take them outside. Grit your teeth, Sabbath said, and cry or display anger out of sight.

"It's so frustrating when you miss," Sabbath said. "I try to leave the arena before I start cursing."

As the calendar flipped to August, July buckle winners were presented awards by Nikki Tate on the arena floor.

Wyoming cowgirl Carol Bachman was a late comer to the sport but performed well throughout the 2014 season (photo by Lew Freedman).

Ethan Hecht won bareback, Daryl Lamb tie-down roping, Carol Bachman breakaway roping and Corey Terry saddle bronc riding. The team roping header was Colby Gines, Codi's husband, and the top heeler was Harold Adema. Jennifer Lewis won barrels and Curry Fiedler won the bull riding. The All-Around cowgirl winner was Tara Edwards and the All-Around cowboy was Legend Mills.

Mills was surprised by the honor.

"I didn't even know I was up for it," he said. "I've got a bunch of them, buckles and saddles, so I can say that I got something besides a beat-up body."

Hecht said the only saddle he ever won was in high school rodeo, but felt he was on a roll in 2014.

"This year I've got six buckles so far," he said.

Bachman had been riding Stewart the horse, but changed his named to Slick and then back to Stewart. She was perhaps the most pleased winner in the bunch. The monthly victory was special since she was older and often reminded herself of her late rodeo start.

"I am very happy," Bachman said. "This is the first time I've had the opportunity to win one."

Bachman could also appreciate something few others at Cody Nite Rodeo could this late in the season. Her body was in one piece. They probably should have given her a trophy for that.

August

SURVIVAL OF THE BEST AND THE FITTEST

Zack Oliver was almost Lane Frost, but in the wrong way.

On June 13, 2013, competing in the bulls at Cody Nite Rodeo, Oliver, 19, was thrown off and then caught by a horn. The bull stepped on his chest twice, proving that while a protective vest might be helpful, it is not infallible.

Oliver is from a rodeo family – his grandfather is Al Schultz, the Stampede board president. He rode steers as a kid, won the Cody Nite bulls title in 2012 and has a PRCA card.

None of that background made an iota of difference when the bull came after him. Oliver's heart stopped beating for 45 seconds.

"They pronounced me dead at the scene," said Oliver in a matter-of-fact tone so casual it seemed as if he was talking about what was for dinner that night.

There was nothing casual about Oliver's on-site medical treatment, however. It was very urgent. He passed out and revived, waking up on a stretcher while coughing up blood. The plan was to life flight Oliver to Billings, Montana for more treatment, but bad weather forced the journey into a drive.

"Two ribs bent across my heart and collapsed my lung," Oliver said.

Oliver suffered a broken collarbone, bruised lungs, and cracked ribs. Yet after the in-the-arena fright he grew stronger. One minute he was dead and the next he was going to be OK. Oliver said he may have turned 20 years old, but "I was born on Friday," meaning the day he was revived following the rodeo accident.

Six weeks after his stomping, Oliver rode a bull again at Cody Nite Rodeo. A one-time roper who turned to bull riding because he thought it would be more exciting, Oliver did not ride very much in Cody in 2014. On August 1, roughly the anniversary of his return to bulls, Oliver won the bull riding with a fabulous score of 87 points.

The lucky young man lived to ride again.

Early-season pickup man Luke Newsom was back from his tour of the region roping and picking up cowboys in North Dakota, South Dakota, and Oklahoma. He also competed in ranch rodeos and a peculiar event that combined cow milking, a four-man relay, passing a bottle of beer between riders, and roping in pairs, two steers at a time. After his current two-week sojourn in Cody, Newsom was scheduled to go sheep hunting in Alberta.

"I like to keep it mixed up," he said.

So does Jordan Couch, who wore a brown sport coat when he scored 79 points in ranch broncs. A sport coat in rodeo?

"I wanted to look flash," Couch said.

Couch, from Idaho, said he came to Cody because "I heard about 90 days of rodeo." He was rebounding from an accident that broke a couple of ribs and his right arm. So he switched to holding his rope with his left hand.

He was urged to trade in the brown sport coat for a white sport coat and a pink carnation, but it wasn't clear if he had even heard of Jimmy Buffet, never mind the song's lyrics. Couch waved and snapped a rope like a whip, making a pistol shot sound. Told he did his wardrobe proud, Couch said, "Thanks, boss."

It was not clear if Couch was to be believed, but when asked what he liked best about bronc riding, he said, "It's a rush. I've tried every drug there is and nothing compares to bronc riding."

Either because he didn't quite catch the Buffett reference or hadn't made it to a Goodwill store, Couch stuck with his brown sport coat.

Codi Gines, 35, wife of Colby and mother of 10-year-old Caden in junior steer riding, struggled while sidelined from breakaway roping because of hand problems. Yes, it was true, she said, Maury Tate was forced to cut her wedding ring off a couple of weeks earlier when she caught her finger on a rope. She bandaged it up and kept roping, winning four nights in a row before she smacked her hand on a saddle horn and broke a bone.

Gines said she was six years old when she first attended Cody Nite Rodeo as a spectator and living 25 miles away in Powell has made it easy to keep coming for the next 29 years. Ordered to rest her injuries for two weeks, Gines was impatient to get back into the mix and qualify for the season's finals.

"I might be able to come back for the finals, but the odds are slim," she said.

Corey Terry, the season-long top saddle bronc rider hangs on as he is bounced all over the arena by an aggressive horse (photo by Jason Koperski).

Gines said she loves roping and hates to miss out because of injury. About five years earlier she had recorded a 1.9 time in breakaway, so Gines knew how good things could be.

The latest clown on the scene was Jesse Larson from Duluth, Minnesota. Unlike other clowns that tote in anonymous dummy figures to woo a wayward bull away from hitting a person, Larson brought a lookalike of himself that he called his "mini-me." The message to the bulls was a simple one: Hit the dummy, dummies. While the little stuffed Larson did get bashed periodically, bulls did not always fall for the trick. Larson was creamed in his barrel once and yelled to the bull fighters, "Protect me! That's what you're supposed to do!"

The can protected Larson that time and a second time the next night when another bull took a run at him and blasted the can. "I feel a little twisted," Larson said after being bounced around for a second night in a row.

August 2 was a dark and stormy night, with lightning in the distance and sprinkles in the air. Naturally, as it had previously, the weather saved its absolute worst for the barrel racing when rain began to fall in buckets. Bailey Stenger, 16, of Warden, Montana won in 17.42 seconds over a muddy course not at its finest.

Andy Mumm was back from a little road trip highlighted by rodeos in Basin, Wyoming and Worland, Wyoming. He won about $300 and believed he got his bareback riding groove back. However, for a change of pace, Mumm entered bull riding – unsuccessfully.

"I got thrown off like a fat lady," Mumm said.

K.C. Jones, who had already somehow broken a rope, looped a rope over a calf in tie-down, but then signaled for assistance. The black calf was down, possibly because of a broken leg. Normally, when a rope is loosened, freeing the calf's legs so it can stand again, it jumps up and runs out of the arena through an open gate. This calf did not get up. It took four men to carry it off.

Coleman White was still out there for tie-down and putting up with the exas-perating age jokes. Jesse the Clown joined in, though with a compliment of sorts on the theme, telling fans of age 53 and above, "You couldn't tie your shoes in less than 20 seconds."

★★★

MAKING SURE TO MAKE THE FINALS

Carol Bachman sat atop her horse Stewart, AKA Slick. Actually, she had finally decided on Slick Stewart, which seemed an appropriate compromise. But the horse and her roping were both improving. On an early August night she clocked a breakaway roping time of 2.3 seconds, one of the swiftest of the season and her best. Sitting atop her own horse next to Bachman was Jalissa Klassen, one of Cody Nite Rodeo's best in the event. The women high-fived as they watched the last of the event unfold and Bachman's time hold up.

"I needed that so badly," Bachman said. "I knew I had a good calf. I had to get the rope out of my hand."

The three-month Cody Nite Rodeo culminates with a three-day summer championship, the last three days of August. The important thing for competitors on the bubble, who may not have done well enough to score big or may not have shown up for enough rodeos, was to pile up points in the standings throughout the last month.

Rodeo clown Jesse Larson from Duluth, Minnesota (photo by Lew Freedman).

Riders accrue points for competing, even if they are thrown off their bucking horses and bulls, but to ensure a finals slot it is necessary to record official scores, win nightly events, or place high in them.

Barring injury, it was starting to be obvious who some of the end-of-year competitors would be. Andy Mumm was a sure thing in bareback. Colt Chlarson and Corey Terry were safe in saddle bronc. Curry Fiedler was leading the pack in bulls. Anna Allshouse just kept scoring points in barrel racing, and Coleman White's steadiness was going to uplift him. But many spots were open.

The weather was also changing. At 5,000 feet of elevation summer began petering out in August with temperatures slipping into the 40s. The 2014 summer brought more inconveniently timed rain than expected, too. Periodic wind storms ripped across Cedar Mountain right through the open-ended west side of the rodeo grounds.

In other parts of the country the National Football League was getting underway. On a coolish night Maury Tate broke out his New York Giants coat. When asked if that was in honor of training camp opening, Tate said, "That's because I think it might rain."

Jesse the Clown conjured up some elaborate acts and some required volunteers. For one act he enlisted Skeet Chadwick. While Chadwick did not have a speaking part, he did play a cowboy, something easy enough for him, although he had never acted before.

As part of his new role, Chadwick was fake shot and had to be carried off on a stretcher. "I laughed a couple of times," he admitted later when he officially came back to life. "Acting was different." He awaits an Academy Award nomination. Chadwick did the whole thing again a day later and Jesse hammed it up a little more, providing a eulogy. "Let's have a moment of silence for Skeet," the clown said. "He was a good cowboy."

For some reason in his bronc busting, if only to provide a photogenic moment, Colt Chlarson lathered up heavily in baby powder. Cowboys do use some baby powder to improve grip, but Chlarson pretty much started a snowstorm. White flakes surrounded his head as he rode, but it didn't interfere and he won the saddle bronc night with 76 points.

"It was in my mouth," he said. "I could taste it."

The bulls kept up their winning pace. They were going to the finals regardless of who the riders were. Jesse the Clown looked askance at some of the behemoths and said, "I like my hamburger on a bun."

Andy Mumm studied the bulls once more and said, "I've got a better kinship with horses."

For nearly two months either Kade Rogge or Ty Miller had been telling rodeo fans that bull rider Jeff Gideon was going to become a first-time dad and was expecting twins. It seemed as if Gideon's wife had been pregnant for a year. However, the real due date was fast approaching and except for the eight seconds it took for Gideon to record a 74-point successful ride on August 6 he kept his cell phone close and turned on. Sure enough, immediately after his good ride the phone buzzed.

"The Mrs. is calling," Gideon said and then ran for the exit. A few hours later, at 2 a.m., Gideon's wife gave birth to twins.

K.C. Jones, 47, had seen changes in ropes during his long career, which in a way began when he was five years old and he was one of the kids dashing onto the Cody Nite Rodeo arena floor for the calf scramble. He seemed less shocked than others about his rope breaking in half.

"There are different fibers in ropes," Jones said. "The weather affects them."

A good roper realizes different ropes work best at different temperatures and so bathes them in linseed oil, according to Jones. Ropers arrived at the grounds carrying ropes inside cases with handles that resembled those used for musical instruments or for machine guns toted by gangsters in movies.

K.C. Jones, a Wyoming cowboy who is a five-time world champion in timed events, carries his rope to work in a spiffy case (photo by Lew Freedman).

"You want an extra soft rope at night," Jones said. "If the temperature is 90 degrees or it is 30 degrees, I'll be using a different rope. Nylon is better than hemp. Hemp ropes, they'll break. But it still happens with nylon."

Jones excelled competing against the clock and never had much interest in bull riding or the like.

"Nah," he said. "I like the roping end of the arena."

Chaz Arthur, 36, of Powell, has roped for 16 years. He carried his ropes in a case that was like a violin case only rounder. The ropes sat inside in powder.

"One tends to be softer and one tends to be stiffer to me," Arthur said. "The powder, for lack of a better word, is in case the rope gets dirt on it and feels slick."

Although Jones was nonchalant about his broken rope, Arthur was nonplussed at the sight of Jones' and Legend Mills' ropes snapping in half during competition.

"I don't think I've ever had it happen to me," Arthur said.

A couple of nights later the wind blew at what seemed to be hurricane force. People walking around couldn't stand up straight. Even the best-fitted cowboys had trouble holding on to their hats.

As Skyler Erickson prepared for bronc riding he took off his hat, picked up a couple of softball-sized rocks, and put them inside. He rested the hat on the planking behind the bucking gates, crown down. Yet as Erickson readied for his ride his hat began to move slowly, but steadily away. The wind was probably blowing at 50 mph. Someone else's hat blew off his head and rolled like tumbleweed into the legs of other competitors. If not for a wall or two, the hat may not have stopped flying until it reached Old Trail Town down the block.

Erickson noticed his wiggling hat and placed it under the platform, rocks still in it, until he was ready to go. This seemed to be one night his hat was bound to fly off on the dirt. Yet amazingly, Erickson's hat remained on for the duration of the ride, an irony that did not escape him since he did not stay on the horse.

The wind was so strong that ropers like Legend Mills, riding in the direction of the breeze, believed their ability to lasso calves was impaired. "With the wind blowing as hard as it is from behind," Mills said, "it affects it."

Bull riders had their hands full without high winds. Tossed-off Wyatt Lehman just about landed on his head. "I bet he knows what it's like to be run over by a train," said Jesse the Clown. Lehman pretty much admitted so. "He stepped right on me," Lehman said of his bull.

Corey Terry, the saddle bronc regular, showed up in the bulls and pulled out an 84. Where did that come from?

"I've been riding bulls since I was eight years old," Terry said. "I've just been working on my saddle bronc."

The barrel racing course was readjusted to lengthen it. The idea was to shift away from the well-used sand of the same area. Where were Al Schultz and his tractor when you really needed them?

Terri Kaye Kirkland was back from Montana for a cameo and rode 18.90. Jennifer Lewis rode 18.47. They were usually a second or so faster.

In a rarity, a barrel racing horse took a tumble. Kayla Fielder was rounding the first barrel when her horse stumbled and went down. Fielder also hit the ground and could not get up Bull fighters and medics ran out to provide aid. Fielder left the grounds leaning on a shoulder, one jeans leg slashed from her hip to her ankle as if a knife sliced it.

Although Fielder rested her horse, she was back in competition one night later. Using a different horse, Fielder went out and won. "I have a huge bruise," Fielder said of her leg. Unlike James Greeson, she did not roll up her pants leg to show it off. "I just started to walk normal today."

Fielder used her phone to take a picture of her torn jeans and then messaged her mother in Arkansas if sewing could repair the pants. The return note was not encouraging.

"The jeans could not be saved," Fielder said.

Many a night over the summer Andy Mumm was disappointed at the shortage of bareback riders signed up, but not on Aug. 11, which featured the best field of the season. The five riders were all experienced and all made the eight seconds for a good score. Alex Christofferson won on Hot Mama with an 81. Toby Collins notched a 79. Skyler Erickson's mark was 77. Mumm's was 75. And Luke Wasney scored 70 points. Many nights Wasney's 70 would have won.

"We all drew nice horses and we all covered," Erickson said.

In much calmer weather, Erickson lost his hat during his ride. It seemed astonishing how much of a sweat bareback riders could work up in eight seconds. "It's like being put in a blender," Erickson said.

Of course, riders do not cover every night. One night later Erickson was tossed and while jogging out of the arena he hit himself on the side of the head, a reminder that he had made a mistake.

Daryl Lamb kept doing well in tie-down roping, but his long days of work followed by competition and then putting away livestock, were telling.

"I shoe horses all day, pick up at night, and then rope," Lamb said, admitting to getting worn down as the end of the season approached.

It had to happen to somebody. Lamb came out of the chute chasing a calf and roped himself. The rope did not loop the way it should have. On the other hand, once while buffalo hunting General George Armstrong Custer once accidentally shot his horse, something a bit more embarrassing.

Kooper Bott, who had thrown away her crutches, decided not to follow through on her college plan for the fall. Her hip was still bugging her, so she was going to have surgery and take a year off from school. This decision made Kade Rogge's repeated announcements retroactively true.

Colt Chlarson kept up his steady riding and earned praise from Ty Miller. "He's a cowboy's cowboy," the young announcer said. "Rancher by day, cowboy by night."

Jennifer Lewis, skin specialist by day, cowgirl by night, spent the summer riding the same horse, a small one, but now switched up and she was nervous. The new horse passed the test, though, winning two nights in a row.

After being outed by a long-time rodeo person, Lewis admitted she had left one part out of her tale of rodeo beginnings. Lewis' dark secret was that she had once been a rodeo queen.

"Oh yeah," she said. "I had the big hair and everything." Lewis also produced a reasonable, if out-of-practice facsimile of a pageant wave. Yep, it's all in the wrist.

★★★

CULLING THE COWBOY HERD

Coleman White did everything right. He spent the entire Cody Nite Rodeo season competing and collecting points. He won his share of tie-down roping events and he placed highly in many others.

He built an insurmountable lead in the season-long points category so he was sitting pretty on his horse Speedy as the regular-season drew to an end. Then everything fell apart.

White tore something in his right, roping arm. The first-blush diagnosis was torn tendons. He went doctor shopping in Cody, trying to find a doctor who would give him a good prognosis, like rest, so he could still enter the finals. No dice. Then he went doctor shopping for surgery, a procedure that would end his season, keep him sidelined during the finals, and leave him walking around in a sling.

Coleman White led the tie-down roping event all season but couldn't compete in the finals because of a torn tendon in his right arm (photo by Lew Freedman).

The only good news for White was that he may have totaled so many points that even without competing over the last couple of weeks of the season and in the finals he might still hang on and take home the championship buckle for 2014.

White was not the only casualty going to be shut out of the finals. Codi Gines could not recover and qualify, her hand prohibiting it.

Skyler Erickson was thrown in the bareback event of August 16. After being helped from the arena he lay down on the ground behind the bucking gates, shirt off, with a bag of ice soothing his right shoulder. Things did not look good. When it was time to go home Erickson could not lift his arm high enough to pull his shirt back on without help. A doctor visit confirmed the worst.

"I tore all of the ligaments," Erickson said.

That same night the electricity abruptly died in half of the arena. This was no clown gimmick or act. It was a real blackout. It was 100 percent dark on one side and the usual artificially lit brightness on the opposite side. Team roping continued in semi-darkness.

"It was OK," said Jimmy Morris. "It was half-light. It's not exactly Shea Stadium bright here anyway. It wasn't that much different from what we're used to."

For the third time over the summer Tim Ditrich got injured. This time he was finished for the year with cracked bones in his left cheek and mouth.

Jordan Couch was bucked in the saddle bronc, and he did not move after landing hard on the dirt. A hush enveloped the crowd as medics treated him at the scene and then he was carried off on a stretcher board. Colt Chlarson was there and said while Couch was being carried out he said, "Where are the girls?"

Couch was taken via emergency vehicle, one of the rare ambulance pickups all season, to West Park Hospital. He was diagnosed with a punctured lung and a broken back, but no paralysis.

This was Couch's planned last ride of the season and relatives from Idaho were present at the arena and at the hospital, including his mother. Supporters joined Couch throughout the night at the hospital and into the next morning. Couch's injury was not as bad as it looked and his back was expected to heal within six-to-eight weeks. But the sight of him immobilized on the ground was one of the scariest moments all season at Cody Nite Rodeo.

Shortly before Jordan and Skyler's seasons concluded, they, along with Chlarson and Skeet Chadwick, made a boys road trip to Rapid City, South Dakota, where they entered a rodeo and visited Mount Rushmore. Erickson said the four of them garnered considerable attention wearing cowboy hats and people kept asking to take their picture. Chlarson somehow lost his gear bag, but it had some identification in it. Authorities found it, called the rodeo office, and it was returned to Cody.

Since the quartet kept repeating, "Hey, blonde girl" as the theme of the trip there was apparently an untold story out there. Nobody was arrested, but it almost seemed as if that was an accidental circumstance.

After Couch's injury, the show went on and Cody Culver turned in a bravura bull riding performance. Drawing a bull that tried everything in its repertoire to unseat him, Culver's glorious effort earned him 84 points.

Zack Oliver scored 77 points on his 21st birthday, definitely an acceptable present.

Jeff Gideon was back in the house, with his wife Brandi, and his week-and-a-half-old baby boys in bassinets. The cowgirls all cooed over the babies.

Kacee Nesius, the 2013 breakaway champion from Minnesota, who did not have as good a year in 2014, turned in one of her best go-arounds with a 3.4-second clocking.

Late in the season Britt Givens, 59, who had made cameos all year, but not competed consistently, started winning regularly. It was almost as if he was replacing Coleman White as the old guy of tie-down roping.

An Arapaho from Riverton, Wyoming, Givens won the National Indian Rodeo Championships once. He followed older brothers into rodeo, starting in high school, worked rough stock, competed in calf roping and bull riding after growing up on a ranch. He was quite lean and hard-muscled for a man of his age. His hot streak was notable, but Givens was one of those ah-shucks guys who didn't brag, nor hardly take credit for his accomplishments.

"They still let me win," Givens said. "I get a check now and then."

Givens has debated retirement from rodeo many times, but couldn't stay away.

"Every year I think I'm gonna stop, but here I am," Givens said. "This is a good place to be in the summer."

Even if he did not say so, perhaps Givens was winning because of a good horse. The horse he rode out of the chutes every day was named Mr. Miracle.

Despite Givens' self-effacing comments the competitors in tie-down roping weren't letting him win. Daryl Lamb had worked too hard to ease up. Lamb grew up on a ranch in Australia where his father worked. He was 15 when he began working with livestock, and in 1989 Lamb came to the United States, combining ranch work with rodeo in Montana.

At one time the broad-shouldered Lamb was a bareback rider, taking advantage of more rodeos in the U.S. than in Australia. These days, after 20 years of roping and soon to turn 51, Lamb, who spends non-summer months in Texas, said he felt old.

"My body aches and I'm getting arthritis," said Lamb, who has not lost his Australian accent.

Yet Lamb has kept pace with the younger competitors – as well as his contemporaries like White and Givens – even if his work pace threatened to exhaust him.

Ty Miller, at the opposite end of the age spectrum, and not yet a high school graduate, showed no signs of flagging. In fact, Miller did not plan to finish school in Pennsylvania, but polish off his senior year through cyber space.

Now that he had a major taste of rodeo announcing Miller wanted more. He hoped to travel through Oklahoma and Texas over the winter gaining more experience.

"I'm having a blast," Miller said. "I love it out here. I'm getting better every night."

Miller did make his share of announcing mistakes, misidentifying a competitor or providing erroneous information, but he had definitely improved since Kade Rogge split following the Cody Stampede.

Miller's family has a background in rodeo and he attended his first rodeo when he was three years old. He first roped off a horse at six, and something tickled him when he heard a rodeo announcer's voice describing the action. Just like that he decided being the master of ceremonies, the man on the microphone, was for him.

Miller hoped he could return to Cody Nite Rodeo for the entire 2015 season and then parlay that into a PRCA card and a full-time career on the circuit.

Zack Flatt knew that the final night of his evaluation period for a PRCA card was in mid-August. He scheduled some freestyle matches in Oklahoma, Utah and Texas for after the Cody Nite season concluded, and while he enjoyed Cody he hoped his next step as a bull fighter would be in bigger arenas.

A couple of months later, in early fall, Flatt got the word. He qualified for his card.

As if the spate of injuries wasn't sufficient to identify something weird in the air, near the end of August it rained so long and so hard in Cody that three straight Cody Nite Rodeo performances were called off. That was unheard of and unprecedented given the track record of two cancellations in 10 years before 2014.

There were puddles the size of the Pacific Ocean on the grounds. The dirt was mud. One day alone two-and-a-half inches of rain fell.

"It was unbelievable," said Nikki Tate. "We would have had to call it off the next night too if we didn't replace the dirt. It just wasn't safe."

Belt buckles were awarded for August, the end of the Cody Nite Rodeo regular season. Cody Culver won the bulls title. Kayla Fielder, despite her accident, won the barrels crown. Willy Gould was the top heeler. Colt Chlarson won the saddle bronc buckle and in honor of the difficulties Ditrich faced, Chlarson called it "The Tim Ditrich Memorial Belt Buckle."

★★★

TONY THE CLOWN

The end of his 35-plus years as a rodeo clown came for Tony Martoglio near the end of August.

At 60, the Cody rodeo clown was told by his doctors that he had to quit. As the survivor of a stroke, Martoglio was on medication, and they told him that one minor calamity in the arena could trigger a serious, life-threatening issue.

Martoglio's last day was in mid-August and Sid McFarland was back to partner with his friend to wrap up his career in style. The duo that had first clowned together about four decades ago was giving a command performance.

Martoglio gave much thought to the occasion. His three kids, an aunt, an uncle and a niece planned to come out. His sons were in the back country, but they were coming back to town for dad's last performance.

"It will be my saddest day in 38 years," Tony the Clown said. "I'd love to keep doing it."

Rodeo clowns and friends for more than 30 years, Tony Martoglio of Cody, Wyoming (left) and Sid McFarland of Montgomery, Alabama (right).

Tony let it out a few days early that he was retiring under pressure.

"I have to because of my health," he said. "I had a stroke, you know." Asked if he was alright, Tony said, "I'm here, aren't I?"

He and McFarland, who had worked together in Cody and nearby Jackson Hole, as well, bantered.

"I've known Tony for 40 years," Sid the Clown said. "He started me clowning in rodeos 37 years ago."

"He needed some help," Tony needled.

Martoglio knew what he wanted to do on his final night: "Leave 'em laughing."

Once the rodeo began Tony and Sid shared the clown role, blending their specialty acts. Tony did his boomerang hat routine, the one with the "$10,000 cowboy hat." Sid took a shot at it (with blanks). "Oh, no," Tony said. In retaliation, Tony shot Sid in the behind and sparks flew.

Ty Miller chimed in: "You're on fire, Sid."

Sid and Tony did an explosion routine, much like one of Sid's prior acts. Make that a fake explosion routine. They called it making a Texas Firecracker. Tony said that the recipe called for a pound of TNT, bottle rockets, five Roman candles, and two pounds of horse manure.

"You light it, I'll throw it," Tony said to Sid.

Then Sid sneaked up on Tony from behind and threw the concoction down his wide clown pants as it exploded.

Sid also interrupted the proceedings to inform fans what was going on. He gave Tony a send-off speech.

"Tonight, ladies and gentlemen," Sid said, "you are witnessing the end of a clown's career. Tony has pulled many a bull off of me. Tonight, I'm having the greatest honor I've had as a rodeo clown. Thanks for always being there, brother." Sid tipped his hat to Tony and they shared a hug.

As the nightly rodeo was nearing its end, Tony dabbed at his eyes with a red handkerchief. No, he wasn't crying, he insisted. "It gets dusty in the arena."

Tony had already let it be known that he was not going to do anything bizarre or spectacular like burn his clown gear in the middle of the arena on his way out the door.

"My kids want me to frame my clown pictures," he said.

Tony kind of liked that idea. He said he did not picture spending free time during the summer of 2015, or beyond, attending Cody Nite Rodeo. For him it was more about being a rodeo clown, not about sitting in the grandstands cheering during the saddle bronc riding and barrel racing.

When the last bull rider ate dust, Sid and Tony said their farewells in the arena. Tony the Clown walked out and mingled with fans at the front of the grounds as they walked to their cars. Then he doubled back, still wearing his clown outfit, to depart the grounds from the rear of the grandstand.

The stroke had injured Tony's health, but as he put it, "I'm still here." The last show had come and gone and now Tony Martoglio was no longer there at Cody Nite Rodeo. He was a civilian for the first time in ages.

★★★

THE FINALS

Before the rodeo began Skeet Chadwick stood behind the bucking gates drinking energy from a can. He was asked if it was Red Bull so he could ride a bull.

"No, it's Rock Star, so I can feel like one," Chadwick said.

A short while before the first of three nights of the Cody Nite Rodeo 2014 Finals started, James Greeson came running up to the back gate, huffing and puffing. "I made it," he said.

Greeson hadn't been around for weeks, or since his magnificent leg bruise hindered his self-propulsion. It turned out he had tried other rodeos and even begun the college school year in Texas, but he hustled back to Cody for the championships. It took a 21-hour ride for Greeson to make it to Wyoming from Sam Houston State, though he was flying back out of Billings, Montana, 100 miles away, after the rodeo.

Up to 10 competitors qualified for the finals per event at the cost of a $200 weekend entry fee, although some events did not have full fields because of injuries. At stake was prize money of $77,000. Al Schultz delivered a little speech about the payouts and said that $45,000 of the finals money was contributed by the Stampede. Rodeo contestants could win a nightly round, a weekend title, or a season championship.

As a nod to ceremony and showmanship – it was actually a Buffalo Bill kind of thing to do — all the competitors rode into the arena on horseback, even bull riders who borrowed horses, and then lined up facing the crowd. Then the cowboys and cowgirls tipped their hats. Some let out a "yippee ki yay" as they bounded out the gate.

Riding Shasta, Andy Mumm was first up in the bareback riding. Mumm turned in an excellent ride and standing behind the gates watching was Jesse Nelson, whose ride on Boogie Man was still to come. "He beat us," Nelson said.

Nelson was one of six out of eight riders who scored, but he was right. No one topped Mumm on Day One. On some days during the season there hadn't been close to eight entries in bareback. Mumm took a victory lap with his fist in the air.

The most important thing that a rider or roper had to do during the three-day event was post a time or a score because the three-day aggregate total was paramount. In the tie-down roping only Bryce Bott missed. That meant he could not win the title, but would be competing only for day money the next two days. Britt Givens walked off with the first-day crown.

The opposite occurred in breakaway roping. Five women missed altogether and two incurred penalties. That left Carol Bachman's 3.3-second time tops and gave her the first-day championship lead.

All five of the kids in the junior steer riding were presented buckles for their seasonal efforts, including Lukasey Morris, Caden Gines, Zain and Kade Fitzgerald, and Jaysen Lowden. Morris won the first night with an 86 and only Gines, with an 83, also scored.

The girls in the junior barrel racing were also recognized, including Abi Dawson, McKinzie Connor, Lauren Shepperson, Ta'Lynn Paul and Cammi Gerhardt. Anna Allshouse, who was able to double all season in the junior and open categories, collected so many points before the finals she was already the season-long winner.

A number of contestants in the open barrels knocked over barrels, including Allshouse, and were slapped with costly time penalties. Raelyn Gould won the night in 17.75 seconds with Jennifer Lewis second in 18.21 and Kayla Fielder third in 18.24.

The energy drink did not help Skeet Chadwick survive his bull ride on Prime Rib. Just as they had all summer long the bulls mistreated the humans. The only rider to make the eight seconds was points leader Curry Fielder, who scored an 83 and then embarked on a reckless, jubilant fist-pumping victory lap that was almost as exciting as his bull ride.

Rain returned to mess things up for Day Two. There were puddles galore around the grounds and the temperature was in the 50s. Many people wore jackets, even though it was supposed to still be summer. Sid McFarland's clown outfit was accented by rubber boots.

Sid the Clown tested the ground. It wasn't quicksand because he didn't sink. The conditions reminded him of another rodeo long ago when horses were on the loose and he got run over. He spent five days in the hospital with multiple broken ribs. He was not interested in a repeat.

Shanni Shipley, she of the 1.9-second breakaway time earlier in the season, topped the field on Day Two with a 2.6-second clocking. Carol Bachman was not as sharp with a 4.8, but still led in combined time after two rodeos.

Toby Collins (80 points on Comanche) topped Greeson (74 points on Alabama) and Corey Terry (72 points on Trixy) for day money in the saddle bronc riding. Colt Chlarson was thrown. So was Lukasey Morris in the junior steers. Coming on strong, as he had during the latter stages of the season, Caden Gines notched a score of 88, the highest point total of the year. The bulls once again wiped out the riders, with only Tylor Bird, with an 81, covering.

The puddle next to the third barrel looked deep enough to house aquatic life. There was no way to avoid it if the rider came in from the right side. The only way around the water was to approach from the left and swing wide, which might cost time. Allshouse rode 18.07 to win.

Givens won the tie-down roping again, in 10.5 seconds. This was an upset in the making, the oldest guy in the field leading after two rounds, with some of his top foes more than 35 years younger.

The bareback competition continued at a high level, but again, although five riders scored, Mumm was first with a by-far best score of 81 points.

There was a sense of melancholy on the back gate as the competitors led their horses into the arena and others carried saddles over their shoulders on Day Three, the final night of the 2014 season.

Harold Adema led his three horses for pickup duty past gate man Dwight Cabra and shook hands with him.

"Hi partner," Adema said. "Last night."

When Curry Fielder entered, his eyes on the prize in the bull riding, he said, "I've been on 10 bulls in the last couple of days." His right cheek was stepped on at a rodeo in Red Lodge, Montana. "But I've been doing great. Tonight, I'm gonna win."

Britt Givens had been on fire, but on Day Three when he tossed his rope it bounced off the calf's head: No score. End of that dream.

Coleman White had accumulated enough points during the year to capture the season-long title without competing in the finals. He won a shiny pair of ornamental spurs, but when he rode out on his horse, his right arm still in that sling, he couldn't grasp his prize because he held the reins in his left hand.

Legend Mills finished first in average, ahead of K.C. Jones.

Shanni Shipley won breakaway for a second night, but Bachman won the finals crown and Kooper Bott grabbed the season title. Alas, on the final night of the finals, Molly Jo Collins chased a calf all over the arena on her horse which then screeched to a halt, throwing her over its head.

"And she scores 25 points in the bronc riding!" Sid the Clown yelled.

The saddle bronc riding was intense. Even though Corey Terry ended his ride airborne and splatted into the mud on his butt, he scored 77 points. Ricky Warren on Cherry Chip scored 78 to win the night. James Greeson scored 75 points and won the weekend. Colt Chlarson was good for 74 points. Goldman Realbird and Cree Minkoff also covered with 71 points each.

Terry won the title and when presented with glittering trophy spurs, he said, "I needed a pair of these."

For the second night in a row Caden Gines scored 88 points in the junior steers. Although they didn't win any other hardware, Bill Parker and Jace Crabb's 6.3-second time in team roping won Day Three and the old cowboy Parker became the year-end header champion.

Jennifer Lewis won the last go-around in barrel racing at 17.20 seconds, but Raelyn Gould won the weekend by placing fourth.

True to his prediction, Curry Fielder, riding T-Bone, capped his marvelous summer with a championship bull ride of 85 points. Nine other bull riders struck out with no scores. The final day of the finals was consistent with the theme of the summer – the bulls started out ahead and finished ahead. Fielder was No. 1 for the season.

For all of his aches and pains Daryl Lamb won the All-Around Cowboy award for the year and Tara Edwards won All-Around Cowgirl. Edwards lifted the leather saddle off the fence where it rested and immediately placed it on her horse. A leather worker by trade, Edwards recognized good workmanship. Neither Lamb nor Edwards had a good finals weekend, but were rewarded for their season-long performance.

Later, Edwards said, "It's a good saddle."

Many of the bareback riders saved their best for last as they challenged Andy Mumm. Seven out of the eight riders earned points, Shane Morin, Jesse Nelson, and Toby Collins all scored 74 points, Alex Christofferson scored 73, Naudy Esposito scored 72, and Robbie Cobbler 71.

"These guys came to ride tonight," Sid the Clown said.

But none rode as well as Mumm.

"Mr. Mumm, it's your time to shine," Ty Miller said over the microphone.

Shine, he did. Mumm scored 82 points to break the field. It was a heck of a weekend for Mumm. He won all three nights of the finals. He collected the most points in the regular season. He took home about $3,000 for the finals alone.

The Cody Nite Rodeo 2014 bareback champion in every measurable way, Mumm improved on his runner-up finish of 2013 and he did not expect to be back for 2015, at least not full-time.

"Time for the PRCA," Mumm said.

In his mind Mumm was ready to rodeo around the country on bigger stages for more prize money. Mumm figured to join the legion of former Cody Nite Rodeo cowboys who started in the Rodeo Capital of the World, and then blazed new trails.

Not that Andy Mumm imagined ever completely abandoning rodeo in Cody.

"Even if we do go pro," he said. "This is home base."

Epilogue

Buffalo Bill Cody died on January 10, 1917 at the age of 70. The cause of death was listed as kidney failure and he had been in failing health for some time. He passed away at his sister's home in Denver.

Cody always expressed his desire to be buried in Cody, Wyoming, the city he helped found. He wished to be buried on Cedar Mountain overlooking the community. Indeed, he wrote his preference for burial in Cody into his will.

When the world-famous Buffalo Bill died, his wife Louise and other family members announced that William F. Cody underwent a death-bed change of heart and wished to be buried in Colorado. This news infuriated citizens of Cody. They believed the change-of-mind statement was a flim-flam.

What followed was a bizarre story with alternative endings. To some extent the controversy still flares up nearly a century after Buffalo Bill's death. Buffalo Bill fans must make up their own minds about what really happened.

Soon after Cody's death and the changed burial plan was revealed, it was announced that his body would be kept in hibernation for the rest of the winter because it was too cold, snowy and stormy to conduct a funeral on Lookout Mountain in nearby Golden, the burial site his sister Mary Decker chose.

It is alleged by some that during this period a small contingent of angry, but determined Cody citizens stole into Colorado and swiped Buffalo Bill's body, quietly burying it atop Cedar Mountain as he requested. Supposedly, a drifter of some resemblance to Cody was placed in the coffin in Buffalo Bill's stead.

Rumors surfaced that Louise, who was at odds with Buffalo Bill for many of their 51 years of marriage, had pretty much literally sold his soul. The story goes that the *Denver Post* and other business interests paid Cody's widow $10,000 for the privilege of holding a public Denver funeral and then interring the body in Colorado for the benefit of tourism. As winter raged in the Rockies, Cody reposed.

On June 3, months after Cody's death, a public funeral, with an open casket, was conducted on Lookout Mountain. Thousands attended and saw the great Buffalo Bill in death, which would seem to be at odds with any belief that Cody's body was snatched in the intervening months. No one blew the whistle after looking at Cody by saying that he did not look like himself.

The burial site left room for Louise to be buried beside her husband, and she was interned there when she passed away in 1921. By then the burial site was also being turned into a museum. Johnnie Baker, for decades Buffalo Bill's right-hand man with his Wild West exhibition as well as his foster son, donated personal artifacts to open the museum, also in 1921.

Fears remained that raiders from Wyoming would dig up Buffalo Bill and move him to Cody. Eventually, the burial site was covered with tons of concrete to ensure against forcible removal. The Johnnie Baker-founded museum and the burial site are part of the same tourist visitation location on Lookout Mountain, an attraction that lures in about 65,000 visitors a year.

Meanwhile, Cody, Wyoming remains the heart of Buffalo Bill's legacy, with the Buffalo Bill Center of the West being the focal point and a museum many times larger than the one in Colorado.

Not even Bruce Eldredge, the executive director and CEO of the Buffalo Bill Center thinks that Cody body-snatchers were successful or that they even tried.

"I personally believe that Buffalo Bill is buried outside of Denver," Eldredge said.

However, he noted, every few years he and Steve Friesen, the director of the Golden museum, do engage in debate about the Cody burial site. "One of us starts the controversy again and it gets attention," Eldredge said. Eldredge winked as he said that. He meant that the controversy could be good for business.

Friesen has no sense of humor whatsoever about the issue of where Buffalo Bill is buried.

Buffalo Bill Cody's grave site at Lookout Mountain in Golden, Colorado, outside of Denver. Some Cody residents believe that his body was secretly transferred to Cedar Mountain overlooking Cody as his will stipulated (photo by Lew Freedman).

"He is and always has been," (buried on Lookout Mountain)," said Friesen, the director of the Buffalo Bill Memorial Museum since 1995. As for stories about the stolen body, Friesen said, "That is just the biggest pile of BS. The fact of the matter is he was under armed guard in a room until he was lowered into the ground."

Friesen got more worked up as he continued. "It's cockamamie, sour grapes, an outright lie," he said. "There is no good evidence. When it comes to debate on where he wanted to be buried, that's open for discussion. There is no letter in his own hand saying he wanted to be buried at Lookout Mountain. Twenty thousand people walked by his body. He was a well-known person. The statute of limitations on grave robbing is up. It's the myth of Buffalo Bill. It is hearsay."

Friesen does admit to "good-natured discussion" with Buffalo Bill Center officials on this topic, but does not waver in his argument. When Buffalo Bill died, his wife, daughters and sister were with him. "They participated in the choice of the spot. It is the preponderance of the evidence. I don't know about a bribe. He was getting a free burial plot. We are delighted when this comes up. It makes for good public relations."

Rather astonishingly, Buffalo Bill, who gained fame in the Indian wars, late in life provided employment for Native-Americans by the dozens in his Wild West.

He needed Indians for authenticity in his productions, and although he had to haggle with the U.S. Department of the Interior to get his way, he took responsibility for Native-Americans who would otherwise have been confined to reservations. Cody used his clout with top military men in Washington, D.C. with whom he had served and knew to hire them. Indian Tail became a close friend and trusted advisor to Cody and was paid more than the other Native-American performers. Cody then opened the door of opportunity to Sitting Bull.

It was almost inconceivable to imagine Sitting Bull, the revered Lakota chief and one of the architects of the Battle of the Little Big Horn resulting in George Armstrong Custer's death and the massacre of his troops, as an actor. Actually, Sitting Bull didn't do much besides play himself during his six-month stint with the Wild West in 1885. His assignment was to ride around the performance arena once. For that he was paid $50 a week.

During this period Sitting Bull met Annie Oakley, one of the biggest Wild West attractions, and as was just about anyone who ever saw her pull a trigger was dazzled by her shooting. Sitting Bull named her "Little Sure Shot."

Annie Oakley, a tiny woman, spent 16 years with the Wild West and she and Cody were friends and business partners. Oakley always said that Cody offered her a square deal, and she had great respect for him. Oakley, who always traveled with husband Frank Butler, was a rare Wild West performer who got star billing. When she and Cody parted in 1902, there was no animosity.

Oakley always called Cody "Colonel" and he always called her "Missie." Cody, who preceded Oakley in death by nine years, was highly praised by his one-time shooting star when he passed away. "...the whole time we (the Wild West) were one great family loyal to one man," she said. "His words were better than most contracts."

Citing Buffalo Bill's innovative nature, his sympathetic stance on Indian treatment and his support of women's suffrage, Eldredge believes that if Buffalo Bill was alive today he would enthusiastically endorse the Internet and social media, especially for use by the Cody museum, and he would be driving around in a hybrid fueled car.

"He was a person really ahead of his time," said Eldredge, who would love to meet Cody, via séance or any other means. "All of the time. I wish I could ask a series of questions."

The summit of Cedar Mountain is not open to automobile traffic. There is private property involved. However, a bronze buffalo stands on the spot where Buffalo Bill Cody stated in his will that he wished to be interred.

Cody Mayor Nancy Tia Brown likes the fact that the buffalo is atop the peak.

"One can't contain someone's spirit," Brown said. "Buffalo Bill had connections to lots of places, but his true love, from everything I've ever read, was right here in Cody. The spirit is here. It doesn't matter where the body is."

Informed of Brown's comments about Buffalo Bill's spirit being in Cody, Friesen offered this rebuttal: "Buffalo Bill's spirit is everywhere," he said.

Through rodeo, the ongoing mystique of the Old West and the cowboy, it is difficult to argue that Friesen is wrong.

A visit to Cody, with all of the photographs and posters of Buffalo Bill Cody on the walls of business establishments, the Irma Hotel that he built as the centerpiece of downtown, and the Buffalo Bill Center of the West being the premier attraction, indicates it is also difficult to argue that Nancy Tia Brown is wrong either.

Once, William F. Cody was simply a youngster hustling to make a living after the death of his father left his family poverty-stricken. He went West and made much of himself, through his horsemanship, innate scouting ability, his stature as an Indian fighter and as a buffalo hunter supreme.

He met the rich and famous and developed friendships or acquaintanceships with powerful generals and fortuitously hooked up with Ned Buntline. That connection put Cody on the stage and that led to his creation of the Wild West.

In an article that appeared in the October 5, 1873 edition of the Galveston (Texas) News, Cody said, "I'm no scout now. I'm a first-class star."

He was and remained so for the rest of his life and apparently for eternity.

Friesen calls Cody, "America's first superstar. He rubbed elbows with Mark Twain, Oscar Wilde and James McNeil Whistler. We have a time in our history that is fascinating to people. He built the myth around that time. I would say that yes he is a beloved figure from the past. For the most part he is. We have people who come here to the museum and the grave site that are dressed like him and there are people who leave flowers on the grave."

Scholars and museum authorities like Friesen proclaim Cody the first American superstar, at a time when the word had not yet been coined. Author Larry McMurtry lumps Cody and Annie Oakley together in this realm. In his book, *The Colonel and Little Missie*, McMurty stated flat out that was his opinion. "...at the height of their fame," he wrote, "their images were recognized the world over. Buffalo Bill was probably the most famous American of his day; he was easily more famous than any president, more famous even than Theodore Roosevelt."

The man who helped settle the frontier, who hunted buffalo, won the Congressional Medal of Honor, and perpetuated the glories of the Old West, lives on in so many ways in so many places that it seems as if the great Buffalo Bill Cody never died at all.

If that is so, it shouldn't matter where he was buried, because the man, the myth and the legend cannot be contained by mere earth. And if credence may be given to another story, Buffalo Bill Cody still may just be dancing in the living room at the Caroline Lockhart Inn.

It was often said that Buffalo Bill Cody was born to ride a horse. The legend of one of the chief propagators of cowboy lore remains alive nearly a century after his death (photo courtesy of the Buffalo Bill Center of the West McCracken Library).

A large percentage of the 90,000 or so fans that attend Cody Nite Rodeo each year are coming from or going to Yellowstone National Park, located 50 miles to the west. A common sight they see are buffalo (photo by Lew Freedman).

Sources

American Rodeo: From Buffalo Bill to Big Business, Kristine Fredriksson.

Buffalo Bill's America: William Cody and The Wild West Show, Louis S. Warren.

Buffalo Bill's Life Story: An Autobiography, By William F. Cody.

Caroline Lockhart, Her Life and Legacy, By Necah Stewart Furman.

Gold Buckles Don't Lie, By Fred Whitfield and Terri Powers.

Rodeo: An Anthropologist Looks at the Wild and the Tame, Elizabeth Atwood Lawrence.

Steamboat: Legendary Bucking Horse, Candy Vyvey Moulton and Flossie Moulton.

The Colonel and Little Missie, By Larry McMurty.

The Hero of a Hundred Fights, Ned Buntline, editing and introduction by Clay Reynolds.

The Lady Doc, By Caroline Lockhart.

Author Lew Freedman did sit on Mongo's back, but here he merely pets the giant bull.

About the Author

Lew Freedman saw his first rodeos in the early 1960s at the Boston Garden. He saw about 80 rodeos during the summer of 2014 in Cody, Wyoming. When he was growing up in Massachusetts watching every western show on television he wanted to be a cowboy. Instead he became a writer.

A veteran journalist, Freedman is the author of dozens of books about sports and Alaska. During his career he has worked on the staffs of the *Philadelphia Inquirer, Chicago Tribune* and *Anchorage Daily News*. He has won more than 250 journalism awards.

Freedman currently writes for the *Cody Enterprise*, a newspaper that Buffalo Bill Cody founded in 1899.